Richard Sims was born in Crewkerne, Somerset, where his interest in railways and their history developed during the last days of steam. In 1976 he moved to a teaching post in West Dorset, which allowed him to focus on its railway history, especially that of the GWR's route to Weymouth.

He moved on to study Bridport's industrial past in the 1990s. He has produced a series of leaflets on the Industrial History of Bridport for the local museum, which were illustrated by Marion, his wife.

Early retirement from teaching has given him the time to concentrate on researching the history of Bridport's textile industry. He has contributed some of the research for *Bridport and West Bay, the buildings of the flax and hemp industry*, published by English Heritage, as well as supplying additional text for the reprint of the late Anthony Sanctuary's book *Rope, Twine and Net Making*. His research into the history of Palmers Brewery was the main source used in their recent book, *Palmers, the Story of a Dorset Brewer*.

Following page
Mrs Crabb braiding at her home in Uploders in 1948.
Note the photographs on the mantlepiece of her sailor son.
This is the first of 6 photographs in this book taken in 1948 by the Central
Office of Information to help publicise the Bridport net industry. 'Wherever
in the world there is a fishing industry,' went the caption on the back, 'a
traveller from one of the Bridport firms pays his calls.'

Rope, Net and Twine

The Story of the Bridport Textile Industry

RICHARD SIMS

THE DOVECOTE PRESS

Netting made in Bridport is used throughout the world, often at the cutting
edge of science and manufacturing. This photograph of the NASA space shuttle
shows Bridport arrester webbing used to help slow the shuttle during an
emergency landing.

First published in 2009 by The Dovecote Press Ltd
Stanbridge, Wimborne Minster, Dorset BH21 4JD

ISBN 978-1-904-34972-3

Typeset in Georgia
Printed and bound by KHL Printing, Singapore

A CIP catalogue record for this book is available
from the British Library

Contents

Introduction

Bridport has been a centre for the rope, net and twine industry for centuries, probably since the foundation of the Saxon town in the ninth century. That the industry is to be found here is the result of the juxtaposition of topography, climate and geology, all of which proved ideal for the growth of hemp and flax.

It has been the industry's ability to adapt to change that, together with the presence of good transport links, has allowed it to survive to the present day. The town was already renowned for its production of ropes, cables and hawsers by the 13th century. When the Royal dockyard took over production in the 17th century Bridport soon filled the gap by making lines and nets for the nascent Newfoundland fishery. These soon became the dominant products and were exported all over the world. During this time sailcloth gradually expanded in importance and by the end of the 18th century Bridport and South Somerset were suiting all the revenue boats, packets and smacks of Great Britain, as well as exporting canvas to the American navy; sails for the Royal Navy came later!

The industry served this market until the depression of the latter part of the 19th century when it turned to producing nets for the rapidly developing sports of tennis, cricket and football. The end of the 19th century saw the industry re-enter the production of nets for the military. While this protected them during times of trouble it did allow competitors to take some of their traditional trade away, especially after the Second World War. This was countered by making cargo nets for the developing aviation industry. These, over the years, have become the dominant products, with the result that Bridport Gundry came out of its traditional markets all together. This left a gap in the market which a number of firms stepped in to fill, leading to the formation of the dozen of so firms to be found in the town today.

The final section of the book looks at the individual histories of the firms concerned. The reason for this is to allow the reader to understand the overall history before looking at the firms in detail. In addition, treatment of the story in this way means that I have not seen the need to include an index as the table of contents effectively serves the same purpose.

This photograph of North Mills shows the factory in an early state of development. The tall chimney was built in 1861 on the introduction of steam into the mill. A second chimney was added in 1867, which dates this photograph to the early part of the 1860s. An 1841 map of Bridport, in the possession of AmSafe Bridport, shows the mill to have changed little in the intervening 20 years.

Acknowledgements

It was the late Anthony Sanctuary who was instrumental in ensuring the survival of so many of the records of the rope, net and twine industry. Without his foresight this book could not have been written.

The Museum of Net Manufacture holds a significant archive of original documents and photographs and Mrs Frances Sanctuary and Jacquie Summers have kindly allowed me access to these.

Likewise the Dorset History Centre holds the other major archive relating to the industry and Hugh Jacques and his staff have provided much assistance in accessing these and other documents at the centre.

The Bridport Museum Trust, through curator Alice Martin, has provided a great deal of help in allowing access to its collections, as has the staff at the Bridport Library in allowing me to use the microfilm copies of the Bridport News and other resources.

The Guildhall Library, London, kindly provided copies of the Sun Insurance records for a number of the Bridport manufacturers and the National Archive provided Wills through their online service

Past chairmen and managers of Bridport Gundry have been kind enough to provide information of the history of the firm from its beginning. Special mention must be made of Bill Budden, Pat Darley, Bob Holder, John Bowden, and Geoff Dilbey.

James McLeod and Walter Hay helped provide the detail for the Irish and Scottish side of Bridport Gundry, while Lawson Lyon did the same for Pearsalls.

Malcolm Brooks and Louise Samways (of AmSafe Bridport) have provided information and photographs .

Archie Barclay, Alan Nute, Toby Eeles, Richard Connolly and Chris Louden have provided much help in detailing the history of the firms since 1997, while the owners of the smaller businesses have done the same for their firms.

Thanks also go to Allan Hall of York University, who

Anthony Sanctuary (1926-1991)

provided the evidence on the origins of hemp and flax in Britain; to Mike Bone, for his help and advice, and likewise to Mike Williams of English Heritage and to Pat Slocombe for help with Gundry's Swindon factory.

Thanks also to David Burnett and Elizabeth Dean of the Dovecote Press for their patience and help in turning a very raw manuscript into the final article.

Finally to Marion for her help, encouragement and support over the past years while this book was being rsearched and written.

PART ONE

The Growth and Development of the Industry

An aerial view of Bridport, looking north in about 1954.
The Saxon town is centred around St. Mary's Church in the middle
distance. The medieval extension of East and West Streets can
clearly be seen running across the photograph. The factories follow
the River Brit which runs to the west of the town, once using its
water to turn the machinery.

ONE

Flax and Hemp in Dorset

CULTIVATION

The geographic origins of Flax, *Linum usitatissimum*, are unknown but it was already an important crop in Biblical times and is mentioned by Homer and Pliny. It arrived in Britain during the Bronze Age, where it is recorded in sites from Wiltshire to Suffolk.

Hemp, *Cannabis sativa*, was a later arrival and its geographic origins are better understood. The species is a native of western Asia where it seems to have been cultivated from around 900BC. Its use spread to Italy in 100BC and it arrived in Britain with the Romans. It was not until Saxon times that it became important, coinciding with the increased cultivation of the heavier soils. By the 14th century its cultivation was widespread and it was grown all over Dorset, apart from the high chalk downland.

By the 18th century the growth of both hemp and flax had become limited to the 13 parishes around Bridport. Even then there was a subtle pattern to their distribution. Less demanding of soil conditions than hemp, flax was

Flax and hemp. Flax, on the left, grows to a height of about 1 metre. Hemp is taller, growing to 2-4 metres, and also has separate male and female plants.

primarily grown in Symondsbury parish, in an area centred on Broadoak. Here the Middle Lias beds of marls and clays, with their deep moist loamy soils, contain the organic matter required by flax.

Hemp flourished in Bradpole and Loders on an outcrop of Upper Lias known as the Bridport Sands, and growth of the plant followed this outcrop through Beaminster to the Crewkerne and Yeovil areas, another important region of textile manufacture. These well structured soils, usually on the gentler slopes, provide the fine, firm seed bed hemp needs, there being little risk of waterlogging or the soil drying out.

Flax could be grown after a winter root crop and before a late summer catch crop. Unlike hemp it was often grown on freshly broken ground. The seed bed was prepared early in the year as flax does not like newly manured soils, preferring a certain amount of folding of sheep prior to the single ploughing. A firm warm seed bed, free of weeds was ideal, as cold and wet conditions delayed germination.

Sowing occurred in March or April at a rate of around 70lb per acre (13kg/ha), enough to leave the stems about 1 inch apart, and was often under sown with clover. If the seed was collected from the crop it usually had to be changed every two or three years due to contamination from competitive weeds. Weeding had to be carried out by hand as flax is surface rooted and suffered more from competition than hemp, especially as it only reaches a height of one metre. Flowering occurred in June, colouring the fields a pale blue.

Harvesting the plant for fibre took place in early August before the seed set. The whole plant was pulled, a task which, although more time consuming, was made easier due to its shallow roots. As with hemp some of the crop was left to provide the next year's seed, although by the mid-19th century the Pymore Mill Company was selling seed imported from the Baltic port of Riga. For many years seed from this source had been widely regarded as being of the best quality.

If the seed was being collected the crop was left on the ground and turned once or twice before being threshed. The seed was collected for use the following year, for crushing into oil or as cattle feed.

Contemporary early 19th century accounts describe the cultivation of hemp in the Bridport area. Hemp was usually grown as a fallow crop to be followed by wheat or barley. Preparation of the soil began in February with the first

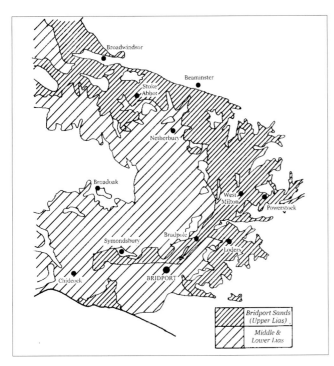

The distribution of the Middle Lias and Bridport Sands in the Bridport area. The bounty returns of the late 18th century show that the centre of flax production was in Symondsbury parish, on the soils derived from the Middle Lias. Hemp production centred on Bradpole and Loders, on soils derived from the Bridport Sands.

A map showing how the outcrops of Middle Lias and Bridport Sands link the textiles industries of West Dorset and South Somerset.

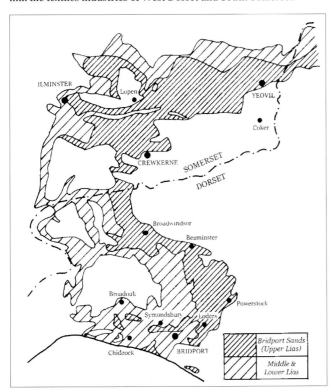

ploughing, which was later heavily manured; it needed to be the equivalent of a good garden soil. Second and third ploughings were carried out in May, after which the seed was sown, late enough to avoid the frosts, and at between 2 - 4 bushels per acre. Once established, hemp suffered little from competition with other plants. The initial growth was concentrated in leaf formation to be followed by stem

Bales of flax seeds, which were collected after flax had been scutched, were sold and made into linseed oil or cattle food.

growth, with the plant eventually reaching a height of 2-4 metres. Hemp is dioecious, having both male and female plants, and flowers in August just when the day length falls to 15 hours. The male plants, which account for a quarter of the crop, were harvested after flowering, some six to nine weeks after sowing. Since they occurred amongst the female plants narrow paths were cut at 30 ft intervals and the male plants cut out.

The female plants remained until September before being harvested, which for fibre was done prior to the seed being mature. The yield was normally some 512lbs per acre (92kg/ha). If seed was needed for the next growing season a stand of plants was normally left until seed formation was complete.

THE WORK FORCE

A letter of 1808 written by Henry Saunders of Bridport gives some idea of the costs involved in raising a hemp crop:

'Of the Male Hemp fifteen women will draw one acre per day; that cost will be, including liquor, £1 2s 6d. Speading Male Hemp, turning and taking up ditto, about 7s 6d per acre. Ten women will draw one acre of Seed Hemp in a day; cost, including liquor, 15s. Thrashing out the seed, and winnowing, reckoning two men and five women per acre, cost, including liquor, 13s per acre. Spreading, turning and taking up the Seed Hemp, 7s 6d per acre.'

'There is no machine for dressing the hemp; the process is performed by women and children, who scale it by hand and are paid 1d per lb for the Male Hemp, and ½ d per lb for the Seed Hemp. It is then fit for market and the manufacturer buys it at about 16s 6d or 17s per weight; present price about 18s'.

At around 18s per weight of 32lb, and 15 weights per acre in Dorset, this produced an income to the jobber of £13 10s per acre against an expenditure of £13 5s 6d even before scaling is taken into account. Clearly the jobber made very little money at these prices.

Traditionally the person who owned or farmed the land was only responsible for its preparation and sowing the seed, for which he was paid from £4 to £9 per acre. It was the jobbers who organised the care of the crop and its harvesting. Belatedly their role was taken over by the manufacturers.

It was bought by the merchant around whom the trade was based, and who used warehouses and yarn bartons as temporary stores; those of Joseph Gundry in 1772 were located at the top of St. Michael's Lane.

After purchasing the hemp and flax from the growers, carefully weighed amounts were put out to the artisan workers. Here the family was the normal working unit, the men carrying out the initial process of dressing the crop, the women spinning the yarn and twine, assisted by children who turned the spinning wheel. The men also carried out the line and rope-making. Weaving was carried out on hand looms, either at home or in weaving shops.

Often one family would work for a merchant down though the years, as was the case with Matthew Powell who worked for Joseph Gundry in the late 18th century and for whom Matthew's grandson was still working 80 years later. Mechanisation meant that the work gradually became centred in the factory mills rather than in the homes and walks of the artisans.

In other cases one person would organise a group of people to work for him and contract with the merchant to produce the items he needed. John Crabb was Gundry's line-maker in the early 19th century and his son carried on after him and eventually running the new line-walk at The Court in the 1860s.

The completed articles were returned to the merchant who paid for the added value, checking that the weight returned was within the normal agreed limits to ensure that none was being skimmed off and sold elsewhere.

The graph below shows late 18th century production of hemp and flax and the link between production and spring rainfall. Flax, with its shallow roots, is more affected than hemp by a dry spring.

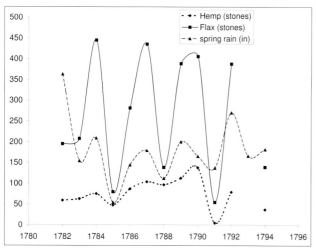

PRODUCTION

The level of production until the 15th century was never very high. Demand increased as sailing rigging improved and both the merchant and naval fleets grew larger.

The imposition of a bounty on the growing of flax and hemp in 1769 has allowed some estimates of the crops in the county. Table 1 below shows the data for the years 1782 to 1794, during which the production of hemp increased for much of the period, with only small decreases every three years until a significant fall in 1791.

Year	Hemp (stones)	Flax (stones)
1782	5,911	19,500
1783	6,271	20,771
1784	7,489	44,458
1785	4,754	7,943
1786	8,658	28,114
1787	10,356	43,506
1788	9,645	13,818
1789	11,245	38,827
1790	13,750	40,555
1791	443	5,435
1792	7,899	38,769
1793		
1794	3,321	13,861
Average	7,510	26,298
[14lbs = 1 stone]		

Table 1. Hemp and flax production in Dorset from 1782 to 1794, based on the bounty returns. Taken from Stevenson's *Agriculture of Dorset,* published in 1812.

With flax a distinctive three year cycle is seen throughout the period, with two good years followed by a poor third season. These cycles in both hemp and flax coincide with those years having a dry spring. Flax with its shallow rooting system was particularly prone to dry soils in the early stages of growth and would also suffer from increased competition with the deeper rooted weeds.

By the time these figures were recorded the cultivation of both hemp and flax was restricted to the 13 parishes around Bridport. Even here there was some differentiation which is illustrated by the figures for 1794; over 50% of the hemp was grown in Bradpole and Loders, in fields which had been unofficially enclosed and which seems to have been advantageous to the culture of hemp. Symondsbury accounted for 17% of the flax grown, and within that parish flax production centred on Broadoak, while Netherbury accounted for another 17%.

With productivity of the crops being around 34 stones per acre the 1794 figures translate to some 110 acres of hemp and 410 acres of flax being grown in Dorset. Of that

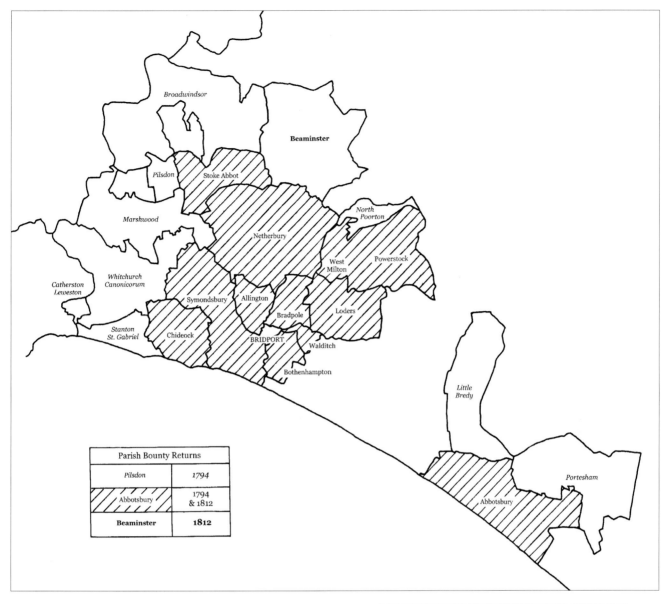

The distribution of the production of hemp and flax, based on the bounty returns of 1794 and Stevenson's Agriculture of Dorset (1812). Between the two dates the area under these crops was reduced significantly. As more of the demand was met by imports through Bridport Harbour the growth of hemp and flax was increasingly centred on Bridport.

1783-90 Bridport	Hemp (tons)	Flax (tons)
Locally grown	451	1487
Imported	2339	2051

Table 2. The origin of flax and hemp used in Bridport between 1783 and 1790.

total, Bradpole and Loders grew around 50-60 acres of hemp, while Symondsbury grew about 100 acres of flax.

By 1805 William Fowler noted that large amounts of hemp and flax were being grown in this area along with East and North Devon and Somerset. He gives figures of 1,006 tons of hemp and 500 tons of flax. These figures equate to 4,500 acres of hemp and 2,300 acres of flax and contrast with figures of 400 - 500 acres of hemp and ten times that amount of flax being grown in Dorset around the same time, given in Stevenson's *Agriculture of Dorset* (1812). According to Fowler the crops gave a return of around £20 per acre but he commented that the bounty, at 4d per stone for hemp and 3d for flax, had not materially increased the size of the crop.

However by this time the locally produced crops had been overtaken by imports from Russia and the continent, as seen in Table 2.

Demand had begun to outstrip production in the 15th century and as a result hemp and flax had to be imported. Nationally the figures for flax show that 495 tons were imported in 1695 and this had increased to 2,576 tons from Russia alone in 1765.

During the 19th century the decline in local production of flax and hemp continued so that by the early 20th century none was being produced in the Bridport area. With the demands of two World Wars some cultivation was again undertaken but it did not survive long into the peace that followed the end of the Second World War in 1945.

Unpacking the raw hemp, probably at Pymore in the 1940s. The stems had already been crushed. It was then taken to be hackled before being spun into yarn.

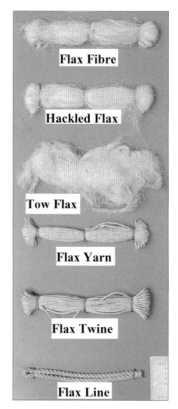

Flax seen at different stages in the production sequence. From top to bottom-
1) Raw flax fibres before any treatment.
2) The flax is then hackled to product line, or hackled, flax.
3) Tow flax is the flax left in the hackles after combing.
4) Flax yarn, produced from spinning the flax.
5) Flax twine, produced by spinning strands of yarn together.
6) Flax line, produced by spinning strands of twine together.

Loders Mill in 2009, this is an example of a bolling mill where the hemp stems were crushed by water-powered hammers. Gradually their work was taken over by roller mills located in the factory mills.

PROCESSING THE RAW MATERIAL

Right up to the mid-19th century the Bridport textile manufacture was little more than a cottage-based industry, with only flax spinning mechanised. In the 1850s nearly all the processes were mechanised and moved into the factories, leaving the spinning walks to be turned into gardens and the workshops into sheds. Mechanised braiding was only suited to long nets, so the smaller and more complex shapes continued to be handmade by female outworkers in Bridport and the surrounding villages.

Retting. In order to facilitate the removal of the fibres from the stem the harvested plants were allowed to undergo partial decomposition. In **dew retting** the plants were placed in thin layers on grass and the dew allowed to assist the fungal decay, a process which took around 20 days. An alternative, rarely used in the Bridport area in the late 18th and early 19th centuries, was **pond retting** where the plants were placed in slow moving water for around 15 days.

Scaling was the stripping of the hemp or flax from the remainder of the stem and was carried out by women and children. The scalings were collected and burnt and the ash spread on the fields.

Bolling or breaking. The stems of the plants had then to be broken to help remove the unwanted woody parts. This process was mechanised from an early date by using the power of the water wheel. Most mills had bolling machinery, that at West Mill, Bridport dated from 1735. The water wheel tripped a number of stamps which hit the stems thus

A traditional spinning walk, part of a series of murals painted by Francis Newbery for Bridport Borough Council in the 1920s. They can be seen in the Town Hall.

breaking them while the elasticity in the fibres prevented them from being torn. The stems were placed under the stamps by young boys who had to be agile enough to get the work done and not crush their hands.

During the 19th century ribbed wooden rollers began to take over from the stamps in the bolling mills providing a more controlled means of breaking the stems.

Scutching. The woody part, having been broken, had to be removed. This was achieved by an action akin to flailing in which a wooden baton, attached by a short chain to a handle, was beaten over the stems. This provided much needed winter employment for both men and women who were paid 4d to 6d per day. This process was mechanised locally in 1803 by Richard Roberts of Burton Bradstock, but the machinery was dangerous and many people lost their fingers.

The flax and hemp imported from Russia had already undergone this preliminary treatment.

Spinning walks were the working units for the family and were designed to allow the processing of the raw material. At the bottom of the walk was the turnhouse which consisted of the wheel-house where the spinning wheels were housed while above this was the combing shop.

The walk ran up to the family's house and would be up to 100m long. It was often tree-lined, providing attachment for the skirders which supported the spun yarn and shade for the spinners in summer.

Hackling. The raw fibre consisted of fibre cells of different length and alignments. The task of the hackler was to produce a sliver with the fibres separated and all aligned in the same direction. Hackling was also called dressing or combing, the latter name deriving from the process itself.

A hand of raw fibre was taken and thrown onto the hackle, a wooden board with numerous upturned pins sticking out. The fibre was then drawn back though the pins, a process which was repeated a number of times. To start with coarse hackles were used before progressing through those with finer pins. In this way the fibres were 'combed' out in one direction. Those remaining in the hand being the better 'line' fibres while those left in the hackles were the shorter 'tow' fibres used for coarser yarns.

Spinning converted the weak fibres into a stronger yarn by giving them both overlap and twist, thus increasing the friction between them. The yarn was then spun into twine made up of two or more strands of yarn.

The spinning wheel stood at the bottom of the walk and was attached to the framework of the turnhouse. It consisted of a wheel to which was attached a pole handle whose other end was placed through a hole in a piece of wood. The rate of turning could be altered by gripping the handle nearer or further from the wheel.

Reg Perrott hackling hemp at Pymore Mill, c1950. This was piece work and Reg worked here part time. He kept a fishing boat at the Harbour, where he was to be found when not at Pymore.

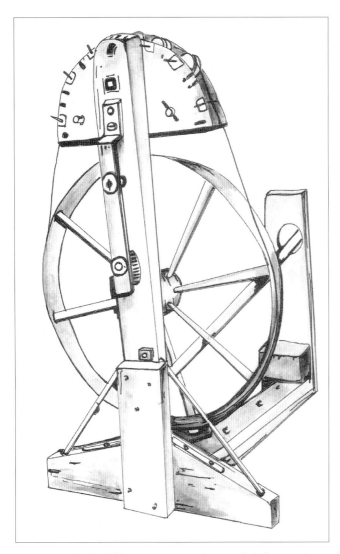

A spinning wheel. Children as young as six spent their days turning the wheel on the command of the spinners. The speed of the wheel could be altered by changing the position of the hands on the pole, which runs from the wheel to the hole in the backboard. The further they were from the wheel the faster the wheel turned.

The wheel turners were children who started at six years of age and worked from seven in the morning to six at night, for which they would be paid 6d per week in 1830.

The spinners, the older girls and women, carried the prepared fibre in bunches around their waist, attaching a portion to a hook on the spinning wheel. As the wheel turner began spinning the wheel, the spinners started walking backwards, letting out the fibre as they went. Every so often the spun yarn was hooked over the skirders to keep it from the ground.

The yarn produced would sometimes be knotted together and the spinner walked back down the way spinning this knotted yarn into a strand of twine, which could be used for braiding straight away, otherwise it was taken off and stored for further use.

It should be remembered that there were numerous types of twine, each suited to a particular function be it for weaving, shoe thread, braiding or one of the many different types of fishing line. It was said the spinners could recognise their own yarn from that of other spinners.

Line Walk at Rendall and Coombs West Allington works. The cart is in the process of being pushed along the length of the walk paying out the strands that will make up the line. Henry Rendall is credited with inventing the modern linewalk.

Lines and ropes were made by a variation of the basic spinning process. Although carried out in a line or rope walk there was little outward difference between the spinning way and rope walk.

Longfellow's contemporary poem *The Ropewalk* provides us with a picture of the ropewalk:

In that building, long and low,
With its windows all a-row,
Like the port-holes of a hulk,
Human spiders spin and spin,
Backward down their threads so thin
Dropping, each a hempen bulk.
At each end, an open door:
Squares of sunshine on the floor
Light the long and dusky lane;
And the whirring of a wheel,
Dull and drowsy, makes me feel
All its spokes are in my brain.

Both rope and lines were made by spinning strands of twine together, the main difference between the two being size and use. Lines were usually smaller and largely intended for fishing and were the main product after much of the rope-making moved to the naval dockyards. After which the ropes made in Bridport were for local use, typically for the ships being built at the harbour.

At the bottom of the walk was a revolving hook or sledge affixed to a wall or post. A spike was inserted to stop it revolving at the start of the laying of the rope or line. The warping boy placed three strands of twine on the hook and the other ends to different hooks on the rope jack, a type of spinning wheel of heavier construction and placed on wheels. A grooved wooden top was placed between the strands and against the sledge. The rope maker then turned the jack in the opposite direction to the twist in the twine, which caused the twine to shorten and moved the rope jack forward. Weights were added to the jack to increase the

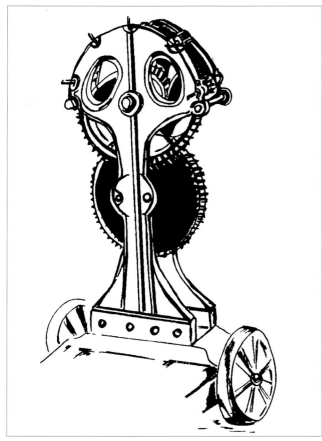

Rope Jack, the yarn was attached to the hooks on the jack and to a hook on the wall. The yarns strands were placed in the grooved 'top'. The turning of the jack imposed a twist to the yarn. When the right amount of twist had been added the hook on the wall was released. The strands of the rope became entwined as the 'top' was moved up the walk.

tension needed for different types of rope.

After imparting the requisite amount of twist the spike was removed from the sledge and the rope maker moved up the walk pushing the top as he went. Behind the top the strands, now free to turn, wrapped themselves around each other forming the rope. The rope jack continued to be turned during this operation to ensure the right amount of twist remained in the strands.

The ropes and lines could then be tarred or tanned to increase their working life, although this tended to make them more brittle.

Braiding was largely done by outworkers in the local villages, helping to supplement the meagre agricultural wages. Over the years each village specialised in producing certain types of net. Although much reduced from the peak some braiding is still carried out at home in order to make the nets a machine cannot handle.

In many ways braiding is much like knitting, as the net can be increased or decreased in size as it is produced. The braiding needle is designed so that it carries the twine and was loaded by the children ready for the braider to use. In nets each mesh is knotted into position, either by the fisherman's knot or the Bridport knot, both forms of sheet bend. The latter is made in one movement by looping the braiding needle around the fingers of the left hand and has

Above Pricilla Hodder braiding outside her cottage at Eype in about 1900. This scene was a feature of the Bridport area for centuries, being remarked upon by the Swedish writer Angerstein on his travels though West Dorset in the 1750s.

Below Mrs Judy Greening, in the background, making a pig net and Mrs May Poole a rick net behind their homes in Loders in the late 1940s. Between them lies the 'Bridport Cross' or swifter, which they used to refill their braiding needles. Outworkers were an essential part of the netmaking workforce.

the advantage that the knot lies flat thus reducing slippage. The gauge of the mesh is checked by the lace or measuring stick.

Weaving. While ropes and nets are most associated with Bridport, the town's merchants were exporting canvas to the eastern USA in the 18th century and the making of sailcloth remained a major industry until the days of sail were over. Whilst sailcloth normally used flax, the coarser hemp fibre was being used to make sacks, bags and webs.

Weaving was either contracted out to individual hand-loom weavers, often as far away as Beaminster, or it was carried out in weaving sheds owned by the merchant,

This second of Francis Newbery's Town Hall murals in the book shows a braiding scene. The braider by the door is making a fishing net, the meshes of which were diamond shaped.

such as those that were to be found in Wykes Court and 18 South Street. The only possible site remaining is the brick building occupied by Oxenbury's in St. Michael's Lane, with its large upper floor windows typical of weaving shops.

Traditions. As with other industries, the Bridport industry had its own traditions and celebrations.

Celebrations to mark the feast day of Queen Catherine, the patron saint of ropemakers, took place on the 25th of November. In 1856 the *Bridport News* records the Pymore Mill Company treating their flax and hemp dressers to a meal of roast beef and bread, while the Dolphin was the venue for those of Bridport.

The 'Lantern Festival' was held in the first week of October and marked the lighting of the spinning walk for the winter, enabling work to be carried on into the evening. Even so some walks were so dark that it was necessary to use candles all year around, these being carried on the shoulders of the spinners.

On Pancake Day the spinners received 3d and the wheel turners 1 ½ d, while at Whitsun the workers ate treacle rolls.

Mrs Olive Legg braiding in her cottage at Loders in 1948. The photograph shows the tools of her trade. The braiding needle is in her right hand. The swifter, seen on the table, was used to fill the braiding needle. The 'lace' or measuring stick, seen in her left hand, was used to ensure that the mesh was of the right size. The name derives from its use when lace was knotted rather than woven.

TWO

The Bridport Story

THE NINTH CENTURY TO 1740

Bridport was one of the fortified burgs established in the late 9th century by King Alfred. In addition to being a place of refuge, it was also an administrative and economic centre from the outset. The Saxon burg covered a surprisingly small area of around 25 hectares, while of the surrounding parishes many occupied well over 1,000 hectares. As a result the new burg was dependent on these parishes for food and timber. This meant that it had to develop an economy able to provide goods or money in exchange for its own needs. In other words a craft-based trading structure had to be established.

The cultivation of hemp had increased from the mid-9th century and by 888 the high quality of English rope was already being noted. Here was a commercial activity suited to Bridport. The local soils and climate were ideal. There were good transport routes, either over the dry chalk ridgeways to the east or by sea. The exporting of the finished ropes by sea led in due course to the next logical step, that of making ships' ropes and cables and the weaving of sailcloth.

The town was clearly prospering, a mint had been established in the mid-10th century and the level of taxation seen in the Domesday Book shows that this prosperity continued into the next century.

The first documentary evidence of the nascent industry dates from 1211 when the Pipe Rolls for Somerset and Dorset include the order for 3,000 Dorset weights of hempen thread. Just two years later King John ordered:

'to be caused to be made at Bridport, night and day, as many ropes for ships both large and small cables as you can, and twisted yarns for cordage for ballistae.'

This was presumably in advance of the raid on the fleet of King Philip of France by the English fleet led by the Earl of Salisbury.

Clearly the town had already gained a reputation for producing high quality hemp ropes and yarns. This new prosperity fostered the medieval expansion of the town in the mid-13th century. Hitherto Bridport had been restricted to the Saxon burg centred on St. Mary's Church. By 1240 a new alignment to the north had developed along what is now East and West Streets, with three chapels soon established along this new road. Reported as one of the towns noted for cord and hempen fabrics, Bridport's increased wealth resulted in the granting of its first Charter in 1253 by Henry III, by which time the town included a small Jewish community.

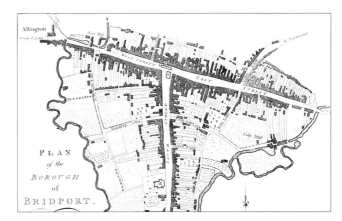

John Hutchin's map from his *History of Dorset* shows Bridport as it was in 1777. The original Saxon town was centred on St. Mary's Church in South Street. East and West Street were part of the 13th century expansion of the town.

It was at this time that the shape of the town was set. The wide streets, although used for the drying of yarns, were probably the result of the market shambles that were to be found in the middle of the streets. Those in East and West Streets survived until the late 18th century, when the new Town Hall was constructed. Even today, in the gardens of East Street, can be seen the echo of the long spinning walks that were to be found behind most of the town's houses and have long since been out of use.

Further evidence for the demand of Bridport's hemp and ropes is seen late in the 13th century. In 1266 hemp was sent to furnish a siege engine at Kenilworth and in 1276 there was a dispute concerning non-delivery of ropes to Plympton.

The 14th century gives us our first insight into the names behind the industry, their products and wealth. In 1315 the town's leading merchant was William Bume, whose goods were valued at £9, among which were sailcloth, girth webs and twine valued at 40s as well as rope, flax and hemp to the value of another 40s; the same textiles that were being made centuries later. The absence of any mention of nets is probably explained by their being made by the fishermen for their own use.

This series of taxation returns also lets us see the vicissitudes of the market: just four years later Bume was worth only 25s, although this had increased by 1323 to £3. By now the wealthiest person was Edward Renaud whose goods were valued at £8. Just as happened in later years there were good and bad years in the industry. The tax return of 1315 shows that out of 180 burgesses only 44 were able to pay the tax levy of 6.67%, while four years

Bridport Coat of Arms was first given in 1623. It shows three spinning 'cogs', indicating the importance of industry to the town's economy.

later only 67 could pay the 10% rate being levied.

The importance of the textile industry to the town can also be gauged by the municipal gifts made by the Borough to those they wished to influence. These included webs, reins, horse nets and girths. At the same time many assessments and inventories include cords and yarns, while the Bailiff's accounts record instances of the forfeit of yarn and hemp.

Another instance of the industry's importance is the incorporation of the three 'cogs' or hooks used in ropemaking into the town's seal, the first mention of which is in the 17th century.

At this time the organisation of the industry centred on the factors, such as William Bume. They purchased the hemp and flax from the farmers and sent it out to the artisans, who worked it up into the yarn. Finally it was delivered to the rope makers or weavers to be made into a finished product, before being returned to the factor for marketing.

In 1322 six ropers were sent to Newcastle to instruct the local merchants in the arts of ropemaking. In was no coincidence that ropes were being introduced into the coal mines of County Durham a few years later.

As trade increased it came under the influence of the Craft Guild who controlled the market in medieval times. The master rope maker owned the tools and materials and received the income from the sales, but much of the work was done by apprentices who, like the orphan John

Baillie in 1683, were bound to the master rope maker, in this case John Keich, from the age of about seven until they were 21 years old. In return they were given their board and lodging and taught the trade. After training the apprentice became a journeyman who was paid for his work.

In 1348 and 1349 the Black Death swept through Dorset, following its arrival in Britain by a ship that had docked in Weymouth. Bridport was not immune, and perhaps a third of its population succumbed to the plague, including William Bume. Trade gradually recovered, and a 14th century cordage account for the King's Navy gives a further insight into the industry. The Navy then numbered around 20 ships, for which Bridport ropemakers provided the majority of the cordage.

1361	£165	hempen thread at Bridport for the King's ships
1363	£81	for black and white thread at Bridport
1364	£70	for Robert Budden and Associates at Bridport

Table 3. Thread provided from Bridport for the King's ships in the 1360s. Black thread had been tarred while white thread was the natural, untreated colour.

It also gives the names of various merchants, including William Hychecoke, Edward Coterich and John Tracey. The use of the word 'Associates' suggests that they were representatives of the Ropemakers Guild in Bridport. The reappearance of the plague in Bridport during 1361 claimed the lives of Hychecoke and Coterich, although Tracey survived until 1384. It would seem that Robert Budden took over the position of representing the Guild by 1364.

Table 4, shown at the foot of the page, lists ropes marketed in three types – white, bastard and black. The last named was tarred and the cheapest, because the tar affected the quality of the rope. Bastard rope was a mixture of white and black, whilst pure white thread was the most expensive and the best quality. On shipping, white rope was used for anchor cables and hawsers, bastard for hawsers, and black cord for hauliers and shrouds.

The following century however saw the end of

Table 4. The expenses paid in 1361 for thread provided from Bridport. £1 in 1361 is worth £342 today, based on the retail price index.

Expenses to William Hychecock, John Tracy, Edward Coterich and Associates at Bridport					
1361	cost per 100lb	rope (lb)	cost of rope	thread (lb)	Total (lb)
White thread	32/-	14,912	£238 11s 2d	2,400	17,312
Bastard thread	20/-	18,812	£188 3s 9d	3,908	22,730
Black thread	10/-	2,700	£ 13 10s 0d	400	3,100
			£440 4s 11d		43,142
					(19.26 tons)

Bridport's near monopoly in supplying the King's Navy, though such was the quality of Bridport cordage that the local ropemakers were little affected. It was the 16th century that saw significant changes, for when Henry VIII became king in 1509 his Navy consisted of only five warships. He was determined to increase the fleet lest the French threaten invasion or attacks on coastal towns, and by his death in 1547 the Navy could put 52 warships to sea. Combined with the increasing needs of the merchant service, the demand for hemp outstripped production. In 1533 Henry VIII passed an Act of Parliament requiring that for every 60 acres of arable land a ¼ acre of hemp should also be grown.

The increased demand for hemp may be the reason for the 1530 Act of Parliament ordering all the hemp grown within five miles of Bridport to be sold at Bridport Market. This has been taken as an illustration of Bridport's monopoly in providing the cordage for the Navy. Another interpretation is that it protected the local industry from competitors who were buying up the crops and manufacturing the ropes elsewhere. It ensured that Bridport had first choice of the hemp grown on the land most suited without having to add additional transport costs to the final price. Around the same time a set of weights was leased to an official of the market, whose duties also included keeping an accurate record of all the hemp grown within the five mile limit.

In 1563 Elizabeth I modified the 1533 Act to ensure that for every 60 acres a full acre of hemp had to be grown. While her Navy, at just 27 ships, was smaller than that of Henry VIII, she relied in times of trouble on armed merchantmen or privateers.

When the traveller John Leland visited Bridport in 1542 he described it as a fine large town. He noted its lack of a harbour, but did think there was a suitable site for one to the south of the town. Clearly the River Brit was navigable from where it entered the sea, but by 1594 it had almost become blocked with sand, causing economic difficulties by reducing commerce and trade. The need to reverse the town's fortunes was one of the main reasons for applying successfully to Elizabeth I for a new Charter, allowing an additional market day and three additional fairs.

By this time the town was also becoming famous for another of its products – the hangman's rope, which was often called 'the Bridport Dagger'.

The bulky nature of the ropes and cables meant that they were expensive to transport to the naval dockyards. The establishment, in the early 17th century, of ropewalks at Woolwich and Portsmouth dockyards meant that Bridport could no longer compete economically and removed, at a stroke, a major source of the town's wealth.

But as one door closed so another opened. The year 1600 had seen the setting up of the East India Company, which in turn was followed by the gradual development of overseas trade. Bridport was ideally placed to supply the rigging and sailcloth needed. Indeed the description

The Salt House at Bridport Harbour used for storing salt for curing fish on the voyage back from Newfoundland.

of Bridport given by Michael Drayton in his epic topographical poem of 1612, *Poly-Olbion,* shows that the town's cordage was still highly regarded:

'Bert-port which hath gain'd
That praise from every place, and worthilie obtain'd,
Our cordage from her store, and cables should be made,'

Of greater significance to Bridport was the discovery of the Newfoundland fishery. Although the fishery was initially exploited by other nations, by the late 18th century, only the English remained. These fishermen, who came from the counties of Devon, Somerset and Dorset, initially returned home after the end of each season, which started in the early summer. Over time, however, colonies were established on the coastal fringes with each one being home to a specific group of fishermen, those from Dorset inhabited Trinity and Bonavista Bays.

The English fishermen concentrated on the inshore fisheries, using lines to catch cod. The knowledge of the fishery took several years to acquire, as it required an intimate knowledge of the waters as well as the migration patterns of the cod, from their off-shore feeding grounds to the breeding grounds.

They also developed a new way of preserving fish by salting, washing and drying them. The outcome was what became known as the triangular trade. Every spring the West Country fishing fleet headed west across the Atlantic, their holds laden with good and supplies for the settlers. The dried cod catch was then either shipped to the Caribbean for the slaves on the plantations, or – more commonly – to Catholic Europe (Portugal, Spain, Italy) from where the fleet returned home with either Caribbean rum and sugar or Mediterranean wine, olive oil and dried fruit. The Salt House at Bridport Harbour stands as a reminder of this trade, for it was here that salt was stored before the annual voyage to Newfoundland.

The development of the fishery, which peaked in the 1880s, saw Bridport merchants move away from ropes and sailcloth to develop the manufacture of fishing lines and nets. It was this trade that was to shape Bridport's fortunes through the next two centuries. Every March,

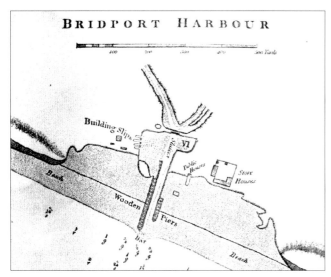

The 1787 map of the harbour shows 'Good's' warehouse next to the Bridport Arms public house. Both were built soon after the completion of the harbour in the 1740s. Curiously both are measured in 'goads', an archaic unit of length.

until the late 1880s, one or more ships sailed from Bridport Harbour carrying the lines, twine and nets needed by the fishermen. While the firm of Joseph Gundry figures large in this export the Hounsells were also involved.

1740 – 1790

Early 18th century Bridport was recorded by two travellers. Thomas Cox (1720) in his *Magna Britannica* depicts a town which has lost its monopoly but was still in vogue for hemp and flax manufactures. Around the same time

Daniel Defoe in his *Tour of the Whole Island of Great Britain* was depicting the Corporation as poor with the loss of the hemp and flax manufacture, the result of the harbour being closed. This closure of the anchorage and loss of the piers is mentioned in a petition to Parliament in 1721. The provision of a suitable harbour was central to Bridport's future development.

The River Brit reaches the sea at West Bay, some 1½ miles to the south of Bridport and passing through a shingle ridge or storm beach, to the east and west of which lie cliffs. Over time the gap in the ridge became blocked by sand and gravel, causing the river mouth to migrate to the eastern end of the ridge. A similar process happened at Seaford, East Sussex, where in 1533 an artificial cut was made at the western end of the ridge to let the River Ouse exit to the sea, the new harbour being named Newhaven.

It would seem likely that a similar artificial cut was made at Bridport Harbour at some time in the past. As there is no evidence for a true harbour until the 18th century it is likely that this early 'harbour' was no more than a pair of piers or groynes forming a channel through the shingle ridge by which ships could reach the River Brit.

However these piers did not prevent the accumulation of sediment blocking the channel. With the small ships in use at Bridport at this time it may not have been a problem but as ships became larger access to the haven

The Whit Tuesday Fair, Bridport Harbour, 1860. As well as the Bridport Arms and 'Goods's' warehouse, Elias Cox's boatbuilding yard and slip are visible top right. Note how much erosion of the cliff has taken place over the last 150 years.

would have been prevented. The frequent reports of the blocking of the haven by sand and shingle shows that the town's economy was being affected and that a longer lasting solution had to be found. The Town's Charter of 1594 granted the right to have additional markets and fairs, the profits from which belonged to the Bailiffs and Burgesses, and was one attempt to find alternative income to help restore the haven. While further attempts were made in the 17th century these were to no avail.

In 1721 a second petition from the town resulted in an Act of Parliament for the building of a harbour but it was not until 1740 that a working harbour was finally completed. Sluices were used at the high spring tides to scour the accumulated sand and shingle from the harbour, a method still being used today. At last Bridport had a proper facility by which goods could be transported both nationally and internationally and between 1743 and 1753 some 24 ships berthed there each year.

The effect of the new harbour on the town can be seen by the accounts of three travellers. In 1750 Richard Pococke in his *Travels through England* reported that the town was the site of great manufactures in twine, cables, sailcloth and coarse cloths. Just three years later the Swedish writer, Reinhold Angerstein, in his *Illustrated Travel Diary* reported on the large trade in cordage, sailcloth, nets and lines. He noted that in all the cottages in the surrounding villages women were spinning twine and braiding nets. He also records the use of water powered stamps for breaking hemp – a bolling mill, one of which was in operation at West Mill, Bridport in the 1730s. John Hutchins was researching for his *History and Antiquities of the County of Dorset* around the same time and he commented that the staple trade was in the making of net, seines and other hemp manufactures.

In 1793 John Claridge in his *General View of Agriculture in the County of Dorset* noted that Bridport manufactured all sorts of twine, thread, string and cordage. From the first named were made nets, for use

A 19th century view of the harbour. Each March, one or more ships set sail for Newfoundland, carrying nets and lines for the communities there. The last direct voyage sailed in 1885.

both in Newfoundland and locally. Sailcloth, tarpaulins, sacking and bags were also manufactured.

The decline in West Dorset's woollen cloth industry in the late 18th century produced a pool of weavers who could now use their looms for making sailcloth which was then fast becoming a major manufacture in Bridport.

By the end of the 18th century the number of ships using the harbour annually had risen to 125, a clear sign of the prosperity of the staple trade, which in no small part was due to the improved harbour. This increase in imports was helped by the manufacturers insisting that locally grown flax should be only 1/3rd of the total amount needed.

Between 1777 and 1784 hemp was imported directly by the merchants through Bridport Harbour after which it was normal practice for factors to take over the

At 'Good's' Warehouse, dating from the 1750s, the ground floor has a vaulted ceiling which supports the upper floors. Much of the warehouse's walls were made from Blue Lias stone, brought in from Lyme Regis, rather than the local Bothenhampton stone.

Located on the property of John Ewens, this was probably used as a weaving shop during the first half of the 19th century. The large upper floor windows provided the light needed by the weavers. The use of English bond, with its alternate layers of header and stretcher bricks is rarely seen in Bridport.

importing. The result of this activity was the construction of warehousing at the harbour, the first of which was that currently known as 'Good's Yard'. The earliest surviving lease refers to 1775 but the building is likely to have been earlier as it and the nearby Bridport Arms, whose leases date back to 1750, were measured in 'goads' rather than in feet and yards.

The organisation of the industry was still based around the merchants, who bought the flax and hemp and marketed the final products. Manufacture was carried out in the spinning ways, the family-based working units, where the men prepared and dressed the raw material and the women spun the yarns using spinning wheels operated by children. The additional preparation needed by the sailcloth manufacturers meant that it became centred around the 'yarn bartons', a cluster of buildings including the bleaching or 'bucking' house, a combing house and warehousing. Joseph Gundry's yarn barton was in St. Michael's Lane and can be seen in the 1777 map of Bridport, as can that of the Tucker family a little to the south.

Whilst weaving was often carried out in the outworkers homes, which could be as far away as Beaminster, a number of weaving shops were set up in Bridport and these could be seen in Stake Lane, behind St. John's, and near the Ropewalks where John Ewens' shop was located. Currently Oxenbury's repair shop in St. Michael's Lane is the only possible survivor of these once numerous buildings.

The names of the manufacturers can be seen in the directories and insurance records of the late 18th century. Based on their stock and utensils valuation the most important manufacturer was Joseph Gundry and Co., twine spinners and sailcloth makers, who had considerable property at The Court and in St. Michael's Lane and were valued around £2,000, peaking at £2,500 in 1778. Robert Gummer and William Stone ran them close, for in 1779 their valuation was for £1,750, increasing to £2,950 four years later. They were twine spinners, sailcloth makers and carpet weavers with premises centred in Pink Mead, behind 103/5, East Street, and with a yarn barton at Walditch.

The third merchant was George Golding. In 1780 his own valuation was for £1,800, whilst in partnership with Nicholas and John Bools, as twine spinners, net makers and sailcloth manufacturers, he had a share in an additional £1,000 worth of stock and utensils. William Fowler was another sailcloth manufacturer and whose stock was valued at £1,000 in 1785. Other insurances include the Tucker and the Hounsell families, names to be famous in later years but their businesses at this time were significantly smaller.

In all cases the valuations increase from the 1770s into the 1780s, showing the healthy state of the industry as the century closed.

1790 – 1860
THE MARCH OF MECHANISATION

Until 1790 the only machine in operation was the bolling mill which had been added to many corn and grist mills during the 18th century. In that year Matthew Murray, of the Leeds firm of Marshall and Co., patented a flax spinning machine and just four years later one was built in West Dorset. Built not in Bridport but at Burton Bradstock, the three storey mill was owned and operated by Richard Roberts who used the yarn to make all manner of linen woven goods, including sailcloth. In 1803 he built the first swingling or scutching mill in the area, adjacent to the Grove flour and grist mill.

Burton Bradstock Tithe Map of 1843 showing the Burton Spinning Mill straddling the mill leat between fields 6 and 7.

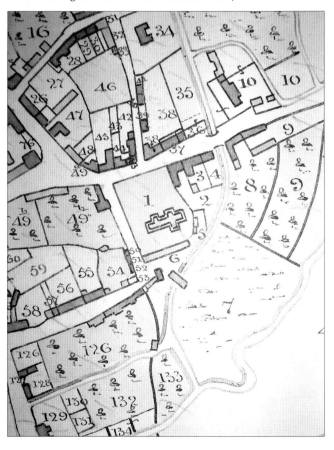

It was not until 1800 that Bridport had its first flax spinning mill, the product of a partnership between four Bridport merchants. In 1790 William Fowler had purchased the freehold of Pymore Mill, a grist and oil mill on the River Brit, just to the north of the town. In 1799 he formed a partnership with fellow merchants Joseph Gundry and Joseph Gundry Downe, the two partners of Joseph Gundry and Co., and Samuel Gundry. The new company traded as the Pymore Mill Company, producing its first twines early the next year.

The third mill, the Bridport Flax Spinning Mill or Ewens and Golding's Mill, was built at the junction of the Rivers Symene and Brit by John Golding in 1804, who formed a partnership with John Ewens shortly afterwards. Both partners were sailcloth manufacturers in their own right and this gave them access to the twine needed to compete with the other manufacturers.

In 1806 Joseph Gundry and Joseph Gundry Downe, again in partnership with Samuel Gundry, built Slape Mill, on the River Brit between Netherbury and Pymore. This was a swingling and flax dressing mill and in 1808 Thomas Fox of Beaminster and Henry Saunders of Bridport were added to the partnership. Unfortunately the mill burnt down in 1814 and was not rebuilt until the 1830s.

The increased production of sailcloth allowed by these spinning mills complemented that of nets and lines and together formed the bulk of the goods produced by the Bridport manufacturers, although sackcloth and webbing were also being produced in significant amounts. In 1802 unsuccessful trials using Canadian Hemp were made in an attempt to increase supply and by 1806 such was the demand for canvas that delays of several weeks were experienced in completing the customer's orders.

By the 1790s as well as supplying the south western counties and other areas of the UK there was a significant amount of export trade with North America. The position was summed up by William Fowler in a letter dated 1805.

'We have extensive manufactories of hemp and flax into fishing lines and twines for nets of all descriptions for the use of the fisheries, at Newfoundland, Nova

Above Aerial view of Pymore Mill c. 1952: this should be compared to the 1835 and 1887 plans on pages oo and oo. The original mill, by the river, has been extended to the east. The newer spinning and winding mills are seen to the north east of these. Allotments are on the site of the lower reservoir. The Mill manager's house is the double eaved building opposite the older spinning mill.

Priory Mill and Ewens and Goldings Mill in about 1860. The former, the nearer of the mills in this historic but sadly poor quality photograph, was the first purpose built steam powered spinning mill in Bridport. Ewens and Goldings Mill was the first water powered spinning mill. Note a treeless Colmers Hill in the distance between the two mills.

Scotia, Canada and the West Indies and in general for all our colonies and settlements abroad where there are fisheries as well as for those on our own coast and great quantities of these are annually exported to the U.S. of America'
'The manufacture of sailcloth and sailcloth twine, both for the Navy and Merchant service, sackings for the bags etc. are very considerable.'
'At present we have but one person in the ropemaking business (excluding fixing seines and nets) and what he does is wholly for the Merchant service'.

This golden period for the Bridport manufacturers led to some diversification. The profits being made were put to work by the opening of private banks in the town. In 1791 the Bridport Bank was opened by Joseph Gundry,

Above A Bridport Bank £1 note issued in September 1815. Joseph Gundry was a partner from the time the bank opened in 1791 until his death in 1823. Samuel Gundry, who had been a partner for many years, then became the senior partner until bankruptcy forced the bank to close in 1847.

Below Ewens and Gundry's warehouse at Bridport Harbour. The land for this was leased from the Pitt Rivers estate in 1770 by Samuel Cox, sailcloth manufacturer of Beaminster. In 1792 he sold the land to Kenway and Downe who built the warehouse two years later. Ewens and Gundry took over in 1797. A number of surviving warehouse ledgers, dating from 1805 to 1883, are held by Bridport Museum.

Samuel Downe, Joseph Pike and Samuel Farwell. In the early 1800s William Fowler opened the Dorsetshire Bank in partnership with William Good.

In order to accommodate the orders increasing amounts hemp and flax had to be imported via Bridport Harbour. Between 1783 and 1790, on average, 337 tons of Hemp and 293 tons of flax were imported annually, and by 1806 this had increased by between 25 and 33%. At the harbour a series of new warehouses were built to accommodate the increased trade. The first was built in 1794, behind the current George Hotel, to be followed by others along George Street in the next decade.

In 1819 an Act of Parliament was obtained to build a new road to the Harbour, branching off the Burton Road where the Crown Roundabout now lies. With trade developing the opportunity was taken to improve the harbour and this was undertaken by Francis Giles in 1825, creating the harbour basin that is still being used to day, although the piers have recently undergone major alterations.

Many of the ships serving Bridport Harbour were owned by partnerships of local merchants. Often seen as competitors, they co-operated here as they did in the large investments such as spinning mills. Ships sailed from its harbour to Cornwall with cargoes of herring, mackerel and pilchard nets, the hemp for which was always Bridport grown, and from 1811 Bridport herring nets were being sold to Scottish fishermen.

While many of the ships served to transport the goods to other ports for onward transport there were regular voyages to Newfoundland, returning with salt cod. By 1809 Joseph Gundry and Co. were trying to establish a base in Liverpool to better serve the eastern seaboard of America, which was made difficult by the prejudice against Bridport products at the port. Development of foreign trade was not being helped by the war with France, which saw Gundry's ships sailing in a convoy with a Naval escort.

Land transport was provided by Russell's Waggons from their office at 28, East Street. They ran a thrice weekly carrier service between London and Exeter with onward connection to Cornwall. The reliability of this service meant that the reason for any delay greater than 30 minutes had to be explained to the partners.

The next innovation to be introduced was the use of steam power in the spinning mills. The mills needed a regular supply of water to ensure their efficient working and by the 1830s this could no longer be guaranteed. The Pymore Mill Company had already built an additional reservoir to counter the problem but this was only a partial solution. The final outcome was the installation of a steam engine at Pymore Mill where the 20hp engine supplied by the Neath Abbey Company supplemented the 30hp water wheel, providing the consistency of power

Bridport Harbour in 1928, the year in which the last cargo of hemp was landed.

Thomas Russell and Co. were carriers who ran a thrice weekly service between London and Exeter, via Bridport. While most of the nets and lines were sent by sea, both Richard Roberts of Burton Bradstock and William Fowler of Bridport used them on occasions.

T. RUSSELL & CO.
BELL, 12, FRIDAY STREET, CHEAPSIDE, LONDON.
WAGGONS TO AND FROM
SALISBURY, SHERBORNE, EXETER, PLYMOUTH, AND FALMOUTH.

required. Other steam engines were installed at Ewens and Golding's Mill and at the Burton Mill of Roberts and Darby around the same time.

Until 1839 all weaving was carried out by handloom weavers in cottages or weaving shops. In that year Whetham and Sons opened Priory Mill, a steam powered spinning and weaving mill, although the latter still used hand looms.

In 1857 the Bridport Railway opened, linking the town to the rest of the country. Its impact in relation to the textile industry is uncertain. The raw materials probably still came in by sea, at least to start with, and it was probably the same with finished products destined for export and to English coastal ports. What it did allow was the use of Somerset coal for the steam engines rather than Welsh or Durham coals. It also made easier the transport of new equipment for the developing factories. The boilers, steam engines and spinning machines were freighted in by rail from now on.

Further innovation did not take place for almost two decades, but when it arrived it dramatically changed the face of Bridport in many ways. The first arrival was the hemp spinning machinery, which marked the end of the spinning walks and the beginning of the factory mills, a move which was hastened by the introduction of cotton yarn, spun in the mills of Lancashire, for nets and lines.

At this stage the final movement of the hemp dressers into the new factories took place. This was done partly to get all workers under the same roof but also to provide less opportunity for theft of hemp and flax, there being an upsurge in this activity in the late 1850s.

The second innovation had been awaiting its call for many years. Braiding machines date back to the examples of Patterson of Musselburgh in the 1820s and are thought to have been introduced into Bridport in the 1840s. However these 'Jumper' looms needed strength to operate them and were the preserve of men, and since all the braiders in the 1851 census were women it must be assumed that there were few braiding machines in Bridport at this time. The expansion in the use of braiding machines needed two developments; firstly the increased abundance of yarn which could only come about from machine spinning of hemp, and helped by the introduction of cotton yarns. Secondly it needed the presence of experienced and innovative iron founders who were not seen in the town until this period.

The use of braiding machines, initially those of Henry Parris and Thomas Helyear, allowed large volumes of standard nets to be made, ideal for herring, mackerel and pilchard nets. Hand braiding continued as this was essential for shaped netting. Joseph Gundry and Co. followed a different path when it came to braiding machines. They entered this market in the early 1860s, being supplied by John Payne of the Perry Street Works, Chard. Whilst Payne was developing his models Gundry's workers were sent to Chard to operate them.

This period also saw the emergence of what were to

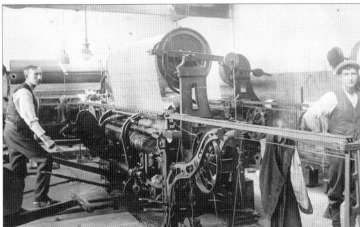

Top Bridport railway station in the late 19th century. The railway allowed the use of coal from Somerset, as well as making it easier to bring machinery to the mills.

Centre The Jumper braiding looms needed strength to operate them and were the preserve of men for many years. While looms such as these had been invented in the 1820s it was not until the 1860s that they became common in Bridport. The long extensions to either side of the loom carried the tensioning weights.

Bottom The carding shop, Pymore Mill, in about 1925. The raw fibres can be seen being fed into the left hand side of the machine. The carding machine prepared the fibres for spinning by separating and paralleling the fibres. This produced the slivers, which can be seen hanging over the edges of the stacked containers.

Nonconformity was a feature of many industrial towns and Bridport was no exception. The Unitarian chapel of 1794, one of many Nonconformist chapels to be found in Bridport, was built as a result of a split in the Nonconformist community who worshipped in the Barrack Street chapel of the 1740s.

The 1858 notice warning workers of the consequences of theft of material, following a spate of thefts. The hemp and flax was weighed out before being given to the hacklers. It was reweighed on its return to the merchants, less an allowance for wastage.

become, along with Joseph Gundry and Co., the major manufacturers of the 19th century. The Hounsell family quickly developed along two family lines, William Hounsell and Co. and Joseph Hounsell; the Tucker family again developed along two family lines, with Thomas Tucker specialising in the traditional sacking goods and Richard Tucker initially in sailcloth but later moving into nets and lines. Stephen Whetham started in partnership with the Tucker family before branching out on his own around 1830. Like Richard Tucker, the Ewens family started in sailcloth but moved over to produce lines and nets and a similar story is seen with John Pike Stephens and Co. who built Asker Mill in the 1830s.

While these formed the backbone of the manufacturers the spirit of the time led to the emergence of a new set of entrepreneurs, men who started off as artisan workers but by their efforts climbed up the business and social ladder. Robert Hounsell who started his net making factory in North Allington around 1850 was one of these, as was Henry Rendall who, on the retirement of his father, set up in partnership with Charles Coombs. Initially producing woven goods like sacking they later moved into lines and nets when the former market declined. What helped in this spirit of enterprise and self help was the fact that most of the Bridport manufacturers were Nonconformists.

Dissenters were prevented from civil and military service by the Test and Corporation Acts of the 17th century and, as a result, they made a virtue of science and practical skills which in turn encouraged economic development. Consequently Nonconformists were a major force in the Industrial Revolution and Bridport was no exception to this. However, and perhaps uniquely, the Bridport Nonconformists formed a majority of the Burgesses from 1720, in defiance of the 17th century Acts, and were in charge of running the town for over 100 years before the first elections, at which they were returned by the new electorate.

The economic position of the Bridport industry

through this period saw the town prosper but there were a series of downturns which had to be overcome. One such happened in 1816 when 1,200 of the 4,000 population were without employment and 1,770 were supported by the parish. Fluctuations in trade could happen quite quickly, as in 1829 when an abundance of work at the beginning of the year turned to a shortage just five months later. The 1830s and 1840s generally were good times with the manufacturers increasing wages in 1836 without being asked! In the mid-1840s while trade was not as brisk as before the town was still prosperous and had full employment, with production limited by the availability of the raw materials. However by 1852 the town was being described as at a low ebb with several houses shut up.

Trade was not helped in the late 1850s by a number of high profile thefts of materials. In 1858 Charles Foan was tried for the receiving of stolen hemp, while John Newberry absconded to the Army in India when his theft was discovered. The last of the major trials was in 1862 following the discovery by J. P. Stephens and Co., on the introduction of power looms to Asker Mill, that canvas and twine had been stolen over a number of years.

The *Bridport News* published accounts of these trials and these allow an insight into the operations at the various manufacturers. Each had their own peculiarities of manufacture which allowed an experienced eye to recognise the different twines. For example, Thomas Ewens and Son produced rope of three strands each of eight thread twine. The only other eight thread manufacturer was Joseph Gundry and Co. but the colour of this twine was different, while William Hounsell and Co. was the only firm to produce machine spun and polished twine.

They also showed that very little of the production was being used locally and was normally either for export or sold to customers many miles from Bridport. Herbert

Hounsell was selling cod-net twine to Chichester, Essex and Suffolk, while W. Hounsell and Co. sold their products at a distance no less than 70 miles from Bridport.

Thus by 1860 manufacturing in Bridport had changed from an outworker based to a factory based industry, powered by both steam and water. No longer were the walks the hive of activity of the '*human spiders*' of Longfellow. Instead there was heard the steady tramp of the workers to the factory in the early morning and their return in the late evening. The change was so complete that in 1861 the *Bridport News* was calling for the old walks to be turned into gardens.

Passages drawn from two sources give the impression of the conditions in a spinning mill. One is the *Bridport News* of 1861 and the other Eden Phillpots novel *The Spinners* of 1918. Both convey similar impressions of dust, noise and the never ceasing machine-driven work.

Bridport News
'You will observe that the atmosphere is of a very peculiar kind. Having in its composition constituents unknown to the air out-of-doors, it is visible. On being analysed, it would prove to be composed of nitrogen, oxygen, carbonic acid and hemp or flax dust in different proportions.

Happy is the man that hath a moustache which may catch the floating particles.'

'We read of a darkness that may be felt. Surely here is a noise that may almost be seen. The English language cannot do justice to a description of the pandemonium of noise.'

'Now, friend, are you tired? Of course your head aches and your throat is dusty. But before you go just observe how the power of the 60 horse power female friend (the steam engine) is distributed over the building.'

'The huge flywheel turns and you see that, by a simple arrangement of two or three wheels, several other shafts are made to partake of its motion. From these shafts others branch along the ceiling of each room and, from almost every foot of the ceiling shafts some band conveys motion to one machine of one kind or another.'

'(The bands) look almost as numerous as the threads in a cobweb and cross and re-cross each other in every conceivable way.'

The Spinners (Eden Phillpots, 1918)
'The general blurred effect in Raymond's mind was one of disagreeable sound, which made speech almost impossible. The din drove at him from above and below; and it was accompanied by a thousand unfamiliar movements of flying bands and wheels and squat machinery that convulsed and heaved and palpitated round him.'

'With swift and rhythmic flinging apart of her arms over her head, Sarah separated the stricks into three and laid them overlapping on the carriage. The ribbon thus created was never ending and wound away into the torture chambers of wheels and teeth within, while from the rear of the spreaders trickled out the newly created sliver. Great Scales hung beside Sarah and from time to time she weighed fresh loads of long line and recorded the amount.'

This East Street garden was the site of a spinning walk. The long, thin gardens to be found in Bridport have their origin in their use as spinning walks, which were usually some 100 metres long and generally sloped downhill. The machine spinning of hemp from the late 1850s resulted in their conversion into gardens.

'Mrs Northover started to see the nature of the spiunner's duties and the ease with which she controlled the great, pulsating, roaring frame of a hundred spindles. Sabina's eyes were everywhere; her hands were never still; her feet seemed to dance a measure to the thunder of the frame. Now she marked a roving reel aloft that was running out, and in a moment she had broken the sliver, swept away the empty reel and hung up a full one. Then she drew the new sliver down to the point of the break and, in a moment, the two merged and the thread ran on. Now her fingers touched the spindles, as a musician touches the keys, and at a moment's pressure the machine obeyed and the yarn flew on its way obedient.'

1860 – 1900
A PERIOD OF ECONOMIC DIFFICULTIES

The final years of the Victorian period were typified by a series of economic swings but with an overall downward trend in business. The good times were over and the end of this period saw the first significant bankruptcies to happen for many years, even Joseph Gundry and Co. were not immune to the troubles.

At the start of the 1860s the factory system of working was getting into full swing. New factories were being built, such as Herbert Hounsell's Sparacre spinning and line walks and his Pelican Net works. His was the also the first Bridport firm to take advantage of the new limited liability status recently allowed by Parliament.

In 1861 the American States began their Civil War which removed Bridport's source of cotton, causing the Bridport manufacturers to return to their traditional hemp yarns for the nets and lines and resulted in the spinning walks coming back into operation so that by 1864 nearly all were fully occupied.

This upsurge in trade saw Charles Hoare, the foreman of North Mills, set up on his own at the Burton Spinning Mill which he re-equipped with the latest machinery.

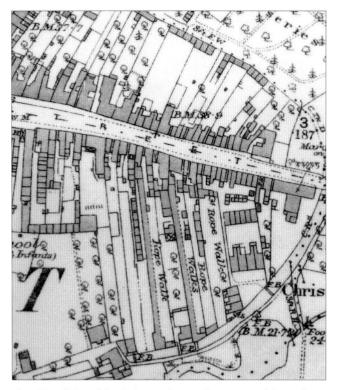

The 1887 edition of the Ordnance Survey shows some of the gardens in East Street, all of which were once used as spinning walks. A number continued in use as linewalks until the early 20th century. Those marked here were being worked by James Dyke Symes.

	Bridport area population	textile workers	textile workers as % of population
1851	12,074	2,040	16.9
1861	12,130	1,976	16.3
1871	12,642	1,537	12.2
1881	11,052	1,291	11.7
1891	10,457	990	9.5

Table 5. The figures for the number of textile workers in the Bridport area, taken from the census returns. The percentage of those employed in the industry declines firstly as a result of mechanisation and secondly due to the effects of the recession.

Opening in March 1865 he made a profit of £400 in the first year but with the end of the Civil War his business steadily declined and he became bankrupt in 1869.

The restoration of cotton supplies saw the final closure of many of the spinning walks. The few that were left specialised in lines and small cordage, such as those of James Dyke Symes at 90/92, East Street, whose walks were marked on the 1887 O.S. map.

The end of the Civil War saw a severe depression fall on Bridport and by 1868 this was sufficiently bad for the manufacturers to hold a meeting to discuss the distress of the poor. Although they had little control over the situation a relief fund was set up and by April the following year it had reached £1,500.

Trade picked up again in the early 1870s but this was short lived. In 1873 the Gas Company was reporting that local trade was depressed and just three years later it was remarked that the course of action taken by many manufacturers had driven the trade to Belgium and France.

Trading difficulties brought about the closure of Ewens and Golding's Mill, while the death of Alfred Stephens saw the closure of Asker Mill, with the business transferred to the Stephens family mill at Bristol. Both of these Bridport mills produced flax yarns, mainly for the sailcloth industry. As a result of these closures Stephen Whetham and Sons, with their London Office and good connections, had a near monopoly for sailcloth in Bridport which ensured that their trade was still profitable, although they too sought to diversify into nets and lines as their canvas sales declined.

With its broad base Joseph Gundry and Co. were initially able to cope with the vagaries of the market. The overall trend in their asset value was upward, reaching a peak of £103,000 in 1877. However over the next decade the economic difficulties caught up with them leading to a fall in their profits from the mid-1880s, while the firms of Stephen Whetham and Sons and H. E. Hounsell were making losses.

The impact of these periods of recession can be seen above in Table 5 in the population returns for the area, which includes Bridport and its surrounding parishes.

While the population continued to rise into the 1870s there was a fall in the number employed in the industry. The sharper fall in the 1880s was due to the recession and caused an increase in emigration from the town as people sought work elsewhere. In the town itself schemes were put in place to try and alleviate hardship where possible. In the mid-1880s the building of Victoria Grove, a road linking Bridport's West Street with Pymore Lane, gave work to unemployed mill workers and labourers, with the land being given by J. T. Stephens.

Table 6 below provides the changes in work patterns affected by mechanisation and recession.

The fall in the number of spinners in the 1860s represents the introduction of hemp spinning machinery and the use of cotton in nets and lines. Initially the fall in the number of weavers was due to the introduction of

Table 6. The breakdown of the occupations of the textile workers from 1851 to 1891, taken from the census returns. Once again they show the affect of mechanisation on the industry.

	1851	1861	1871	1881	1891
Fibre preparation	215	213	149	122	96
Spinners	789	729	344	245	91
Linemakers	18	19	23	26	7
Ropemakers	28	40	40	49	30
Weavers	160	90	52	14	13
Braiders	378	404	386	359	223
Total	2040	1976	1537	1291	990

A group of Gundry's machine braiders photographed in 1910, prior to the emigration of Mr Wallbridge (second from left, front row).

Flax spinning machine needed constant attention to make sure that any broken threads were mended and full bobbins replaced.

power looms and was followed by one caused by the fall in demand for sailcloth as steam took over from sail.

In contrast braiding held up well until the 1880s recession hit the fishing industry hard, causing employment to fall by some 40%. Both the Newfoundland and the UK fishing industry had declined, due in part to over-fishing following the introduction of trawl nets, which began to take the place of the traditional fishing lines. This resulted in reduced catches in later years, added to which fish was not yet a food favoured by the British people.

With Bridport dependent to a large extent on the Newfoundland trade things did not bode well. In 1882 Moses and James Harvey Monroe had set up the Colonial Cordage Company of St. John's, Newfoundland, to manufacture the nets and lines that had been previously imported from Bridport. Monroe had approached Joseph Gundry and Co. with an offer of a partnership but this was turned down. With these locally manufactured goods being protected by import bounties and with tariffs on imported foreign goods it meant that trade with Bridport was reduced. The result was that W. Hounsell and Co. and Joseph Gundry and Co. were now sending just one ship to Newfoundland each March. Long credit was being reduced and it was said that thousands of pounds of debt was not worth the paper on which it was written.

Trade recovered in the early 1890s with employees now asking that the wage cuts imposed in the 1880s be ended. By 1893 things were on the up and Bridport was thought to be better placed than others. Bridport manufacturers had taken the opportunity to modernise their netmaking equipment, with Gundrys using the new Zang multi-shuttle braiding machines.

The following year it was clear that there was increased competition from abroad but it was thought that Bridport was equal to it as its goods were superior to those of its competitors, which now included cotton fishing nets from the USA. However it was recognised that conditions were not conducive to trade and once again the manufacturers tried to treat the workforce sympathetically during these difficult times.

However the end of 1894 was to produce a crisis for

Bridport manufacturers from which few would emerge unscathed. It was a financial crisis in Newfoundland that was to be the trigger. It was here that Hounsells and Gundrys had much of their business and the tradition of advancing credit to vessel owners who paid off their debt when the catch was brought in did not help matters. Once again Bridport was plunged into recession and this time it brought down two manufacturers, S. Whetham and Sons and Richard Tucker and Sons. While both were finally precipitated by the fraudulent activity of their solicitor Richard Tucker jnr., the principal cause for the downfall of R. Tucker and Sons was the result of the end of their Australian trade and that for S. Whetham and Sons lay

Changing a shuttle on a Zang braiding loom at W. Edwards and Son in about 1925. These multishuttle looms were introduced around 1900.

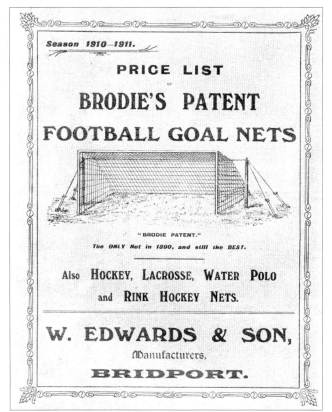

Charles Clarke was one of the smaller net manufacturers of the late 19th century. His business was located in South Street.

Fitting soccer goal nets at W. Edwards and Son in the 1920s. The typical square mesh of the sports nets can clearly be seen. Many of them were exported to South America, encouraging the development of soccer in the continent.

in the difficulties of trading in Newfoundland. Indeed Whetham's concern had been trading at a loss for some years but it was not until the death of Charles Langley Whetham in 1890 that the true figures came to light.

Joseph Gundry and Co. was severely affected. Sales in 1884 were worth around £65,000 but by the early 1890s they had dropped to just £25,000 producing losses running at around £4,000 per year. Luckily the firm was large enough to make adjustments and survive. However a change in the Government of Newfoundland in 1898 saw an end to the bounties and their replacement by increased tariffs leaving the local Colonial Cordage Company without competitors and further reducing the inflow of Bridport products.

The economic situation had one positive effect as it

The W. Edwards and Son catalogue of 1909, advertising the sale of Brodie's patent goal nets. Brodie had invented the goal net in 1890 and licensed production exclusively to William Edwards and Son. It was the sale of these which made the firm's name.

forced a number of the smaller manufacturers to move away from their dependence on fishing nets and lines. The late 19th century had seen an increase in sporting activities, with cricket and lawn tennis being taken up by large numbers of people. As a result many small manufacturers, including Alfred Hussey, Charles Clarke, Walter Tucker and Elizabeth Norman, the widow of Edward, started to supply nets for these increasingly popular activities.

Two more of the smaller manufacturers also underwent significant changes with the retirement of the original founders. In 1895 W. S. Edwards bought out his father's interest. This marked the start of the real development of William Edwards and Son, their six employees of the 1880s grew to over 200 by the 1920s. William Edwards and Son seem to have moved into sports netting on a small scale in 1884, initially providing lawn tennis and table tennis nets before expanding into cricket nets. Then in 1891 J. Brodie of Liverpool patented and manufactured the first football goal nets and assigned the sole rights of manufacture to William Edwards and Son at the turn of the century, providing the firm with a secure future.

When Sidney, Fred and Albert took over from their father the firm of William Gale and Sons moved from twine manufacturers into netmakers specialising in herring nets.

1900 – 1945
THE INDUSTRY DIVERSIFIES

Not only was the Newfoundland market shrinking but Bridport was now facing competition from Lancashire and Yorkshire as well as from Ireland and Scotland. The Gourock Ropeworks Company in Scotland was one such competitor and, following the Scottish fishing fleets as they moved south to follow the herring, the Gourock established a presence in Bridport between 1904 and 1912, thereafter concentrating production back in Scotland.

However help was just around the corner for between 1899 and 1902 Britain was fighting the Boer War. The Army's need for lines, tents and rifle pull-throughs, as well as hay and forage nets, saw an increase in employment in Bridport, allowing a certain amount of relief for the duration of the war. The Boer War also signified a major change of direction for the Bridport industry. From now there was to be a gradual increase in the supplying of the military, a trend which was to continue throughout the 20th century.

In 1904 there was a cotton shortage in the USA which, with cotton now the basis of many of the netting products being made in Bridport, caused a recession in the local economy. The scarcity of cotton had pushed its price up by 50% which in turn produced a downturn in trade. During the worst of the cotton crisis many braiders were on short time, with machines lying idle and a number of factories closing on Saturday mornings.

Heeding the lessons to be learnt from this the manufacturers called for the British Dominions to grow more cotton in order to reduce their dependence on the USA. It was becoming increasingly apparent that the dependence of Bridport on the sale of fishing gear was proving more and more precarious, resulting in further investment in other areas, such as sports nets and military contracts.

While trade started to return to normal towards the end of the decade, such was the competitive nature of the business that profits were low. In 1908 there was a call for the Bridport manufacturers to form a trade association in order to fix prices and reduce competition, although by now most firms had full employment and some were even reporting difficulties in getting enough labour. That the troubles were not yet over is seen by the failure of sports net manufacturer Albert Norman in 1910.

In 1912 a comment was made at a trade dinner that the town had lost certain elements of manufacture through short-sightedness by those with money to invest. One example was the use of manila, where a machine had been invented to process the fibre in the 1870s. However in the ten years it took to make the machine reliable the trade had passed from Bridport with little manila being used in the town.

With trade being good for a number of years there was an ever increasing problem of recruiting sufficient labour. Joseph Gundry and Co. responded to this by setting up a factory in Swindon in 1915. A more significant was the takeover of William Hounsell and Co. by Herbert Hounsell Ltd., thus forming Hounsell's (Bridport) Ltd. and becoming the largest manufacturer in Bridport in the process.

In July 1914 the Marine Biological Association visited Bridport to look at those firms making small meshed nets and the report produced provides a snapshot of the industry on the eve of World War One. It comments that most of the netting from Joseph Gundry and Co. was machine-made cotton fishing nets which were then

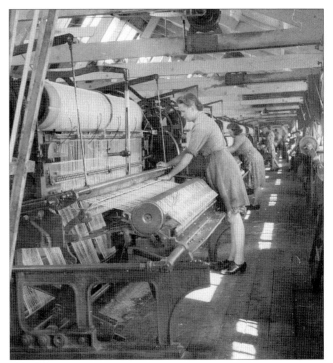

Braiding looms at W. Edwards and Son in about 1950, attended by Nancy Jeans.

tanned and treated with the preservative copper sulphate. While hand nets could be made the firm would not give a definite delivery time for them. They also had an extensive business in fishing lines. Stephen Whetham and Sons had been making herring nets for many years and also made large seines for use on battleships, to catch fresh fish while at sea, which doubled as tennis and cricket nets when otherwise not used. Hand-made nets were also available including one for shrimping and catching whitebait. The new firm of Hounsells (Bridport) Ltd. made most types of

Bridport-made nets at Port Harcourt, Nigeria. There was a significant trade to the West African coast.

33

Cod lines being made for Newfoundland in the 1940s, with Alf Read of W. Edwards and Son in attendance.

nets including herring nets. The firm seems to have had strong links with the Coal, Salt and Tanning Company of Grimsby, later known as Cosalt. The final firm mentioned is William Edwards and Sons who continued to specialise in sports nets and made most of those for Gamages, the famous London department store.

The onset of World War One in August 1914 had a huge impact on Bridport, effectively replacing its traditional trade with military products. On top of that some 1,600 men from the town had enlisted by 1916, including a number of the senior members of J. Gundry & Co., T.

Record of the staff of Hounsells (Bridport) on military service at Christmas 1914.

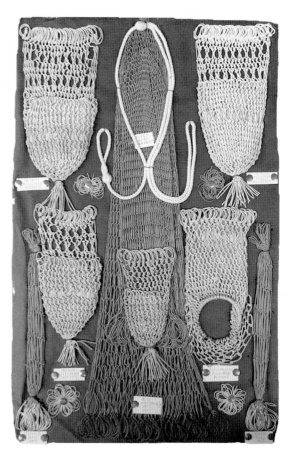

Show case of billiard pockets and tennis ball nets, all of which would have been hand braided. The lanyard was a short length of cord which could be used for a variety of purposes.

Tucker & Co. and Hounsells (Bridport) Ltd. The arrival of Belgian refugees in late 1914 alleviated this to a certain extent, as many of the women were taught the local trade and were able to help in the production of the war materials.

The staple items of fishing nets and lines and sports nets were largely replaced by the production of vast numbers of hemp lanyards, rifle pull-through cords, and hay nets. This last named accounted for 50,000 nets a week at one point! Whip-cord for grenade pins and lines for tents and hammocks were also made. The newly emerging Royal Flying Corps was supplied with cordage as well as the canvas needed to cover airframes. Netting for balloons and airships was also produced, demanding new levels of strength in the cords. From 1917 camouflage netting was needed in large amounts, demand being such that both machine and hand made nets were produced.

Fishing nets were still being made to enable Naval ships to catch fresh fish while at sea. However it was another catch which was to show the co-operation and inventiveness that marks out Bridport from the rest. In 1915 the Admiralty approached the town's manufacturers to enquire if it was possible to make large wire nets for 'catching' submarines. Following a meeting in London with other UK manufacturers W. S. Edwards returned to Bridport and soon produced a trial version.

A submarine would become ensnared by one of these nets, thus giving away its position and allowing it do be

Above W. S. Edwards, drawn by Syd Jordan in 1930. The owner of W Edwards and Son from 1895, he was responsible for the expansion of the business following its concentration on making sports nets.

Above right Bridport Harbour, 1900. At this time the harbour was still receiving regular cargoes of hemp. Behind the ship lie the warehouses built at the end of the 18th century.

dispatched in the conventional manner. The wire mesh was some 10ft to 12ft wide and the nets were made in lengths of 100 yards. Each drifter had 10 of these nets linked together making a span of 1,000 yards. Hollow glass balls were used to keep the nets afloat and an indicator buoy was developed to keep track of the nets after a submarine had been snared. Design improvements continued throughout the war as the Germans sought to nullify their use, with the last of these nets being made in early 1918.

In order to process the military orders as efficiently as possible new techniques of quality inspection were carried out so as to avoid congestion in the War Department stores receiving the products. These stood themselves in good stead in the years after the war.

From the start of the war the supply of hemp from Russia was cut off and was replaced by increased amounts purchased from Italy. Even this was threatened when the Austrian Army approached the hemp growing region around Bologna. From November 1917, in order to overcome some of the supply problems, the Yeovil area of the British Flax and Hemp Growers Society set out to increase the acreage grown in West Dorset. Linen was in short supply and was needed by the Royal Flying Corps as well as for the usual shirts, collars and cloth. A processing factory was set up at Preston in Yeovil and was followed by others, including one at Allington. Locally grown flax was taken to these factories for retting and scutching before being passed on to the manufacturers for processing. This arrangement continued for some time after the war in order to supplement imported flax, which was still below the level needed by the trade.

Peacetime saw the production of the traditional nets and lines re-established. However during the war significant distant markets had been lost to the Americans and the Japanese and it would need much work for them to be regained. These attempts were not helped by difficulties in relations with the workers, both in Bridport and in the North. In late 1918 a strike involving large numbers of cotton workers in Lancashire occurred, to be followed in April the next year by a strike of 900 workers in Bridport over pay and conditions. This culminated in the General Strike of 1926 which resulted in the Bridport factories working a three day week for some time.

The immediate post-war years proved to be difficult ones for the industry, caused by the post-war recession which was hitting the country hard. In early 1920 the poor trading outlook led Gundry to close their Swindon operation and open a new venture in Great Yarmouth, managed by Fritz Dammers, the late principal of William Hounsell and Co. They also consolidated their Bridport business by taking over the Pymore Mill Company and Stephen Whetham and Sons. At the same time they sought to gain access to more distant areas with new bases established Scotland and Canada.

The Bridport businesses now had their own organisation, the Bridport Manufacturers Association, which was first noted in 1919. It was the first sign of the increasing co-operation between the firms, and would eventually lead to the formation of Bridport Gundry many years later. The strain of competition was also seen in 1928 with the agreements set up between the major manufacturers. The first of these was between Joseph Gundry and Co., the Pymore Mill Company and William Edwards and Son by which Edwards would take their twine from Pymore and agreed not to enter the fishing market while Gundry's agreed not to compete in the sports net field. The same year saw an agreement between Gundry's and Hounsells (Bridport) Ltd. in which Gundry Pymore would act as the latter's agent in North America.

However by 1930 the depression had deepened with the factories back on a three day week and over 300 employees working short time. In order to overcome some of the financial problems Hounsells (Bridport) Ltd. came up with an innovative solution, making wooden baskets for fruit growers. This supplemented their traditional markets until 1935 by which time the recession had eased and demand for their nets and lines had increased. Meanwhile Joseph Gundry and Co. went down a different

Hounsells (Bridport) receiving the first delivery of wood for their fruit basket department. To counter the recession, Hounsells (Bridport) turned to making fruit picker's baskets between 1931 and 1935. The Aspen logs were brought in through Bridport Harbour.

Mrs Greening of Loders exchanging her nets for a fresh supply of twine from W. Edwards and Son in the late 1940s. She is to be seen making a pig net in the photograph on page.

route and in 1932 had sought to take over William Edwards and Son in order to improve business.

Increased international competition, especially from the Japanese, meant that costs were becoming critical, needing improved teamwork and the installation of a marketing presence overseas. Matters were not being helped by economic sanctions against Italy, from whom significant amounts of hemp were normally imported. In

Fitting nets at the Court in about 1950. Franka Pinkett, who came from Sicily, was a wartime bride having met her husband while he was in the 8th Army. She returned there after his death. The caption on the reverse of the original photograph says that these are salmon nets for British Columbia. However the square meshes suggest that they may be sports nets.

1939 Donald Cox of Hounsells (Bridport) Ltd. was warning of the need to overcome this increased competition if the good times were to return to the town again.

It was, however, World War Two that was to produce full employment at the factories. For the first time the various firms worked in concert through the Bridport Manufacturers Association. It was the latter that actually sent in the tenders to the military for the various contracts eventually given to the town's firms. This approach was essential if the vast amounts of camouflage net needed were successfully to be produced. However each business still had its specialities with Thomas Tucker producing helmet nets and Rendall and Coombs working on parachute cords.

There were still difficulties to overcome, the labour shortage made it difficult to man double shifts if they were needed, the spinning machines were not adjusted to spin Indian hemp and there was a problem with the forward buying of cotton, needed to ensure that there was sufficient for the camouflage nets. Sisal was used for some hand-made nets but limited availability meant that prices were not competitive.

It was clear that Bridport would find it difficult to compete with other areas on price. However the town had one major advantage – the large number of experienced outworkers on which the trade had always been based. The town was also the original home of the camouflage nets and the two things led to large orders being obtained by the town. So once again the town turned from the fishing trade to the production of war materials. With Bridport seen as a strategic target a number of braiding machines were moved from The Court to Beer Caves for the duration of the war to enable production to continue if Bridport factories were bombed. In the event while Edwards' factory was machine-gunned none of the factories were bombed.

As with World War One wartime conditions saw

Outworkers braiding in the street at Uploders in the late 1940s. Mrs Crabb in the photograph on page 2 can also be seen here. This is one of the photographs taken for the Ministry of Information and accounts for the rather posed image.

the need for more flax to be grown locally and this was encouraged by Rolf Gardiner of Springhead, Fontmell Magna. He formed Fontmell Industries and reopened Slape Mill in July 1939 to process the flax from Somerset and Dorset. The amount of flax grown in Dorset rose from 20 acres in 1938 to over 500 acres two years later, with growers being paid £11 per ton.In 1942 the Ministry of Supply took control of production, offering prizes for the best growth, which was won by Harold Huxter of Broadoak that year. The mill continued to operate throughout the war but return of peacetime conditions saw its closure once more.

As happened in 1918 conditions pertaining at the end of the conflict were to impact greatly on the town. Once again there was increased international competition for the fishing market and it was this that led to the drive to seek the amalgamation of the firms a process which started in earnest in 1943.

Rolf Gardiner in 1935. To encourage the wartime production of flax, he reopened Slape Mill in 1939 to process the flax from Dorset and Somerset.

1947 – 1963

MERGERS AND AMALGAMATIONS

The Report of Edward N. Humphreys

Since the Bridport manufacturers had been co-operating with each other from the start of World War Two it does not seem surprising to see attempts being made to put this on a more formal basis. In July 1943, following correspondence between chartered accountant Edward Noel Humphreys and J. O. MacDonald on the matter of the rationalisation of the Bridport Trade, a meeting was held at former's Chester office attended by James O. MacDonald, Harry Sanctuary and J. H. Senior, representing Gundrys, Edwards and Hounsells (Bridport) Ltd. respectively. A year later following analyses of the companies' accounts for the period 1937-1943 Humphreys produced summaries and analyses for each of the three companies in preparation for his visit to Bridport.

In May 1944 Humphreys held a series of separate and joint conferences with the three firms before returning to Chester where, on the 19th of November 1945, he produced the first report on possible merger strategies and their implementation.

The report made it clear that since they all were long established Bridport firms the proposed merger was sensible but that it would be difficult to find a plan that all companies would accept.The difficulties Humphreys faced included the wide variation in capital investment or the net worth of the firms and the variation in the relative proportion of profits earned.

He estimated that the total assets of new company, based on independent valuations rather than on the capital held, would be £720,612 which was broken down as shown in Table 7 on the following page.

Whilst Gundry's income of was almost double any of the other firms it was producing a smaller return than either Hounsells (Bridport) Ltd. or Edwards, and caused Gundrys to have a lower capital estimate than that of Edwards, with its higher return. He devised 'units of crude

	J Gundry & Co. Ltd.	Pymore Mill Co.	Hounsells (Bridport) Ltd.	W Edwards & Son
Valuation	£309,372	£125,611	£172,527	£113,102
Income	£172,977	£83,333	£89,157	£82,918
Basic return on earnings (%)	2.79	2.46	4.51	7.3
Profits	£4,826	£2,050	£4,021	£6,053
Capital needed to earn data income (at 4½%)	£107,244	£45,555	£89,364	£134,516
Annual net income of equivalence (%)	28.5	12.1	23.7	35.7

Table 7. The estimates provided by Edward Humphreys in 1945 of the total assets of the Bridport firms.

value' to produce a comparison between the firms to which he added a number of statistical analyses, converting the results into a points system to produce a percentage for each company that would reflect its importance in the new single structure (see Table 8).

Cod lines being made for the Newfoundland trade.

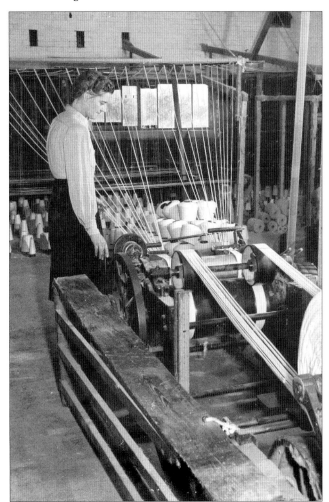

His report proposed that a holding company be formed within which there would be three or four companies, depending on whether the Pymore Mill Company was to be included. Later that month Humphreys returned to Bridport and held a further series of meetings to discuss the report's implications, after which the firms received more information on the holding company, as well as some idea about the treatment of shares.

This led, in January 1946, to discussions on the question of the capital structure of the new concern. Then in July he was asked to produce another scenario which concerned the effect on his initial conclusions of the acquisition of Rendall and Coombs by William Edwards and Son, which was included in his supplemental report of September that year. Two months later he visited Bridport for the third time, holding further meetings with each of the firms, after which he produced a revised set of proposals for the firms to consider.

Then, on the 21st of November a steering committee was set up to discuss the implication of the rationalisation of the facilities required by the new operation. Clearly at this stage the merger proposals were still going ahead, however between the 6th and 8th of March 1947 Humphreys received a bombshell in the form of a letter advising him of the withdrawal of one of the companies – Joseph Gundry and Co. Ltd. On receiving this he returned all the papers in his possession and sent a bill for £1,155 to cover the 176 days spent on the merger proposals.

Table 8. The percentage contribution that each firm was assumed to have in the proposed new company.

	J Gundry & Co. Ltd	Pymore Mill Co.	Hounsells (Bridport) Ltd.	W Edwards & Son
Percentage contribution	39.25	14.5	23.75	23.5
if Pymore Mill Co. excluded	46.5		26.5	27

Freehold	£15,000	(£8,000 on balance sheet)
plant and machinery	£25,000	(£10,000 on balance sheet)
net assets	£13,000	(£18,000 on balance sheet)
Stock	£4,000	
TOTAL	£57,000	

Table 9. The valuation of William Gales and Sons provided by Peat, Marwick and Mitchell in 1944.

	Edwards valuation	Gales valuation
machinery	£20,000	£22,500
freehold	£8,671	£8,671
Stock	£12,676	£12,676
Total	£41,347	£43,847

Table 10. The comparison of valuations of William Gale and Sons, produced during the merger talks with W. Edwards and Son.

The merger, as initially proposed, included only four firms leaving both Rendall and Coombs and William Gale and Son out of the equation. The sales and profits of the former were on a par with both Edwards and Hounsells (Bridport) Ltd. during the second half of the war. Consequently it seemed right to include these firms and this was done by William Edwards and Son buying both at a time when it seemed that the larger merger would go ahead.

The takeover of Rendall and Coombs

The firm of Rendall and Coombs was approached in 1944 by William Edwards and Son with an offer to take them over. The offer was conditional on the acceptance of all the shareholders and it needed the consent of the Treasury to permit William Edwards and Son to issue the further share capital needed to cover the purchase.

After some negotiations, which took until August 1945, the merger was agreed. Managing director Albion Whetham retired after 40 years in the textile industry and Fred Kenway took over as chairman of Rendall and Coombs, which became a wholly owned company within William Edwards and Son. Kenway also took a seat on the board of William Edwards and Son, with Campbell Edwards and Harry Sanctuary joining the Rendall and Coombs board.

The takeover of William Gale and Sons

1944 also saw William Edwards and Son seeking to take over William Gale and Sons, offering £30,000 for the business. However Gales wanted twice that and was given support by the valuation of £57,000 made by Peat, Marwick and Mitchell in November 1944 (see Table 9).

The key to this deal was the additional braiding machines needed by William Edwards and Son to process an order for double knot netting from the York Street Flax Spinning Company of Belfast. Whilst they had a number of Zang double knot braiding machines, many were not in good condition. Gales had six braiding machines, of which two were Zangs, accounting for the interest of William Edwards and Son in the takeover.

In December 1944 Campbell Edwards authorised Harry Sanctuary to put forward three alternative offers.

1. The first was for £48,000, accepting that they would have to pay more for the plant than its proper value. This offer was conditional on the purchase of the netting machines and the goodwill of Gale's business, needed for intended entry into the herring net business.

2. A lower offer of £40,000 to exclude the freehold properties.

3. A third option was for £16,000 which would only include the braiding machines, goodwill and guarantee of the employment of Albert Gale.

By this time Harry Sanctuary was becoming concerned that the take-over was getting out-of-hand, commenting to Campbell Edwards that they had no knowledge of the fishing trade and that they had undertaken to produce 26km of nets for York Street.

A revision of the offers was carried out between the two men which valued Gales at £40,000; £38,000 if the property was excluded and £25,000 for the fixed assets alone. However Gales wanted over £50,000, which William Edwards and Son thought might place their own firm in jeopardy.

Campbell Edwards and Harry Sanctuary then discussed combining a cash and share offer with the former suggesting an offer made up of £32,000 cash with £25,000 in 4% debentures.

The valuation driving this new offer is given above in Table 10.

Gales would be expected to leave 40% in the business at 4%. Sanctuary pointed out to Campbell Edwards that the value of Gales to Edwards' business was:-

1. It was the principal price-cutter in sport nets.

2. The double knot braiding machines would allow them to compete with Gundrys and to supply York Street.

3. If Gales became part of the business it could lead to a merger with Hounsells (Bridport) Ltd. and Joseph Gundry and Co.

Eventually an agreement was made for £50,000, with the Gales leaving from £20,000 to £25,000 in the concern. Peat, Marwick and Mitchell advised forming a new limited company for the take-over and this was carried out with the creation of William Gale and Sons Ltd. which began trading from the 1st of January 1946. The capital of the new company was £50,000 made up of £25,000 ordinary shares of £1 and £25,000 in five debentures at 4½% each of £5,000.

Liabilities		Assets	
Ordinary Shares	£25,000	Plant	£24,049
4½% Debentures	£25,000	Stock	£15,656
William Gale and Son	£816	Debtors	£14,057
Capital	£50,816	Investment	£2,000
Creditors	£3,508	Cash at Bank	£14,519
Extra Profits Tax	£21,915	Land	£21
Deferred Repayments	£500	Miscellaneous	£84
Surplus	£9,211	Property	£15,564
Total	£85,950	Total	£85,950

Table 11. The balance sheet for William Gale and Sons Ltd. on the first day of trading on the 1st of January 1946.

At the start of trading the balance sheet was as above in Table 11.

However when Peat, Marwick and Mitchell provided the final financial analysis of the take-over it was found that the net cost to Edwards was only £1,219! As Table 12 in the opposite column shows.

Thus William Gale and Son Ltd. became a subsidiary company of William Edwards and Son. Both Sidney and Henry Gale retired from the trade with Albert Gale becoming works manager. The move provided entry into the fishing net trade for William Edwards and Son in direct competition to Joseph Gundry and Co.

Further Discussions between Bridport Industries and Joseph Gundry and Co.

Although Gundrys had withdrawn from the merger further negotiations took place to try and get them to change their mind. In June 1947 Price Waterhouse, Gundry's auditors, wrote to Campbell Edwards saying that the offer of 47/6d for Gundry's shares was not sufficient. They thought that there was an advantage to be had by having Gundrys within the group but, while they were in favour of joining on the basis of the Humphreys report, none of the larger Gundry shareholders would relinquish their shares.

In December Ted Gundry met with Keith Cox, the chairman elect of Bridport Industries, to discuss the situation. While they were still amenable to a merger Gundrys, as well as concerns over the financial arrangements, were also demanding 'reasonable stipulations' regarding their role in the new company. This included wanting the same number of Gundry directors as both Hounsells (Bridport) Ltd. and Edwards combined, for Ted Gundry to be the vice-chairman, or managing director if one was appointed, and the continuity of employment of Gundry executive directors in the new board. They also wanted Price Waterhouse, with whom they had a long association, to be the new concern's auditors.

Stock				£9,803
Debts		£15,273		
less bad debts	£110			
Reserve	£715	£862		£14,446
Investment				£2,013
Cash and Interest				£14,541
Unexpired value				£84
Total assets				£40,088
Sundry creditors		£3,508		
EPT reserve		£21,925		
deferred repayments		£500		£25,933
Net Assets				£14,955
Current asset figures		£13,274		
Depreciation	£502			
Additions	£43	£450		£13,756
Net Cost				£1,219

Table 12. The financial analysis of the take-over of William Gale and Sons, provided by Peat, Marwick and Mitchell, showing the net cost to W. Edwards and Son was only £1,219.

In January 1948 Price Waterhouse wrote to Gundrys with a summary of their results over the past few years. Three days later there was a phone call between Ted Gundry and Keith Cox suggesting that they meet with Price Waterhouse to commence negotiations.

Early in February Keith Cox received a letter from Price Waterhouse which suggested that, although Gundrys would accept £37,000 in 6½% preference shares for both Joseph Gundry and Co. and the Pymore Mill Company, the difficulty lay in the ordinary share allocation. Bridport Industries made a profit of £125,892 the previous year which after deducting preference shares and directors' remuneration left £57,250. This meant that the return on their ordinary shares would be double that of Gundrys. As a result the highest valuation that could be placed on Gundrys' ordinary shares was £100,000, although £75,000 was more realistic. Incidentally the letter also showed that Gundrys had invested £20,000 in Bridport Industries when its shares came on to the market in 1947.

The result of this was an offer from Bridport Industries to Ted Gundry which valued Gundrys at £425,250 and was broken down as is shown in Table 13.

Keith Cox pointed out that this was higher than was seen in any firm under the conditions prevailing in 1947 and stating that the shares could be sold at a premium if needed.

After considering this offer Ted Gundry turned it d

37,000 preference 6% shares	@ 27/6	£50,875
100,000 ordinary 4/- shares	@ 13/10½	£69,375
400,000 ordinary 4/- shares	@ 15/3	£305,000
		£425,250

Table 13. The detail of the offer from Bridport Industries to Ted Gundry in 1948 which he later refused.

St Michael's networks of W. Edwards and Son, with the tar house on the left.

own although he kept open the possibility of future co-operation between the two firms. It was clear from the reply however that there were significant differences between the expectations of the two parties and here the matter lay until 1963.

BRIDPORT INDUSTRIES LTD. 1947 – 1963

Bridport Industries Ltd. as a Holding Company

In January 1947 the joint managing directors of Hounsells (Bridport) Ltd., Keith Trenchard Cox and Edward Donald Cox, reported that there was increasing competition to be met by the Bridport firms and that most the production of Hounsells (Bridport) Ltd. was for the export market. In order to meet this competition it had been decided to re-organise North Mills and install new spinning machinery.

At this point it was assumed that the merger would still go ahead. The withdrawal of Gundrys did not stop the process, only changed its point of view. Both William Edwards and Son and Hounsells (Bridport) Ltd. decided to continue on their own, announcing on the 24th of March 1947 that a merger agreement had been made in which a holding company, Bridport Industries Ltd., would acquire the share capital of both firms. The capital to be raised was £250,000, made up of £150,000 in 4/- shares, issued in the ratio of 56:44 in favour of William Edwards and Son, and £100,000 in 6% cumulative preference shares, with £29,762 being exchanged for Edwards preference shares, £44,608 in exchange for those of Hounsells (Bridport) Ltd. and £25,630 being issued for cash. A special dividend totalling £1,693 was made to the shareholders of Hounsells (Bridport) Ltd. in order to produce the required 56:44 ratio of capital.

The directors were to be Campbell Edwards, Harry Sanctuary and Fred Kenway from Edwards and Son together with Edward Donald Cox and Keith Trenchard Cox from Hounsells (Bridport) Ltd., who became the chairman elect.

As Bridport Industries Ltd. was a holding company the subsidiary companies retained their own Boards and continued to trade under their own names and brands. The value of the new arrangement lay in the removal of unnecessary competition and reduction the stock levels.

More significantly it meant that Edwards now received their twine from Hounsells' North Mills rather than the Pymore Mill Company. Each subsidiary was allowed to concentrate on its strengths the whole providing an increased level of competition for Joseph Gundry and Co. Ltd.

In January 1948 the first AGM of the new concern reported a net profit of £42,225, producing a dividend of 20%. 43% of the company's sales were for export with 13% raising hard cash. The following year's figures showed a net profit increase of £5,000 from a gross figure down 10%, leading to a 12½% dividend.

However the year to the end of July 1949 saw Bridport Industries net profits drop to under £32,000, following which attempts to penetrate the American market started in earnest. Fred Kenway embarked on a marketing trip to North America and captured orders worth £0.5m after which the trip became an annual event. In 1950 Bridport Industries set up the Montreal based **Gourock-Bridport Industries Ltd.** in a joint venture with the Gourock Ropeworks Company. There was a significant market in

Below left Campbell Edwards drawn by Syd Jordan. The principal of W. Edwards and Son from 1934, he oversaw the formation of both Bridport Industries in 1947 and Bridport Gundry in 1963.

Below right The tower of the St. Michael's networks, showing the Bridport Industries logo.

An aerial view of the St. Michaels Lane factories of Bridport Industries taken in 1956. The southern ones, on either side of the cattle market, were formerly those of W. Edwards and Son. To the north of these was the factory of William Gale and Sons, this was built on the site of former spinning walks. At the lower left hand edge can be seen Priory Mill.

this region for good quality ropes, lines and nets, with 90% of the boats fishing out of Nova Scotia using Rendall and Coombs Blue Banner cod line.

As a result net profits in the early 1950s began to climb towards the £60,000 level, with one factory working 24 hours a day on the North American orders alone. In 1951 £50,000 cumulative 6% preference shares of £1 were issued to enable the machinery at Rendall and Coombs to be upgraded. The end of the year saw Kenway return with new orders and this, together with various Government orders, gave Bridport Industries Ltd. an order book for 12 month's work.

June 1952 saw the death of the chairman, Keith Trenchard Cox. He had overseen the successful growth of the company with its net asset value rising from around £25,000 to over £45,000, the capital value of the company showing an increase from £250,000 to £450,000. The company was paying a dividend of over 10% and its 4/- ordinary shares were being quoted at between 9/- and 15/-. The Canadian subsidiary had seen a three-fold increase in its value, with the Bridport Industries share being worth £39,369.

Campbell Edwards became the new chairman with Cox's widow elected to the Board. In October Fred Kenway reported that the North American trade was able to keep the order books full for three months at least.

However there were signs of increasing competition with European countries, including Holland, Norway, France and Germany.

1953 saw the take-over of Beeton's Sunrise Works of Lowestoft, founded in the 1930s by E. H. Beeton to make herring nets. The buildings and plant needed a capital injection which the owner was not able to fund, hence the sale to Bridport Industries Ltd. While the year end saw further orders from North America, enough to keep sections of the business busy for 12 months, competition was becoming severe from Germany and Japan and at the same time there were the first signs of the use of man-made fibres, replacing the traditional hemp, flax and cotton.

Turnover, although falling by 30%, was higher than any year other than the previous one. Narrower margins and raw material costs allied to higher wages accounted for the profits falling. The consequence was gross profits falling to £85,748, a reduction in of 40%, but following a stock reduction they still were able to give a 20% dividend.

The Restructuring of Bridport Industries Ltd.

A review of the business was carried out over the following months which led to a restructuring. Bridport Industries Ltd. was no longer to be a holding company but would own the bulk of its assets operating at first hand, although it retained the use of the former subsidiaries trade names for marketing purposes. Campbell Edwards was to remain as chairman, Edward D. Cox and Harry Sanctuary were managing director and executive director respectively. Fred Kenway left the Board but was retained as a consultant.

The restructuring of 1954 came none too soon as the

Beeton's Lowestoft factory was taken over by Bridport Industries in 1953. During World War Two the Beetons moved production to a factory in Wales to avoid the German raids on the East Coast.

figures for the year ending July 1954 showed gross profits falling by almost half to £43,259, due to the decline in Government orders and the increased use of synthetic fibres by other firms. As the current machinery was not suited to synthetic fibres new machinery had to be installed at a cost of £30,000, the benefits of which were not felt until the later in the year. Although Japanese competition was being met it was squeezing margins so that in future the firm had to concentrate on productivity and production capacity to offset these lower margins. Despite this a dividend of 3% on preference and 10% on ordinary shares was declared the following year.

The takeover of James Pearsall & Co. Ltd.

In 1959 Bridport Industries Ltd. took over Pearsall's of Taunton, an old established firm whose origins date back to the late 18th century and had been based in Taunton since 1928. They manufactured silk thread for embroidery, sewing and lace making, later producing silk thread for medical sutures which needed the production of very fine yarns. In the 1950s they were one of the first companies to venture into spinning man-made fibres and it was this capability that interested Bridport Industries Ltd., who already took 20% of Pearsall's synthetic production or 80% of their home sales. The takeover was thus to the benefit of both companies with Pearsall's gaining the extra trade and a new market.

Pearsall's was a smaller business than Bridport Industries Ltd. with assets of £151,000 and the 1958 trading figures reported a gross profit of £24,036 or £11,010 net. The terms of the deal gave five Bridport Industries Ltd. ordinary shares of 4/- together with 2/- cash for each £1 Pearsall's share.

The prime mover from Pearsall's was Reginald Besley who had joined them as director in 1936 later becoming managing director and then chairman. It was he who negotiated the sale of the business to Bridport Industries Ltd. and ensured that he was given a prominent position in the company. The new Board consisted of Campbell Edwards as chairman, Edward Cox as vice-chairman, the joint managing directors were Harry Sanctuary and Reg Besley, while L. Hextall, the former Pearsall's secretary, was also on the board.

The initial effect of this take-over was to boost profits, however by the early 1960s they were on the decline again with the Gourock Bridport returning increasing losses (see Table 14 above).

It was this decline in the trading position that led in 1963 to the formation of Bridport Gundry as Gundry's were finding trading as difficult as Bridport Industries Ltd.

John Thorne Randall moved to 13, West Allington in 1815, adding the neighbouring property in 1848. The following year the site became the base of Rendall and Coombs remaining so until it was converted c1950 into Bridport Industries House, that company's administrative headquarters.

JOSEPH GUNDRY AND CO. LIMITED

1947 – 1963

The end of the war saw Joseph Gundry and Co. Ltd. return to the more difficult trading conditions linked to increasing competition both at home and abroad. Profits in the two post-war years were running at around £60,000 for the combination of Gundrys and Pymore Mill, while those of the Canadian concerns of Gundry Pymore on the Atlantic coast and Gundry Pacific were running at around £5,000. The overall asset value of the company was £256,715, with an issued capital of some £80,000.

Gundrys clearly saw the Edwards take-over of Gales as a threat to their fishing net trade so that when an approach was made by Thomas Tucker and Co. Ltd. asking them to consider taking over their operation J. O. MacDonald saw an opportunity enter the sports nets arena, hitherto almost the monopoly of Edwards.

The final agreed valuation was for £20,112, over half of which was for the stock in trade, with the freehold of the land being retained by Capt. J. A. C. Tucker. The main plant was 10 hand-powered jumper looms, some only 20 years old. The share issue of Thomas Tucker and Co. Ltd. was distributed amongst Joseph Gundry, Edward Gundry

Date	Bridport Industries Ltd. Profit	Gourock Bridport Loss
1958	£37,267	
1959	£68,604	
1960	£56,894	(-£ 600)
1961	£31,372	(-£4,000)
1962	£28,452	(-£5,350)

Table 14. The profit figures for Bridport Industries covering the period 1958 to 1962.

and M. W. Burrough, while Capt Tucker and his partner J. B. Edwards were allowed 5 shares each.

Another development was the acquisition of a 42% holding in Crewkerne Textiles, in 1946. This was a sailcloth and webbing business formed by the amalgamation of Richard Hayward and Son with Arthur Hart and Co., two long established textile businesses who were finding times as tough as their Bridport neighbours.

1947 saw the reorganisation of the Gundry management team; J. O. MacDonald retired with Edward F. Gundry becoming managing director on his return from Canada. His brother, Gerald Gundry became a director while John and Patrick Gundry were both shareholders and employees. On taking charge Edward Gundry set about attacking the problems the company was facing and

Sid Turner baling nets at J. Gundry and Co. in about 1957.

Above The scene of destruction at The Court after the arson attack of June 1949. It took over two years to rebuild the factory and bring production back to its former levels. The arsonist was a former employee.

Right The Court in about 1952 following rebuilding after the fire, the new buildings can clearly be seen.

which had been made more difficult by the decision not to accept the merger offer of Bridport Industries Ltd. in March 1948.

The following year saw the beginning of the invasion of synthetic yarns. As Gundrys were unable to use their hemp or cotton spinning machines, Nylon from British Nylon Spinners and Terylene, made by I.C.I under licence from Courtaulds, were spun into yarn by British Ropes of Leith and Henry Campbell and Co. of Mossley Mill, Belfast. Henry Campbell and Co. were spinners of fine flax yarns, finer than could be obtained from the Pymore Mill Company and the two companies formed a joint subsidiary, Gundry Campbell, to supply Gundrys with fine synthetic yarn for the double knot salmon seine nets destined for the Canadian market. Later Joseph Gundry and Co. Ltd. turned to recycled synthetic fibres as these could be broken down into staple fibres and spun into twines in which the holding qualities of the individual fibres made the yarn stronger.

In June 1949 a serious fire took place at The Court causing £200,000 worth of damage. It was the result of an arson attack for which Stanley Mercer, a previous employee, was jailed the following year. The immediate effects were potentially serious as £150,000 worth of net production was lost. The mending room, Scotch room, fitting room and line walk were gutted and one braiding shop badly damaged. The Company introduced a two shift working pattern, with the first shift running from 07.30 to 17.30 and the second from 10.30 to 21.00. Temporary roofing was erected to allow some production to continue but even so the result was a 50% reduction in output. Although some of the production was transferred to Pymore Mill whilst rebuilding took place, it was not until the end of 1951 that full production returned, over

two years after the fire.

Around this time Gundrys purchased a new double knot braiding machine from the United States. Under the guidance of their chief engineer Mr Brownlee they set about making copies for use in making salmon netting, these machines gained the nickname 'hammers' instead of the more formal 'Solex'.

It may have been the loss of production resulting from the fire, allied to the competition with Bridport Industries Ltd. that caused Edward Gundry in 1950 to set up a Utility Department under Bill Budden, who had recently returned to Gundrys after wartime service in the R.A.F.

This decision was to have a far-reaching effect on the business and was to lead to a significant move away from the traditional fishing net market. The department was tasked with the development of alternative products, which included Brussel sprout nets, rabbit nets and snares, hay nets and fireproof nets for theatres. This was followed in 1951 by entering the sports and agricultural netting

A Solex braiding loom at The Court, these were given the nickname of Hammer looms and were introduced around 1950. The one nearest to the camera is making strips of fishing net.

market in direct competition with Bridport Industries Ltd. By 1954 they were making air freight cargo restraint nets for the Blackburn Beverley. This development proved very successful, with Gundrys receiving orders to supply a number of airlines, including British Airways, British Caledonian, Sabena and SAS, while 1960 saw the introduction of under-slung cargo nets for helicopters.

Even with this diversification business was not easy, but profits were buoyed up by those of the Canadian concerns which were worth $37,135 on sales of $1,201,092 in 1962. Interestingly the Canadian business was always in profit unlike their competitors Gourock Bridport who were experiencing losses year on year.

However the downturn in the traditional fishing market was having a harmful effect on the company finances. From a value of £76,981 in 1959 profits fell to a low of £10,000 in 1961 and it was no surprise to see the initiation of talks in March 1962 concerning a merger with Bridport Industries Ltd (see Table 15).

Profits	J Gundry & Co.	Crewkerne Textiles	Shareholder Profits
1958	£38,566		
1959	£76,981		
1960	£59,303	£10,441	£62,491
1961	£10,434	£4,449	£6,967
1962	£18,123	(-£2,248)	£7,307

Table 15. The profit figures for Joseph Gundry and Co. Ltd. covering the period 1958 to 1962.

It was this increasing difficulty in trading that eventually led to two competitors to seek a merger. Now the financial climate together with the use of an outsider, Reginald Besley, allowed talks to come to fruition. The old firm of Joseph Gundry and Co. Ltd. ceased to exist with the first Board Meeting of Bridport Gundry in December 1963, bringing to an end almost 300 years of a tradition.

PART TWO

The History of Bridport Gundry

Over the years aviation products have been an ever expanding part of the Bridport Gundry portfolio. One of these, helicopter underslung nets which allow the transport of armament, vehicles and supplies, has been an integral part of the UK's Rapid Deployment Force since its formation in the 1990s.

THREE

Bridport Gundry 1964 – 1971

Bridport Gundry Logo, which owes its ancestry from that of Bridport Industries.

THE FORMATION OF THE COMPANY

In early 1962 discussions started between Bridport Industries and Joseph Gundry and Co. The Bridport Industries spokesman was Reginald Besley and in March he informed Campbell Edwards that he had received a favourable response from Gundrys. The merger was desirable because:-

1. Netting sales were diminishing in the UK, due to the development of longer lasting synthetic fibres and the increased competition from Japan.

2. The merger would reduce both wasteful competition and the capital tied up in the duplication of stock.

Campbell Edwards and Edward Gundry c.1965. Campbell Edwards was chairman of the new company, with Ted Gundry and Reg Besley as joint managing directors.

3. There was a limited labour supply at both managerial and shop floor levels.

At this point it seems that Gundrys would be offering their shares for those of Bridport Industries, with one Gundry 4½% preference £1 share for each £1 unsecured loan stock of Bridport Industries, and two Gundry ordinary £1 shares for 15 ordinary 4/- shares of Bridport Industries, plus 2/6d cash.

Campbell Edwards was unhappy about the offer because of the low level of Gundry's profits in 1961. Following a meeting between the two companies in July, it was suggested that the ratio of share exchange, based on recent profits, should be 10 Bridport Industries shares to 9 Gundry shares.

Five months later, Edward Gundry was still suggesting that his company acquire Bridport Industries. However, at this point it, was realised that their combined earnings would not support the proposed share capital of £500,000, on assets of £1.246m. As a result, alternative strategies were considered, including the formation of a new holding company to buy out the two concerns. In February 1963 Edward Gundry wrote to Campbell Edwards suggesting that Joseph Gundry and Co. could become a plc, in which Bridport Industries would be offered shares. Campbell Edwards replied advising that it was Bridport Industries who should offer their shares to Gundrys because:

1. No prospectus need be issued.

2. J. Gundry and Co. did not need to become a plc.

3. Bridport Industries had over 350 shareholders, compared to the 48 of J. Gundry and Co., so there would be no need to explain why a 'smaller' company was being absorbed by a larger one.

Twelve days later, on the 13th of March 1963, Edward Gundry wrote to Campbell Edwards confirming that amalgamation was essential and agreeing to accept Bridport Industries shares for Gundrys. The next month Campbell Edwards wrote to Edward Gundry putting forward the name of **Bridport Gundry** for the new concern. With the major obstacles having been overcome, it was only left to put the final financial details to the merger.

Bridport Industries was offering 15 ordinary shares of 4/-, plus 2/6d cash, for every two £1 ordinary shares of J Gundry and Co. This would be worth £240,000 in shares and £10,000 in cash. It was not envisaged to exchange the Gundry preference shares for those of Bridport Industries.

The combined assets of the new company would be

J Gundry & Co. 4½% preference shares	£140,000
Bridport Industries 6% preference shares	£150,000
ordinary 4/- shares	£490,000
Total	£780,000

Table 16. The proposed share capital of Bridport Gundry.

Chairman	Campbell Edwards
Joint Managing Director	Edward Gundry
Joint Managing Director	Reginald Besley
Directors	
M. W. Burrough	E. D. Cox
J. C. F. Gundry	G. A. Gundry
C. Kennard	A. Sanctuary
L. Hextall	

Table 17. The Board of Directors of Bridport Gundry at their first meeting in November 1963.

£1.5m. The sale of Gundry (Canada) would raise £55,000, some of which would be used to pay off a £30,000 loan. The holding in Crewkerne Textiles, worth £41,061, would be retained, as would that of Gourock Bridport, which was worth £44,500.

The proposed merger was announced to the public in June 1963 and, following the necessary agreements of the individual boards, the amalgamation was effected on the 6th of November, with the first Board meeting of Bridport Gundry held on 3rd of December.

Kenneth Suttill and Harry Sanctuary retired, with the latter being replaced on the Board by his son, Anthony,

Zang Lindemann braiding looms c1968. By this time all braiding looms had been moved to The Court.

who was until then secretary of Bridport Industries. The new secretary was to be Gundry's P. J. Davis.

The first task that was undertaken was the reorganisation of the various factories, which would enable the streamlining of the business, with a concomitant reduction in costs.

BRIDPORT

The initial aim was to reduce the number of Bridport factories. All netting was to be made at The Court, necessitating the construction of a new upper storey on the net braiding shop of 1949. A plan, similar to that of Ederer's of Chicago, was adopted which would allow the hemp and cotton netting to be fitted in paths under the braiding machines.

The first phase was completed in the summer of 1966, with space for 62 machines on the first floor. Following this the Zang shop was emptied for the second phase to start, this being completed by May 1967. The Finn double knot machines from Allington were placed in the old 'Mons' room, with all other double knot machines. This allowed the Edwards and Gales factories in St Michael's Lane to be sold.

During late 1964 the spinning was concentrated at North Mills and a start was made on altering the Allington works so that all lines would be made there, with some of the line making machinery being moved there from The Court.

The next few years saw the increased use of garnetted synthetic yarns. These had the advantage that they could be bought when needed, rather than having to stockpile the natural fibres, necessitated by their annual production cycle.

However, as time progressed, clear trends emerged which required modifications to the Company's plans. In part this was due to the continuing difficulty of getting enough labour. It was decided close the West Allington site and move the twine and cabling machines to North Mills, where two new spinning walks were installed and put into

St Michael's Works, which is now in use as small workshops and artists' studios.

Hackling machine at North Mills c.1968. Hackling produced a lot of dust which was taken away by the ducting seen leading off from the top of the machine

operation during the summer of 1969, after which the spinning of natural fibres ceased.

THE REST OF ENGLAND

The Rochdale cotton spinning and doubling factory was surplus to the new company's needs and was sold to James North and Sons in the spring of 1965.

James Pearsall and Company had two sites in Taunton, one at Silk Mills and the other at St. Augustine's Street, which was used for making twisted, braided or trammed fine surgical sutures and heavy synthetic cord. A new factory at Duke Street was opened in October 1967, while the St. Augustine's Street works was closed a few years later, with the plant being moved to Silk Mills.

Lee Vale Mills, Charlesworth had been part of W. Edwards and Son since 1935 and this link continued during the early years of Bridport Gundry. The same was true for Beetons Ltd. of Lowestoft, which had been acquired by Bridport Industries in 1953.

Binder Engineering had been making valves for central heating systems and metal fittings for buildings at Morden, Surrey since 1960. In 1966 the business moved to Swindon, Wiltshire, where it was purchased by Bridport Gundry the following year. The Swindon site was closed and the business moved to Bridport in 1971.

The Aberdeen base of Bridport Gundry (Scotland). In this early 1970s photograph nets are being loaded ready for delivery.

L. J. Bickham & Company was purchased in 1967, a heating and electrical contractor, it proved to be an ill-starred venture. After losing nearly £38,000 in 1968/9 it was decided to dispose of the concern.

The London depot at Brecknock Road was closed in 1968, following the resignation of the manager.

BRIDPORT GUNDRY (IRELAND) LTD

In 1967 Bridport Gundry sought to expand into the Irish market and did so, in partnership with James McLeod, by opening a net fitting and trawl rigging facility in Killybegs.

BRIDPORT GUNDRY (SCOTLAND) LTD.

Bridport Gundry (Scotland) Ltd. was formed in 1969, to cover the company's operation in Scotland. In 1964 this consisted of the netmaking business at Campbeltown, which had been part of Gundrys since 1926, James Brighouse Ltd. of Aberdeen, which was acquired in 1964, and a depot at Fraserburgh. In late 1967 the operation at Campbeltown was closed and work concentrated on Aberdeen, where a new factory was planned to cope with the expanded business. New netting machines were bought to make purse seine nets for inshore trawlers, while nets and bobbins were made for deep sea trawlers.

OVERSEAS COMPANIES

Gundry Pacific was based in Vancouver, Canada. In 1969 it acquired Bilmac, which provided a complimentary business in marine hardware, with the trading name changing to Gundry-Bilmac.

Another old Gundry company, Gundry Pymore, also continued to trade after the merger, as did the Montreal based Gourock-Bridport-Gundry, the company set up by Gourock Rope and Bridport Industries in 1950.

FINANCIAL PERFORMANCE 1964 – 1971

The first few years saw a very flat performance by the new company, with annual sales running around £2.5m with net profit about £145,000 p.a. This was not what was hoped for when the companies merged in 1963.

FOUR

Bridport Gundry 1971 – 1997

BRIDPORT GUNDRY (HOLDINGS) LTD.

1971 - 1982

1971 – 1976; Reginald Besley, Chairman

Reginald Besley took over as chairman in the spring of 1971. His place as Managing Director was taken by Jack Gobbett, who had joined the board from Pearsalls in 1969. He soon created an impact by reorganising the business, with the formation, in December 1971, of Bridport Gundry (Holdings) Ltd. as an umbrella company for the trading operations. In order for this to proceed it was necessary to create Bridport Gundry Ltd. to cover the Bridport operations.

In 1974 the Bridport-based operations were split into four marketing divisions - Leisure, Marine, Industrial (which included Civil Aviation) and Defence. The mail order horticultural companies, C. Sutton and W. James, continued under separate managements as before.

The country was now entering a period of inflation and, although sales continued to increase, profits remained low as reduced margins were necessary to stimulate this growth. The effect of the recession in the early 1970s can clearly be seen when viewed at constant 1964 prices. From 1973 both sales and profits fell away, not improving until 1976.

During the next few years the nature of the Group Board changed subtly. Campbell Edwards retired as deputy Chairman in 1972, although he continued as a director until 1977. Mike Smith, the General Manager of Bridport

Reg Besley, chairman from 1971-1976, and Ted Gundry. Besley came to Bridport Industries from Pearsall's and helped broker the merger with J. Gundry and Co.

Bob Holder, Bridport Gundry chairman from 1976 -1988. Holder had been recruited from the Fairey Company in 1974.

Gundry Ltd., joined the Group Board in 1974, becoming Managing Director the following year. 1974 also saw the recruitment of R. W. Holder from the Fairey Company. Becoming deputy Chairman the following year, he took over as Chairman in 1976.

1976 – 1982; Bob Holder, Chairman

The recent serious decline in the fishing business resulted in the new executive team of Bob Holder and Mike Smith carrying out a review of operations. This led to another reorganisation, which took place in June 1976.

Four trading divisions were set up;

1. **Netting**, which included Bridport Gundry Ltd., Bridport Gundry (Ireland), Bridport Gundry (Scotland), Jackson Trawls, Sutton and James.

2. **Twisted Products** was made up of James Pearsalls and North Mills Textiles.

3. **Weaving**, which consisted of Crewkerne Textiles.

4. **Engineering** and **Overseas**. The last named was made up of Bridport Gundry (Overseas) Ltd., which owned Gundry Bilmac and Gundry Pymore. Bridport Gundry Inc. was set up in 1977 following the purchase of Brownell and Company Inc. of Moodus, Connecticut.

As well as identifying immediate difficulties, the review was also sought to avoid future problems. Accordingly in June 1978 **Bridport Gundry Ltd.** was split into four trading divisions:-

1. The **Netting Division**, which produced the sheet netting.

2. The **Leisure Division**, which consisted of Edwards

and W. James and produced sports and garden netting.

3. The **Marine Division**, which dealt with the production and supply of fishing nets.

4. The **Industrial Division**, which was a design and inspection team set up to procure industrial, aviation and military orders.

It was expected that the solutions imposed would take 18 months to have their effect.

1979 was to be another difficult year, with sales not progressing as well as expected. This led to the senior management taking a hard look at the Group activities to identify those which warranted future investment. In August yet another reorganisation of the Bridport trading activities took place. Individual companies were set up to run the various trading sectors, allowing a closer appraisal of the performance of each. The companies were: **Bridport Gundry Netting Ltd.**, which was soon transferred to the Twisted Products division, **Edwards Bridport Ltd.**, **W. James and Co. Ltd**. While **Bridport Gundry Marine Ltd**. produced and distributed fishing nets in mainland Britain.

The most significant change was within the Industrial Division, with the formation of **Bridport Aviation Products Ltd**. to manufacture cargo restraint nets and helicopter under-slung nets. Gundrys had started this work in the 1950s now, with the decline of the traditional fishing industry, it was seen as an area in which to move the company forward. This division was completed by the formation of Bridport International Ltd., suppliers of camouflage nets and allied military products.

In the 1980, in order to reduce the working capital needed, North Mills Textiles and Bridport Gundry Netting were placed under a single management team, within the Twisted Products Division. At the same time the Leisure Division became part of Bridport Gundry Netting Ltd., while the goodwill of the loss-making C. Sutton (Sidcup) was sold for £100,000.

However the continued difficult trading conditions led the Group, in July 1981, to report its first loss. This resulted in the resignation of Mike Smith as Group Managing Director, with Pat Darley taking up the post of Deputy Chairman and Chief Executive. Darley had been General Manager at Pearsalls since 1978, joining the Group Board two years later. His brief was to return the Group to profit as soon as possible and not to be affected by the history of its various units.

The result was the reduction of the workforce by over 200, with many of these being at Bridport. In addition much of the plant was concentrated in The Court, allowing the disposal of the North Mills site, while Hayward's sailcloth business, and its Crewkerne factory, were sold.

By now the Group structure had been altered again, this time to allow the Bridport companies to trade under product lines, with smaller management teams. They were placed into four sections:- the Principal Manufacturing Companies, which also included Pearsalls, Bridport Gundry Netting Ltd., Crewkerne Textiles and Brownell's. The

other units were the Marine Companies, the Aviation and Defence Companies and finally the Overseas Companies.

BRIDPORT GUNDRY PLC. 1982 - 1992

1982 - 1988; Bob Holder, Chairman

The Companies Act of 1980 required existing public companies to re-register, resulting in the change of the Company name to Bridport Gundry plc in January 1982. A new company, Bridport Gundry (1982) Ltd., was formed to control the shareholding of the Bridport-based companies. At the same time the subsidiary companies were grouped into Marine, Aviation/Defence, Netting/Cordage/Ropes, Surgical, Industrial Thread and Specialist Textiles.

Bridport Aviation was the star of the Bridport Gundry portfolio, with continued growth year on year; developing further its cargo restraints and moving into the manufacture of camouflage nets. Opportunities were also taken to improve productivity and search for new, innovative products. This new approach had immediate benefits with results improving over the next few years, although the Falklands war also helped to stimulate sales significantly. The financial result was that sales volume increased sharply with profits also recovering, both reaching a peak in 1986. With profits at an all time high, even allowing for inflation, it showed that the drastic action taken had the positive effect predicted.

In 1985 Redport Nets, a small Bridport netmaking business making specialised products such as rabbit nets, snooker pockets and angling nets, was taken over.

Around the same time, a decision was taken for the company to become more self-sufficient. The intention was to gain control of all manufacturing processes, from raw material to finished product, thus gaining a greater financial return. In 1986 the acquisition of Halls Barton Ropery gave Bridport Gundry its own extrusion capability, which was seen as the key to this new direction. Polyform, who made floats for nets and for which Bridport Gundry had been the main agent for many years, became an associated company with the acquisition of 50% of its shares. Finally, on the recommendation of the Board's auditors, Lolift UK was bought from the receivers, making intermediate bulk containers it was seen as complimenting the parent company's business.

Another consequence of this new direction was the strengthening of ties with trawl makers, who were traditionally small firms with less than 50 employees. This policy was set in motion by the acquisition of a 51% holding in Brixham Net Company, the abortive take-over of Marinovich Trawl in the USA, the setting up of Fishkey and the developments with Jackson Trawl and J. & W. Stuart in Scotland.

The mid to late 1980s saw the setting up of additional distribution depots for Bridport Gundry Marine along the southern coast of England, with others in Ireland and America, saving the commission normally given to the agents, who previously managed these sales. In part this was also an attempt to redress the balance, after recognising that the company had become too dependent on the defence industry. In 1987 a new group was made with the separation of Sports Products from Netting, while the Brixham Net Company became a division of Bridport Gundry Marine.

This period also saw changes in the personnel with John Gundry leaving the company to work on his own account. Bill Budden retired from Bridport Aviation Products, which he had overseen since its inception, with his place being taken by John Bowden. The retirement of Anthony Sanctuary also severed another link with the old companies.

The period from 1981 had seen continued growth in sales and profits, but this was now coming to and end. Taken at 1964 prices, the peak was seen in 1986, after which there was a reversal, with the Company reporting a net loss in 1988. The downturn in the traditional fishing business was one cause, but others were the acquisition of Halls, which had not been the success the company had hoped, and Lolift, which was also finding it difficult to produce a good return.

To combat this downturn in business Bridport Gundry sought to move net production offshore, in a joint operation with the Portuguese company Sicor. Bob Holder was not happy about this as he felt it would remove Bridport Gundry's flexibility and ability to react quickly to orders. This and other concerns meant that, although he had planned to remain chairman until 1989, he made the decision to leave the Board in October 1988, with his place being taken by Pat Darley.

Financially this was a very difficult time for the Company as sales were on a downward trend, seen more clearly at constant 1964 prices. Profits dipped, with net losses being reported for the three years from 1988. On top of this there was the increasing danger of a hostile take-over, as Russell Goward's Charterhall plc built up its shareholding in the company, rising from 11.4% in 1987 to 27.1% two years later. This had the effect of pushing the share price up to 300p, making them overvalued by around 30p per share. Discussions were held with Bob Holder and shortly afterwards Russell Goward sold much of his shareholding.

It was during the Chairmanship of Bob Holder that Bridport Gundry moved from being a family run business to one which had a more commercial approach.

1988 – 1993 - Pat Darley, Chairman

October 1988 saw Darley appoint Royston Mountain and David Sebire to the Group Board, in order to strengthen the management team. This was followed in early 1989 by the appointment of Brian Cowley as Group Managing Director and Graham MacSporran as Finance Director. By now only Peter Cox was left from the original Bridport Gundry Board.

A strategic review was soon carried out and its findings

Pat Darley, Bridport Gundry chairman from 1988 – 1993. Darley had been the General Manager at Pearsall's from 1978. He became Chief Executive three years later being charged with returning the Group to profit.

quickly put into operation. The implementation of new targets for earnings growth left a number companies without a future within the Group, unless they could turn things around quickly.

Plans were made to sell Brownells to a management team. When they were unable to raise the capital, the company was restructured, although the Bridport Gundry remained on the lookout for an alternative buyer. Arthur Hart became part of Pearsalls, while Polyform and Halls Barton were sold and Lolift was closed. Once again dependent on others for their extruded yarns, Bridport Gundry looked to Portugal where Sicor was one of their main suppliers.

In 1990 Bridport Gundry purchased shares in the French company Corderie R. Soulet SA., manufacturers and distributors of sports products. The intention was to strengthen the penetration of the sports and industrial markets in the EU. In 1992 the Belgian firm of Stijen Sports was purchased, becoming become part of Soulet.

At the same time, it was planned to move into areas where higher technology could increase the returns made from sales. To this purpose another reorganisation was put in place, with the companies now grouped into five sectors:-
1. Civil Aviation and Defence
2. Specialist Textiles
3. Industrial, Marine and Leisure
4. Marine Distribution
5. North America

Whilst the changes caused sales to fall significantly, as these were in areas of low margins the actual effect was to stabilise net losses, before the company climbed back into profit in 1991. However profits were too low for the Company to relax its guard and the net profit to sales ratio remained precariously low until 1993.

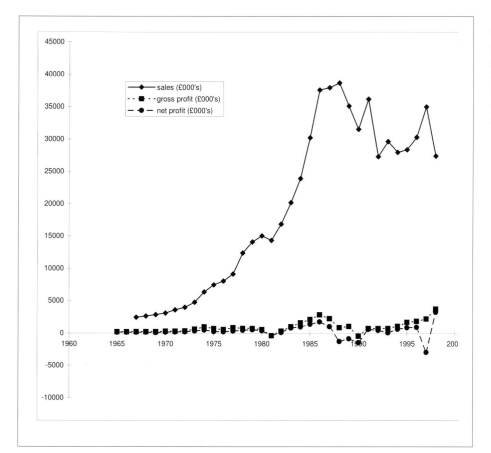

The accounts of Bridport Gundry from 1965 to 1998. While sales increased greatly until 1985, profits were running much below those expected. It was only after the sale of the traditional businesses that returns increased.

BRIDPORT GUNDRY PLC 1992-1997

Increasingly reliant on the Civil Aviation/Defence, Special Textiles and Industrial/Leisure markets, it was decided to streamline the Group accounting by making all companies subsidiaries of one trading company, Bridport Gundry (UK).

The next few years saw the gradual withdrawal from its traditional fishing market, with the sale of Bridport Gundry Ireland and J. and W. Stuart, both to their management teams. The Brixham Net Company was fully merged with Bridport Gundry Marine, and the depots at Padstow and Aberdeen closed. They also pulled out of the North American fishing market around the same time. This left the rump of its traditional Bridport-based netting business with little future within the Group, especially as fishing income was now only 15% of overall sales. It was of little surprise, then, to see Bridport Gundry Netting make its first trading loss for many years, although in part this was due to over-capacity in the European fishing market and the imposition of quotas.

In July 1993 Geoffrey Woods replaced Brian Cowley as Chief Executive and Pat Darley retired as chairman at the end of September, with David Sebire taking over. The new executive carried out a strategic review of the company. The key element of this was the need for each company to maximise its return on investment. There was to be an increased investment in research and development, with Bridport Aviation Products being the first to benefit from the provision of new facilities.

The core areas identified for future development, and in which resources were to be concentrated were:
1. Medical Division
2. Aviation and Defence Division
3. Sports and Industrial Division
4. Marine Division

The following year Sports and Leisure became a separate division, while the Marine Division was absorbed into the Industrial Division. The company was now trading profitably and had acquired two new businesses - Pielenz Flechtgarne of Berlin, which became part of Pearsalls, and Creative Manufacturing Inc. of Canada, which was merged with Bridport Industries of Canada. These changes were part of the general move away from the traditional fishing/bulk netting centre of trade.

With two of the divisions continued to perform well, the Sports and Leisure and Industrial Divisions found life difficult. As a result it was decided to concentrate on three areas - Aviation, Defence and Medical and dispose of the remaining non-core companies. This was done in 1997, completing the severing of the company from its traditional roots. In recognition of this the company changed its name to Bridport plc.

The outcome was that, following the sale of the seven non-core companies, profits gradually improved, with the net profit to sales ratio reaching 11.9% in 1998. Allowing for the disposal costs of these, the ratio was 4.4% in 1997. This clearly shows the correct choices were being made to ensure the survival of the Company, even if difficult decisions had to be taken.

FIVE

Bridport Gundry Companies

BRIDPORT 1971 - 1997

Bridport Gundry Limited

Bridport Gundry Ltd. was set up to act as the trading company for the Bridport-based manufactures. The executive directors were Raymond Keepax, Michael Smith and Bill Budden. North Mills produced the twine for the manufacture of nets, which was carried out at The Court. Reorganisation at North Mills provided the space to house the Engineering Division, which had been formed on the move of Binder Engineering to the site in 1971.

Improvements were undertaken at The Court during 1972, with the building of a bridge to allow access from St. Swithin's Road for the larger road vehicles becoming common at this time. The opportunity was also taken to provide a grassed area for the fitting of very large nets, along with the drying of nets in the summer months. During the next year a new tracked, steam setting machine was installed, to cope with the higher temperatures needed by the new forms of nylon being used for nets.

Netting Division of Bridport Gundry Ltd.

In 1975 the trading operations of Bridport Gundry (Holdings) Ltd. were split into four marketing divisions each under a General Manager who reported to the Group General Manager. Bridport Gundry Ltd., with Michael Smith as General Manager, was placed within the Netting Division, which also included the Scottish and Irish Companies as well as the horticultural mail order companies of C. Sutton and W. James. The last named suffered a downturn in sales that year due to competition

introduced by Bridport Gundry Limited! A decision was thus made to improve the marketing of these two companies the following year.

In its first year of operation within the Netting Division, Bridport Gundry Limited reported a profit of twice the rate of inflation, despite the problems of the fishing industry. This had been achieved by diversifying away from fishing into other markets such as sports, horticulture, industrial and defence. One such example was the securing of a camouflage contract from the Brunswick Corporation for the US military, although this was later cancelled. In 1977 fishing figures held up well, allowing the division to achieve its targets despite camouflage orders from the Ministry of Defence being late. This growth continued into the next year, as these orders came into production. In the Leisure and Industrial sectors the results were patchy, although the improved marketing of the mail order companies had the desired effect and improved their position.

By now it was clear that the organisation of Bridport Gundry Ltd. was rather cumbersome and was affecting its ability to perform. Consequently, in 1978, the decision was made to break up business into four profit centres, each with their own management - Netting, Marine, Leisure and Defence and Industrial. Mike Smith became chief executive officer, with Mike Tuck as production manager. Norman Ollerton and John Lawrence were involved on the sales side, alongside Geoff Dilbey who was looking after the Industrial sales. In 1979 a number of new companies were set up as a result of this change. This emphasis on teamwork and accountability soon had the desired effect of reducing costs and improving deliveries.

Raymond Keepax, Mike Smith and Bill Budden, the executive of Bridport Gundry Ltd. Bill Budden ran Bridport Aviation Products from its formation in 1979 until his retirement in 1985.

Bridport Gundry Netting Ltd

Formed in 1979, Bridport Gundry Netting Ltd. was the centre for the manufacture of nets for all the Bridport divisions, with Norman Ollerton and John Banks tasked to seek alternatives markets for knotted netting.

In 1980 the Bridport manufacturing operations were brought under a single management. Netting was combined with North Mills Textiles and moved into the Twisted Products Division. The aim was to reduce costs and increase machine utilisation. A saving of some £200,000, achieved by the simple expedient of reducing stock levels at Netting, was made available to Twisted Products for the installation of high speed looms, which increased productivity significantly.

Following a poor performance Edwards Bridport Ltd. was rationalised, absorbing the loss making horticultural subsidiaries. One of these, C. Sutton was sold, although the company retained the manufacturing of certain nets and mechanical items. Mike Tuck and John Lawrence combined the sales and production staff to help reduce costs. In 1981 following serious losses, Edwards Bridport Ltd. became part of Bridport Gundry Netting Ltd.

Recovery from this difficult position was achieved by reducing the reliance on the production of low value, primary products like netting, which were vulnerable to competition by low price imports. In their stead the company concentrated on items where service and added value removed them from this competition, a task well suited to the young management team now in place.

The retirement of Raymond Keepax led to M. R. D. Cooper taking over briefly, before John Bowden was invited to join as General Manager, with Richard Connolly continuing as production manager. With the move of Bowden to Bridport Aviation Products Ltd. in 1985, Connolly was appointed General Manager. At the same time Norman Ollerton and David Smith resigned as directors of Netting, the former moving to Bridport Gundry Marine.

During these years Bridport Gundry Netting Ltd. performed well, having to increase capacity in order to meet demand. The acquisition of Hall's Barton in 1986 provided Netting with its own in-house extrusion capability, although this turned out to be short-lived. A new braiding facility was introduced in 1987, when £80,000 was invested in new German high speed netting machines, financed in part by the reduction in maintenance they would need.

In 1988, to allow the exploitation of areas of growth previously neglected, a separate sports and leisure business was created, with Edward Sports Products becoming a separate division within Netting. At this time Netting accounted for some 40% of the Group turnover, with the Marine companies forming by far their largest customer. By comparison Leisure and Industrial, largely safety netting for construction sites, accounted for just 7% each, while Aviation and Defence produced almost 25% of Group turnover.

In the autumn of 1989, with the construction industry showing an upturn in business, the opportunity was taken to re-launch the Industrial Division. The following year industrial netting surged ahead. Orders were up by some 50%, helped by the development of new products, such as the land fill nets made for Somerset County Council. The Marine and Leisure businesses did not perform as well, and the opportunity was taken to reorganise the Leisure business under a new General Manager. Edwards Sports Products, with Hugh Muir in charge, were the nominated suppliers for the Indoor Tennis Initiative funded by Local Authorities.

The following year Edwards achieved a sales growth of 11%. However even this, along with better margins, was not enough to give an acceptable return and led to its re-incorporation into netting. The opportunity was also taken to consolidate the sports and marine distribution businesses in order to reduce administration costs. Around this time Hugh Muir left to be replaced by Richard Storey, with Archie Barclay as his operations manager.

The purchase of shares in the French manufacturer and distributor of sports products, Corderie R. Soulet S.A., in 1990 was an attempt to increase the penetration of Group sales within Europe. Carolisa S.A., who owned the land and buildings of Corderie, was also purchased.

The sale of Halls Barton, with its extrusion facility, allied to the difficult trading conditions, led to Bridport Gundry looking at the future provision of netting supplies. The outcome of this was the formation of a joint company with Sicor of Portugal.

Relocation from The Court

By 1988 it was becoming clear that Netting was unprofitable, a position which was not helped by the wages paid in Bridport being two to three times higher than those in Portugal. Another reason for the move was the challenge of getting the requisite number of staff, there had been a fall in the numbers of 18-25 year olds in recent years.

A plan was devised in which net making would be based in Portugal, with Bridport Gundry concentrating on the assembly of these nets. By relocating to a new purpose built factory in Bridport, the firm would remove the restrictions imposed by the old Victorian infrastructure and cramped nature of The Court site, which would be sold to raise the necessary finance.

The Court, Miles Cross and Gore Cross

In 1990 Bridport Gundry successfully sought planning permission for the building of a new factory at Miles Cross, on land to be bought from Sir John Colfox. In the summer it was announced that The Court site was to be redeveloped by Centros Properties. Planning permission was approved in May 1991, allowing the provision of a supermarket, shops, hotel and a 400 space car park, while The Court itself was to be converted into offices.

In June 1990 Bridport Gundry withdrew the Miles Cross application as it was clear that, due to the recent increase in Bridport Aviation Product's output, the site was too small. Attention moved to Gore Cross, where Westbrook Property Development had submitted a planning application for a business park.

By the autumn of 1991 the recession in the property market was delaying the development of The Court and the move to Gore Cross. In the following year the plans were put on hold and the move to Gore Cross abandoned.

Sicor and Gundry

Founded in 1947, SICOR (Sociedate Industrial de Cordoraria S.A.) had been supplying Bridport Gundry Netting Ltd. with extruded yarns and ropes for some time. In early 1990 a meeting was held between them to discuss how a joint venture might establish a new competitive business in the E.U. Accordingly **Sicor and Gundry** was formed, with Alan Nute recruited from Bridport Gundry as Sales Executive. Bridport Gundry Netting Ltd. was to subscribe 50% of the ESC100m (£400,000), of which ESC25m (£100,000) was paid in November 1990, to allow incorporation later that month.

Land was bought for a netting factory, which would supply Bridport Gundry Netting Ltd., at San Pedro du Sol, Bordonhos, an E.U. grant aided area. Netting machines were sent to Portugal, to ensure the early production from the new factory.

The annual report for the year ending July 1991 stated that the new company traded satisfactorily in its first year. However Bridport Gundry withdrew from the project the following year, after Bridport Gundry Netting Ltd. suffered significant losses. The stated reason being that there was a difference of opinion with Sicor concerning the investment appropriate to the market. Bridport Gundry clearly thought a sourcing arrangement with Portugal was a better way forward than a joint manufacturing project. It was mutually decided to proceed independently, providing each other with technical support.

The disengagement cost Bridport Gundry over £70,000, as well as the netting machines sent to Portugal. In return they received an extrusion machine, which allowed them to produce their own twines. Sicor however went ahead with building the factory and started to produce its own netting, setting up a subsidiary, Sicornete, to achieve this.

1992 –1997
The End of an Era

1992 saw Netting make the first losses for a number of years, in part caused by a reduction in demand by the Marine sector. This led to the restructuring of netting manufacture and a reduction in capacity, in line with the new levels needed. Meanwhile Edwards Sports had managed to penetrate new markets and their products were now sold on commission by Brownell. Soulet continued to perform well and had acquired the Belgian firm of Stijen Sports.

The following year saw mixed fortunes, with some improvement in netting production and further attempts to reduce costs and overheads. This was especially true of Edwards Sports, where production and distribution methods were overhauled in order to re-establish a base from which better returns might be achieved.

The continued poor results, combined with the strategic review carried out by David Sebire and his new executive, led to the major restructuring of Edwards Sports and bulk netting. Preventative maintenance of the machinery had been put place at Netting and Edwards, reducing wastage and allowing more predictable manufacturing times. A three monthly forecasting of production was introduced, which was reviewed every fortnight. The result was that 80% of the manufacturing needs of the business were known in advance, allowing them to meet demands more flexibly. In addition a market survey of customers revealed some areas of concern. These were re-addressed, leading

Redport Nets, 96 East St, on the site of the linewalks of Edward Norman. A small company, it was a very successful part of Bridport Gundry and had the advantage of being able to use netting remnants from the parent firm.

to the production of accurate delivery targets.

This returned both to profit, providing a new platform from which to build the growth seen during the next year. There was also a £200,000 investment in Netting, with the provision of a large extrusion machine, 10 new braiders and two twisting machines.

With Netting unable to provide the returns for which the Group was looking, the decision was made to dispose of it, retaining only that capability needed to source the remaining core business units. Consequently Bridport Gundry Netting and Edwards were sold to separate management teams in 1997.

Redport Nets Ltd.

Redport Nets had been started by John and Alice Norris in 1948, trading from 96, East Street, Bridport on the site of the Norman family's rope and line walk of the 19th century. Around 1963 it passed into the hands of the Dosser family. Making salmon and trout angling nets, snooker pockets and horse blankets it employed seven workers, together with 150 outworkers, and had a turnover of £280,000. Bridport Gundry purchased the concern in December 1983 for £67,000. Peter Cox was brought in from Arthur Hart to become the managing director.

At first this seemed an unlikely acquisition but, because Redport made small nets and could use off-cuts from the Netting Division, it resulted in savings for the company. Consequently in many ways Redport was the 'Jewel in the Crown' of the Bridport Gundry companies, for it performed above budget in every year. In 1988 it acquired Fastnet Products, makers of high quality landing nets.

It remained part of Bridport Gundry until the firm came out of the traditional net making business in 1997.

North Mills Textiles Ltd.

Initially part of Bridport Gundry Ltd., North Mills was formed in August 1975. Part of Pearsall's, it was intended that the new company would seek other markets, thereby making use of the excess capacity at North Mills. In 1978 it, along with Pearsall's, became part of the Twisted Products division. Two years later, following reorganisation, it was given the same management as Bridport Gundry Netting Ltd. in an attempt to reduce working costs.

After a review of capacity in 1981 the North Mills site was offered for sale. The 124,000 sq. ft. of manufacturing space, within the site's 8¾ acres, was purchased by English Industrial Estates for use as small industrial units and offices. The sale was completed in 1983, with Bridport Gundry leasing back two units, one for the spinning of yarn and the other for making man-made fibres for the Netting division.

BRIDPORT AVIATION PRODUCTS

The Utility Department of J. Gundry & Co. Ltd.

Bridport Aviation Products had its origins with the formation of the Utilities department of Joseph Gundry and Co. in 1950. Following Bill Budden's extensive RAF experience in freighting to the forward troops after the D-Day landings, Blackburn Aircraft offered him employment. This was refused but enabled Gundrys to supply the paratroops restraint nets for the Blackburn Beverley in 1953, and also produce the netting required to cover the supplies being dropped from the same aircraft the following year.

In 1956 the Blackburn General Aircraft Company was taken over by Hawker Siddeley, who started using pallets for freight transport, the nets for which were again produced by J. Gundry and Co. The Company also made seat back nets for the growing airline market and, in 1960, produced the first helicopter under-slung nets for the MoD. The supplying of considerable quantities of cargo and helicopter nets to the aviation industry, prior to 1963, bolstered the position of Joseph Gundry and Co. in the merger talks with Bridport Industries.

Aviation within the Industrial Division of Bridport Gundry

The formation of Bridport Gundry saw the continued manufacture of these products, which were placed in its Industrial Division, where Bill Budden was Sales Manager.

Until 1970 Bridport Gundry was reliant on its three main customers for the design and acceptance stages of its aviation products. It was realised that this could not continue, so they hired Geoff Dilbey to head the newly formed Design and Development Department. Coming to Bridport Gundry from GQ Parachutes, Dilbey was an experienced textile engineer and it was not long before he had gained MoD and ARB (Air Registration Board) design approval, allowing Bridport Gundry to tender for contracts on its own. This certification was later extended to FAA and US National Aerospace Standards. The first products introduced by Geoff Dilbey were straightforward replacements, the one ton container net, for the re-supplying forward and parachuted troops, and the parachute troops restraint net.

The breakthrough came in 1971, when Hawker Siddeley Aviation patented Frank Clarke's cruciform net for securing aircraft pallet loads and licensed it free of charge to Bridport Gundry. In addition Hawker Siddeley Aviation gave them space to exhibit these nets at the Farnborough and Paris Air Shows, thereby allowing Bridport Gundry to get International exposure.

Since the knots weakened the twine by up to 50%, the cargo pallet nets had to be hand-made from very heavy braid. This was at the limit of the workforce's capabilities, especially as many were reaching more advanced years, there being few of the younger generation wanting to work from home.

The next development was the invention of the "knotless intersection" by Geoff Dilbey and patented by Bridport

Nets were used to contain the cargo being loaded into this Britannia aircraft of British United Airways in 1966. Cargo nets were developed in the 1950s by Gundrys in association with Blackburn Aircraft and their successors Hawker Siddeley.

Cruciform nets, using the knotless intersection invented by Geoff Dilby, were used for palleted loads. The use of these knotless nets allowed a thinner braid to be used, as they had no knots to weaken the strands.

Gundry in 1974. This allowed much lighter materials to be used, thus reducing the cost and making them much easier to make by the outworkers. To facilitate their manufacture a simple frame or jig was designed on which the net could be hand-made in one piece, incorporating the tensioners and floor fittings during manufacture.

By this time a number of airlines who were using Boeing 707 and DC8 aircraft had adopted palletised loading, allowing Bridport Gundry to sell these nets in large quantities. When Hawker Siddeley ceased to manufacture the pallets they sold the patent for the cruciform net to Bridport Gundry for £250.

The mid-1970s saw Japan Airlines sign a contract for air cargo pallet nets and it was decided to link up with a pallet maker, Nordiske Alumin of Norway, in order to compete in the Far East with their main competitor, Satco of Los Angeles. This was the start of a successful expansion into supplying the Far Eastern Airlines.

The early 1970s saw the entry into airfield arrester netting. Bill Budden went to Boscombe Down on a 'fun' parachute jump with the Army where he met Bill Neale, who advised him that the MoD was having problems with the supply of these nets from Aerazur of France. Beginning with the repair of arrester nets, Bridport Gundry moved on to design a prototype using webbing from Harts, which caused less damage to the aircraft on impact. The design was accepted by the MoD, leading to Bridport Gundry gaining their confidence and later its business. Once the contract had been received a new facility was established within The Court to provide the large area needed for the final assembly of these nets.

As the programme progressed Bridport Gundry were approached by the American manufacturer A.A.I., who made arrester brake systems, asking if Bridport Gundry would manufacture nets for them. A large number of nets were made under this contract allowing the Company to reach a world-wide market.

Bridport Aviation Products

Bridport Gundry's wish to isolate the management and profitability of the Aviation and Defence products from the rest of the Industrial Division, led to the formation of Bridport Aviation Products in 1979. With Bill Budden as the Managing Director, Ken Smith as Production Director and Geoff Dilbey as their Technical Director, the company sought a higher return on investment, aiming to use the profits generated to create and sell textile designs to Aviation and Military customers. They were not afraid to use marginal costing tactics if the competition demanded. The eventual aim was to remove Bridport Aviation Products from control of any other Bridport Gundry unit, although it was dependent on the Group for paying wages, salaries and production space. It also focused on the reduction of costs and overheads and preferred to engage young unskilled staff, who could be trained specifically for Bridport Aviation Products.

In 1980 the RAF, who were buying Chinook helicopters from Boeing, asked Bridport Gundry if they would join a consortium with Spanset, to offer the latter's patented Webbing Slings, which were used to carry the container payload. Bridport Gundry, unlike Spanset, had design approval procedures in place, which could be used to their advantage. In 1983 an Howden Test machine, costing £90,000, was bought to test the slings. Bridport Gundry was also asked to design a 10,000 lb (4,500kg) helicopter net using the knotless intersection. The slings and nets were tested at Boeing's Inspection Establishment at Wilmington Airfield, Delaware. Testing took place over several days, with a light aircraft flying nearby providing the turbulence needed to ensure that the Chinook's flight was not affected when carrying the loaded net. Webbing slings were later used to carry large items such as guns and vehicles.

The Bridport Gundry deputation took the opportunity to visit the US Air Force Development base at Fort Bragg, North Carolina, in order to demonstrate the equipment. This was followed by a trip to the Procurement Office at St. Louis, to try and negotiate sales. While Bridport Gundry was given a small contract, which had to be manufactured in the US, further sales were blocked by the 'Buy American' Act. Additionally a contract, with the

Bridport Gundry developed airfield barrier, or arrester, nets using webbing from A. Hart and Son. These caused less damage to the aircraft than ordinary rope netting.

Camouflage nets were one of Bridport Gundry's staple products and saw use in many theatres of war. The company employed advanced techniques in order to match the colours and reflections of the 'scrim' to the local vegetation, even going so far as to include the correct infra-red spectrum.

Brunswick Corporation of Wolf Point, Montana for the supply of camouflage base net for the US Military, was also blocked. This time Bridport Gundry's competitor, Indian Head Mills of Louisiana, had appealed to the US military to apply the obscure Berry Amendment to the above Act, which had not been exercised since the Second World War. These events led directly to the purchase of Brownell as Bridport Gundry's manufacturing base in the US.

Whilst Bridport Aviation Products was directed to service the Aviation Industry a subsidiary, Bridport International Ltd., was formed to sell its military products, primarily to overseas customers. Initial returns were comfortably ahead of budget and, although Bridport International did not gain any major contracts, it provided a service to Group subsidiaries. In 1982 the Falklands War provided a good platform for its under-slung helicopter nets, with its world wide television coverage. The result was a record year with the innovations and improvements exploited on both sides of the Atlantic. The introduction of container door netting, which increased safety if the load became detached in transit, meant that demand for all types of aircraft netting remained strong.

The following year proved to be even better, with record orders from the Ministry of Defence and the production of a wider range of camouflage nets, sales of which were extended into the overseas market in 1982. Bridport Gundry's first graduate in Textiles, Hugh Muir, was taken on and a photospectrometer, that covered the infra red spectrum, was bought. This was used in the Far East to measure the colours and reflections of the local vegetation, enabling an accurate match for the scrim colours to be achieved. Hugh Muir also introduced a camouflage fabric chemist, Alan Newman, from Bridport Gundry's leaf supplier in Scotland. The result was a considerable and continuous contract for a much higher grade of camouflage net.

Bill Budden OBE retired in 1985 and was replaced by

Helicopter underslung nets being used by a Chinnook helicopter flying for the UN. The payload of these nets was rated at 10,000 lbs, roughly 4,500 kg.

The Falklands War provided world-wide exposure for the helicopter underslung nets. The Sea King helicopter is ferrying goods in San Carlos Bay, with SS *Canberra* in the background.

John Bowden, with Geoff Dilbey taking over Aircraft Sales and Howard Earl managing Design and Development. Bowden had arrived in 1982 and was initially employed as the General Manager of Netting, which gave him the opportunity to see how Bridport Aviation Products was structured. This led to a strategic review being carried out in 1986, which came up with the following recommendations:

1. The upgrading of Design and Development, together with an improvement in quality control.

2. Accounting was to be taken in-house, with the result that Chris Louden was appointed to the newly created position of financial manager.

3. There were to be better financial rewards for employees.

4. The level of military involvement was to remain at the current level. Military orders were not predictable and, while they could provide a very welcome boost to profits, there were often lean periods in between.

5. The development of the civil aviation side of the business.

The key to this last named was again the idea of Geoff Dilbey, involving the provision of underfloor nets for the Airbus A320. Because of the knotless construction, using Hart's webbing, together with the shape and metalwork incorporated in them, the nets had to be made by outworkers, from kits supplied by Bridport Aviation Products.

The provision of these nets meant that Bridport Aviation Products had become original equipment manufacturers for the first time, and this proved to be a most significant point in the company's history. The resulting strong growth continued for a number of years, although there was a downturn in camouflage orders in 1987. New products continued to come on stream, such as the space shuttle arrester nets for the N.A.S.A. and main deck barrier nets for Airbus.

1987 also saw the failure of Bruggemann and Brandt, the original suppliers of underfloor nets for the A300 and A310. Bridport Aviation Products sent a lorry to Germany to recover the Airbus-owned machinery and take it to Bridport, where a new production line was set up to complete their manufacture. That this was achieved, with

Underfloor nets using webbing with the knotlesss intersection from Harts. They were made by outworkers, carrying on the tradition going back hundreds of years.

a final delivery only two weeks adrift of the original date, proved to be of great value in later years, when Bridport Aviation Products were awarded the orders for the A330 and A340 aircraft. These contracts meant that, by 1989, civil aviation sales accounted for 10% of the Group turnover. In addition Defence and Space covered some 14% of Group sales, although a moratorium on Defence spending reduced this the following year.

In 1984 cargo restraint nets were being made at the rate of 100 per week, by the autumn of 1991 this had increased to 1000 per week and they were being used by most of the world's airlines.

Bin visors, which stop passengers' luggage from falling from the overhead lockers, were increasingly being fitted to the major carriers' aircraft, with the first being fitted to a British Airways 747, to be followed by Pan Am and Virgin. After completing the fitting of the 747 fleet, the bin visor range was extended to the 757s.

Military contracts split into camouflage netting, with the market for this mainly in the Far East, New Zealand and Europe, and the helicopter under-slung nets and torpedo recovery systems. In 1992 Bridport Industries Canada started to supply camouflage netting to the Canadian Armed Forces. However this story really starts with Bridport Aviation Products and the 1986 review of military markets. Few of these were suited to Bridport Aviation Products and it was decided to look towards Canada. This was the territory of a Swedish competitor and it took some six years before any headway was made. Eventually Bridport Aviation Products landed a contract worth Can$16m over a four year period. The Canadians insisted on a significant home-based content and were not satisfied with the intention of Bridport Aviation Products to obtain only the scrim from Canada. Since they were unable to source the netting from Bridport it was decided to set up the operation at the Bridport Industries factory at Dartmouth, Nova Scotia. Whilst primarily a Bridport Aviation Products led operation, the moneys were paid into the Bridport Industries account.

The First Gulf war of 1991 led to increased sales of camouflage netting and decoy systems, while humanitarian help to the Kurds saw the deployment of drop nets for the delivery of aid. The channelling of resources into the military saw the reduction in sales of cargo restraints that year, but this still resulted in a 9% increase in overall sales. The following year, with the end of the First Gulf war, saw a downturn but, with the improved control of cost margins, allied to reductions in overheads and stock, Bridport Aviation Products still managed to provide an excellent return. However the downturn in defence orders continued and, to make up for this, Bridport Aviation Products concentrated on providing the consumables for the ever increasing world-wide demands for rapid deployment and relief aid.

By 1994 cargo restraints composed 75% of UK sales, with sale of bin visors being greatly reduced as a result of their fitting most of the UK fleets. Enquiries by two major

Use was made of the aerial delivery system, using drop nets, to provide aid for refugees, especially during the First Gulf War. The photograph on the left shows a load being prepared for dropping.

	1995/6	1996/7	1997/8
Sales	£12.2m	£20.1m	£24.8m
Operating Profit	£1.7m	£3.1m	£4.3m

Table 18. The sales and operating profit figures for Bridport Aviation Products from 1995 to 1998.

airlines resulted in the increased investment in Research and Development, providing a new R&D Centre in the old Carpentry shop at The Court, which was run by Howard Earl, following the retirement of Geoff Dilbey MBE.

Success continued into the following year when Bridport Aviation Products' sales, at £10.5m, accounted for 35% of Group turnover. Air cargo restraint sales continued their strong growth, along with resurgence in the sales of helicopter under-slung nets and slings.

The opportunity was also taken to identify markets on which to focus resources in future, and the decision was taken to concentrate on the provision of spares, maintenance, services and inventory management. These together with the design and manufacture of the textile components of cabin interiors, were to be the new lines to carry Bridport Aviation Products forward.

The acquisition, for £925,000, of Britannic Aviation, who dealt in consumables such as filters and antennae, was the first sign of this change in direction. In June 1996 the business was moved to Albourne, to be nearer to Gatwick Airport. This was followed by the purchase of Militair Aviation, which had been formed in 1990 by David Lock, the company moving to Ringwood shortly after the takeover. In 1997 they were given the Queens Award of Export and in the same year Militair Inc. of Canada was started. In 1996 Bridport Aviation Products acquired Avery Flight International, manufacturers of passenger cabin textiles, and Safetywear Limited, who were distributors of protective clothing for the aviation industry, for £8.25m.

By now 60% of sales were in the civil aviation sector and Bridport Aviation Products exported 65% of its products. The phenomenal growth seen by Aviation and Defence is evident from the figures in Table 18.

For many years Bridport Aviation Products had been courting the American aircraft manufacturer Boeing but to little effect. However in 1998 they received a call from Boeing informing them of the collapse of the firm which supplied their cargo restraint nets. The result was the purchase by Bridport Gundry of Air Carriers Inc. of Seattle for £2.139m, allowing them entry into the American market for cargo restraint nets. When asked why they had made

A cargo barrier net as fitted to a Boeing 737, these helped to prevent damage to the aircraft in the event of the load becoming detached.

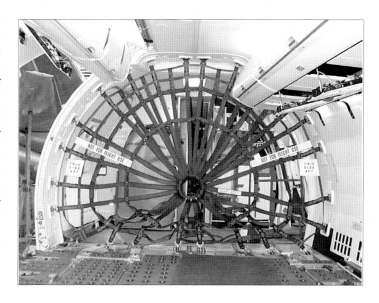

the call, Boeing informed Bridport Aviation Products that they had known about how Bridport Aviation Products had worked with BAe and Airbus Industrie when their German suppliers failed some 10 years earlier!

By now they had a joint venture in Asia based in Singapore, supporting Boeing and Airbus, as well as a base in Erie, Pennsylvania.

John Bowden's long and successful career with Bridport Aviation Products ended with his retirement, his place being taken by Robert McIlwraith. Bridport Aviation Products was to form one of the core businesses for Bridport Gundry after the review of 1993

JAMES PEARSALL AND CO. LTD.

By 1972 production at the Taunton factories had reached capacity and work was being sent to North Mills in order to match demand. The outstanding returns made by Pearsalls over the next few years were the result of the investment made in buildings, plant and machine efficiency during that time.

In 1977 Pearsalls was the best performing member of the Group and had just completed the first phase of expansion into the sewing thread field. The new factory at Priorswood was commissioned, adding some 30,000 sq. ft. of space. It was fitted out with 28 twisting machines for the production of continuous filament yarn, although silk was still being used for most sutures. The following year was not as successful, caused by the recession in their traditional market being stronger than forecast, and by the expansion into sewing threads taking longer to achieve than was hoped.

Pat Darley was appointed General Manager in June 1978. Coming from Tootals, the second largest thread makers in the world, he was appointed to give direction to the newly emerging thread division. With Pearsalls main UK customer having decided to make their own sutures, he arrived to find many of the suture braiding machines stopped. The problem was solved with the help of Lawson Lyon, who was recruited from a Glaxo subsidiary which sold products for operating theatres. With his contacts, he rapidly built up the marketing of the sutures, getting a number of large orders from the Middle East. The result was that the Taunton machines were now working fully employed

The thread market was a more difficult one. Trying to increase sales, in a market dominated by two major companies, was proving difficult for a relatively small company. The decision was taken to become more selective in their marketing strategy. It was realised that there was a niche market in the production of coarse sewing threads, suitable for shoes and heavy industry. Pearsalls set out to capture that market, and were helped by hearing that the West Country shoe firm of C. and J. Clark was having a problem with the threads currently being used. Pearsalls suggested that sutures be used instead and, while this rather expensive solution worked in trials, an economic solution was developed using a nylon and polyester braid. This resulted in the solving of Clarks' problem and Pearsalls finding extra work for their machines.

In 1979 the expected recovery duly appeared helped by the firm's increased involvement in the manufacturing of specialist high grade industrial textiles. Contracts were exchanged for the sale of the Tancred street site, with the money realised being invested in a further extension of the Priorswood site.

1980 saw mixed returns, although some areas of the business were performing well, overall trade was down. Progress was being held back by de-stocking within the Group and customers cutting back on their orders. It was at this time that the decision was made to reduce reliance on Bridport, by the production of more sophisticated products at Taunton.

1981 saw the end of a three year period of reorganisation at Taunton, with Pearsalls moving from being a supplier of sutures, primarily to one customer in the UK, to manufacturers and sellers of branded products. Much of the commission sales on twisted products had been lost in the recession, now the company was supplying most of their sutures to the EU, opening a subsidiary distribution company, Pearsalls SARN of Paris, to service this developing market. When Pat Darley left, to become Deputy Chairman and Chief Executive of the Group, Lawson Lyon became Pearsall's General Manager.

A further reorganisation of the factory site was brought forward by a serious fire in 1982, which resulted in the firm making a loss. However these losses were minimised by the growth in sutures supplied to the EU, together with the increasing sales of bonded nylon thread. This rapid growth had been difficult to manage and resulted in the move of M. R. D. Cooper from Bridport to become Pearsall's Managing Director.

By 1983 the firm had successfully diversified into other products, now only 10% of its business was the same as that produced four years ago. These figures were not helped by production problems, which hounded manufacture for much of the year, nor by a significant stock write-off, caused by the introduction of a more stringent regime of stock ageing.

In 1985 the improving performance in the sales of sutures and the slow growth of sewing threads led to Pearsalls being split into two units, one for industrial thread and the other for sutures. Its market position was further helped by improvements being made in the facilities for suture manufacture. At the same time, problems in the French market led to the sale of Pearsalls SARN.

Over the next few years sales of sewing threads gradually improved, accompanying the growth seen in the sale of sutures. By 1988 Pearsalls accounted for 20% of Bridport Gundry's turnover. Growth continued into the next year with Pearsalls enjoying a 35% UK and 7% EU market share for its continuous filament and braid, which was an essential product for computer-operated sewing

	1971	1972	1973	1974	1975	1976
profit after tax (£)	17,966	26,088	41,168	82,663	96,952	2 months
B-G share of profits (£)	7,693	11,171	17,678	35,396	41,516	7,014

machinery. They had also introduced highly lustrous embroidery thread, designed for use in modern high speed embroidery machines, while 80% of suture production was being sold to the EU.

It was increasingly evident that Pearsalls, as a small player in a market dominated by the large manufacturers, was not getting the returns now expected by the Group. In May 1991 Pearsalls Thread was sold to Barbour Campbell Ltd for £1.65m, a move which allowed Bridport Gundry to concentrate on the manufacture of sutures, these being deemed to have a more viable future. Following the signing of a contract with American Cyanamid Company of New Jersey for the manufacture of suture materials, a new suture plant was installed in the space released from thread manufacture. By the following year sales were up 34%, largely the result of this new investment.

The introduction of a new Laboratory Information Management System meant the streamlining of data collection and reporting. During this period, the focus was on the development of new products, including absorbable suture thread, which necessitated the construction of a special 'dry room'.

Pearsalls gained the Queen's Award for Exports in 1993 and, despite a factory fire in November 1994, the next two years showed strong growth, with profits financing the acquisition of Pielenz Flechtgarne of Berlin, a manufacturer of sutures which was soon incorporated into the Taunton business.

This strong performance saw Pearsalls become one of the core activities of the Group following the strategic review of 1993.

ARTHUR HART & SON LTD.

Initially owned by Sparks and Gidley, Viney Bridge mill, Crewkerne, had been in operation since 1789. Making woollen girth webs and lines, it became Arthur Hart in 1883.

In 1946 it merged with Richard Hayward and Co., an old established sailcloth firm, to form Crewkerne Textiles, with Joseph Gundry and Co. also taking a significant financial interest. When Bridport Gundry was formed Crewkerne Textiles became an associated company, similar to Gourock Bridport Gundry in Canada. Bridport Gundry owned 42.82% of the shares and it made a useful contribution to the company's accounts (see Table 19).

Profits increased sharply during the period shown above although they flattened off in the later years. In 1976, with John and Richard Hayward approaching retirement age after more than 40 years in the business, Bridport Gundry

Table 19. The profit figures for Arthur Hart and Son from 1971 to 1976, showing their contribution to Bridport Gundry's figures.

purchased the remaining shareholding for £194,000. John Hayward became a director of Bridport Gundry and continued running Crewkerne Textiles.

Although the company was too small to have a great impact on the group finances the year 1976/7 started well, with a strong upturn due to increased defence orders and webbing contracts for Bridport Aviation Products. The following year saw a poor summer which affected the sailcloth market, eroding the healthy margins earned by the narrow fabric business. In October John Hayward retired, moving to become chairman, with Peter Cox, a member of the Group Board, taking over as General Manager. Crewkerne Textiles was split into sailcloth and weaving divisions in order to assess the profitability of each. The Hayward Seaspeed sailcloth continued to be improved and modern machinery was introduced into the narrow fabric division. However, in spite of these changes, profits in 1979 were disappointing.

By 1980 it was obvious that the webbing division was supporting the sailcloth side of Crewkerne Textiles. Without embarking on a major investment programme, Bridport Gundry was unable to provide the full range of spinnaker cloth to sailmakers. As a result the business, goodwill and assets of Hayward's sailcloth were sold to John Heathcote and Co. (Sales) of Tiverton for £440,000. Crewkerne Textiles survived but was now trading as Arthur Hart and Son Ltd.

The money gained was invested in the expansion of Harts, who had an increasingly important role to play in production of webbing for Bridport Aviation Products. In addition, Arthur Hart & Son was encouraged to seek new markets for their webbing. Although a small loss of £37,000 was reported in 1982, by the following year the corner had been turned, with the announcement of a £100,000 profit. This allowed an outlay of £72,000 to be made for the purchase of three new automatic looms from Italy, the modification of 28 old looms, as well as overhauling the old fly looms. Other changes allowed the webbing to fall direct from the looms into drum containers ready for transfer to Bridport.

In March 1984 Bridport Gundry was approached by developers, offering to purchase the Viney Bridge site and build a replacement factory in the field opposite. David Smith, the managing director, was asked to investigate the proposal, but reported back advising Bridport Gundry to enlarge the old factory instead.

It was decided to develop the south shed of 1938/9,

Detail of the webbing used for underfloor nets. The metal fittings are incorporated by the outworkers at the time of manufacture.

adding some 9,000 square feet of factory space in the process. For tax reasons completion had to be by March 1985, leading to the contract with R. C. Spiller being signed and building started by the end of September 1984. The new building was commissioned in May 1985, complete with new looms. In 1986 additional looms were purchased from the Healey Narrow Fabrics plant of Levi Jackson, Glossop.

David Smith moved from Harts in 1986 to look after Lolift (Bridport Gundry) Ltd. and was replaced by Ray Fallon. The business continued to expand with a move into the sling webs business and, at the same time, Harts began working in the American fashion trade, with the opening of Hart's Agency in Moodus, Connecticut, which lasted until the reorganisation of Brownell in 1988.

1987 was a difficult year financially following a lack of orders from Bridport, on which they increasingly relied. The next year the Crewkerne Textiles name was dropped and the business was known simply as Arthur Hart and Son, becoming a division of James Pearsall and Co. Ltd in 1989.

As its output increasingly went to Bridport Aviation Products, Harts was concentrating on high performance webbing, such as Airbus restraint systems and Space Shuttle nets, which resulted in an increase in profitability. Further changes in organisation followed in quick succession, with Arthur Hart Webbings acting as a stand-alone business within Bridport Gundry Textiles Ltd in 1991, before becoming a division of Bridport Gundry (UK) Ltd. a year later.

In the early 1990s the general UK recession hit business, with reduced demand from Bridport Aviation Products, as well as lower orders for industrial slings, upholstery and fashion. A review of operations led to changes, which were aimed at putting the business back on track, with Harts becoming part of the Industrial Division in 1993. These changes were clearly successful as the next Annual Report stated that the niche marketing policy recently introduced had paid off, helped by product differentiation and improved cost control. Progress continued with margins improved the following year, producing better profits on lower sales.

In 1995 sales increased 23%, resulting in profits being almost double those of the previous year. The company was now focusing on special webbings for a variety of applications, for both internal and external customers, with nearly 50% of sales deriving from the aviation market, both home and abroad. Its continued success saw it become one of the core businesses in the reorganisation of 1997.

HALL'S BARTON ROPERY LTD.

Hall's ropeworks was founded in 1767, becoming John Hall Ltd. in 1890 and Hall's Barton Ropery Ltd. four years later, having produced its first wire ropes in 1891. It was based in Barton on Humber, which possessed the last natural fibre rope walk in Europe. With the take over of Overton Bros., it expanded to include their Hull and Beverley factories, transferring the wire rope making to the latter. They also leased a depot at Wapping and another at Aberdeen.

The company made extruded polythene and other fibres, which they spun into twines and ropes which, along with wire and combination ropes, were sold to the fishing, shipping, defence and engineering industries. In the year 1984/5 their turnover was £6.98m, producing a pre-tax profit of £236,209 (£227,347 net). Recent results had been affected by a lack of volume of sales resulting in the under-usage of plant.

As part of a general search for growth opportunities and wanting to secure its own extrusion facilities, in order to produce their own twines, Bridport Gundry expressed an interest in acquiring the company. At the time Bridport Gundry was trying to develop along vertically integrated lines and this was seen as a complimentary business which would help in this process and, in some ways, was integral to this new direction. The company was acquired in May 1986 for £2.92m, financed by the issuing of 1,206,300 ordinary 20p shares.

Initially prospects were good, with the Beverley plant heavily booked and the extrusion facilities at the Barton factory being boosted by the Group demand. However the recent increase in imports of cheap natural and synthetic fibres was causing concern. A review of operations saw the closure of the Hull factory, with its work transferred to Beverley, and the re-equipment of the Barton on Humber factory, with better extrusion lines and new synthetic ropewalks in place of the natural fibre walk. As well as costing more, this took longer to achieve than was expected, which resulted in a poor return for the year 1986/7.

The opportunity was taken to strengthen the management, with Steve Rutherford taking over as General Manager, and at the same time the staffing level, originally around 300 strong, was cut by 22%. The reorganisation was completed in July 1988 and shortly after the company was renamed Hall's Barton.

However the firm did not perform as it was hoped and

significant trading losses were being made. With the new Group Board Policy being to concentrate on those parts of the business giving a good return on their investment the closure of Hall's Barton was not unexpected, occurring in October 1989. Bridport Gundry retained the freehold at Barton, Barking and Aberdeen, while selling the Beverley factory and the goodwill to Bridon plc, the Doncaster Wire Manufacturers, for £850,000.

LOLIFT (BRIDPORT GUNDRY) LIMITED

'W' Ribbons (Holdings) plc of South Wales was facing financial difficulties and had gone into receivership in the autumn of 1984. As the firm already supplied Bridport Aviation Products Pat Darley and John Hayward visited them to see if there was any potential in acquiring it. While it was decided not to buy the business, steps were taken to ensure that Harts had the necessary equipment to take advantage of the loss of a competitor.

However one of its subsidiary companies, Mendstyle (Lolift UK) Limited, did show potential and a visit was arranged for early September 1984. The firm had two factories; the larger one at Ripon employed 61 staff, while the smaller factory at Knaresborough employed 86. They were manufacturers of intermediate bulk containers used in the fertiliser and building trades. Pearsall's were already supplying their threads and it was thought that, in future, the webbing could come from Harts. The firm had been trading profitably for a number of years; it was the problems with the parent company that brought Lolift on to the market (see Table 20).

Bridport Gundry had been looking at entering the intermediate bulk container market, which they viewed as being complementary to the products of Bridport Aviation Products and Brownell, but had been deterred by the start-up costs. Here was an ideal opportunity to fulfil that aim and, accordingly, in October 1984 the business was purchased for £1,315,000, later amended to £798,000. In November it was renamed Lolift (Bridport Gundry) Ltd.

After looking at the way the business was conducted, it was decided to close the Knaresborough factory and concentrate work at Ripon, leasing a second factory there. This was estimated to produce annual savings of £70,000, even though it was decided not to make anyone redundant. Once the plan had gone ahead it was clear that the Knaresborough workers, most of who lived in Harrogate,

Table 20. The trading figures for Lo-lift UK prior to their takeover by Bridport Gundry.

	1981	1982	1983	1984	1985 (est)
Turnover (£000)	2,609	6,541	3,771	5,235	6,000
Trading profit (£000)	304	424	335	335	421

did not want to move to Ripon. Labour management in the old company was not strong and, with the concentration of work at Ripon, the employees saw their position strengthened and became more difficult.

However, with a strengthened management in place and production facilities improved, a £208,000 pre-tax profit was posted in the first ten months, the good results continuing into the following year. However in March 1986 it lost its biggest customer of fertiliser bags. This forced Lolift to widen its customer base while steps were taken to reduce capacity in line with demand.

However the continued recession in the fertiliser trade, allied to the over-production of the containers, was causing concern. The decision was made to consult the workforce on alternative working practices, which would allow the business to continue. However, even with the help of ACAS, the employees could not be convinced of the seriousness of the situation and no agreement was forthcoming. Bridport Gundry took the decision to close the factory, even though it would lead to a pre-tax loss of £160,000, and by March 1987 talks were being held with potential buyers.

MARINE COMPANIES

Bridport Gundry Marine Ltd.

Bridport Gundry Marine Ltd was formed in 1978, having been formerly part of Bridport Gundry Ltd. It was a distribution company, selling the fishing products of the newly formed Bridport Gundry Netting Ltd., and was charged with developing new orders for the Company's products.

The distribution network was based around a central supply depot at The Court in Bridport, linked to a number of outstations spread throughout the UK and Ireland. The English depots were at London, Manchester, a relic of Edwards' depot set up there in the 1920s, Whitby and Lowestoft, until the reduction in the East Coast fishing fleet forced the closure of the last named in 1982.

During the 1980s the South West fisherman had taken

Bridport Gundry's Lowestoft depot around 1970, the company relocated here after closure of the Sunrise Works. Note that the Gourock had their own depot, they also had one in Bridport in the early part of the 20th century.

to forming co-operatives in an attempt to force down the price of netting supplies. In order to combat this Bridport Gundry Marine expanded their South Coast distribution network. The formation in 1981 of the Brixham Net Company Ltd., in which Bridport Gundry had a 51% share, saw a new manufacturing and distribution outlet in the South West. This was to have been followed by another depot at Penzance, with the leasing of the old Pickford depository. When this was later deemed to be unsuitable one was purchased in Newlyn, opening in 1984. The following year a new depot was opened at Bexhill, to service the South East. It was during this year that Norman Ollerton took over as Managing Director.

This expansion of the retail distribution network continued in 1986, with the building of a new shop and warehouse at The Court. By now, however, fishing was in decline and Bridport Gundry was looking for new areas of growth. The higher value returns from aquaculture and trawl-making resulted in the exchange of Bridport Gundry's interest in Jackson Trawls for the whole equity of J. and W. Stuart and the acquisition of Net Tec in Padstow.

The continued decline in the fishing market saw the closure of the depots at Bexhill and Newlyn in 1990 and, although a new depot had been operating at Hartlepool for a short while, the closures continued with Padstow and Aberdeen succumbing in 1994.

1990 saw the merger of the Marine division with the Industrial and Leisure Division in an attempt to reduce overheads. Two years later, following the continued decline of the fishing trade and the sale of J. & W. Stuart and Bridport Gundry Ireland, Bridport Gundry Marine was reintegrated with Netting.

No longer seen as a core component the company was sold off in 1997, by which time the only depots left were at Brixham and Bridport.

Brixham Net Company Ltd.
In 1981 a 51% shareholding was taken in the Brixham Net Company Ltd. a manufacturer and supplier of nets for near water and inshore fisheries. Although a small loss

was made in its first few months of trading, its prospects were thought to be bright. It soon became well established and the remaining shareholding was taken over in 1983. In 1986 it had an exceptional year, becoming a division within Bridport Gundry Marine Ltd the following year.

By 1989 it had developed a niche market with profits increasing, whereas elsewhere they were falling. However by 1991 the recession in the fishing market had caught up with it and sales were slowing down. The following year, despite struggling, it met its targets but in 1995 it was fully merged with Bridport Gundry Marine, in an attempt to reduce overheads.

Net Tec of Padstow
In 1988 Bridport Gundry took over Net Tec, who not only serviced the local fishing fleet but also made use of innovative computer software for the design of trawls. Part of the late 1980s expansion in marine businesses, the new company made a profit in its first year despite the disruption caused by moving into a new factory.

However in the longer term the venture was not successful and, as the fishing market contracted, the business was only kept open by the assembly of air cargo nets. This merely delayed closure and the end came in 1994 when the site was offered for sale.

Polyform Marine Limited
Polyform, of Worcester, were makers of plastic floats for the fishing industry, for whom Bridport Gundry became main agents around 1974. In July 1986, as part of the drive to become 'vertically integrated', Bridport Gundry and Dynomar of Norway each took a 50% share in the company. Technically Polyform was outside the Bridport Gundry portfolio and could trade with any other concern, although Bridport Gundry was their preferred customers.

This arrangement continued until 1990, when the re-focusing of Bridport Gundry left Polyform Marine on the edge of its trading area. The result was its restructuring with Norman Ollerton, who had just retired from Bridport Gundry, being called in to look after Dynomar's interest. Ollerton set up Dynomar Marine, running the Bridport agency until 2005, when it was sold to Peter Fanning Polyform Ltd., relocating to Stone, Staffordshire.

The official opening of Killybegs. Left to right are James McLeod, Norman Ollerton, John Gundry, Hugh Norman, Reg Besley and Mrs Besley and Jack Gobbett.

Bridport Gundry (Ireland)
James McLeod was born in Scotland in 1912, later moving to Ireland. Following his apprenticeship in the merchant navy he entered the fishing industry in 1935, buying a boat with Tom Swan the following year.

In 1967 he decided to build a store, which would have space for working on the boat's gear, near his home in Killybegs. Whilst it was being constructed he was approached by Bridport Gundry, whose hold on the Irish market was falling, asking if they could buy it. An arrangement was made whereby Bridport Gundry would purchase it, employing James McLeod as a technical advisor. McLeod was given an option to join the company full-time when he retired from fishing, which he duly exercised in 1971.

Bridport Gundry (Ireland), although registered in Ireland, was wholly owned by the parent company. In April 1967 temporary premises were opened in the Main Street at Killybegs, which allowed trading to take place until the new building was completed. The two storey building provided office accommodation on the ground floor, along with an 80ft working alley and a store room, while on the first floor was a complete working loft. The buildings cost £164,000, with a further £96,000 for machinery. Also included in the sale was the adjoining land, intended for use as a yard for washing nets prior to their repair as well as allowing for future expansion.

Initial staffing consisted of Roger Hutchings, who was sent from Bridport as manager, along with George Gallagher, who was an experienced assistant and fully understood the market for small boat gear. On the opening of the new building, staffing was increased by an office assistant and three netmakers. Nets were sent out from Bridport, to be worked up by the netmakers ready for sale to the fishing trade. The good start was spoiled by the difficulties in the relationship with the parent company, leading to Norman Ollerton, previously the manager of Bridport Gundry Marine, taking over the following year.

Trade prospered and a second two storey building, to the rear of the original, was added in 1971. The ground floor was used for storage and the upper floor was used as an additional work space. Later a tarring shed was also added near the entrance to the yard.

From its initial use as a store, Killybegs developed to manufacture and rig nets for near water and inshore fisheries. In 1982, following the success of Bridport Gundry's partnership in Jackson Trawls, an agreement was reached to sell 49% of the equity in Bridport Gundry (Ireland) Limited to Tommy Watson, an experienced local trawler skipper, who subsequently became its Managing Director.

Expansion continued and necessitated a new store, which was built on land on the Roshine Road purchased from Tommy Watson. The new shed was 40ft tall, to allow work to be carried out on larger trawls, which was further helped by the installation of two gantry cranes. An upper loft was included at the rear of the building. Later another store was built adjacent to the older one and the space between roofed to give an additional working area. The adjoining land was purchased in order to provide a tarred 'runway' for working on the new ultra-large pelagic trawls then coming into use.

Sadly Tommy Watson died in late 1984 and it would seem that his share-holding returned to the parent company, which then held 89.1%, with James McLeod owning the balance. November 1989 saw the issuing 11,250 ordinary shares of Bridport Gundry (Ireland) to Michael Gallagher (7,500) and Joseph Murrin (3,750), the aim being to provide a long term incentive to improve the profitability of the subsidiary company. In order to maintain his level of investment, James McLeod received 120 additional shares.

In 1988 Bridport Gundry Ireland was producing profits of around £150,000 a year. Bob Holder remained as their chairman at their request, despite his leaving the Group. When he resigned from this position in 1990, it was hoped that Norman Ollerton would take over. However he was given early retirement from Bridport Gundry.

The next two years were difficult, with the recession in the trawl making business leading to the closure of the depot at Howth, Co. Dublin. This had the effect of reducing overheads and, with good sales, Bridport Gundry (Ireland) returned a moderate profit in the year ending July 1992. However with the Group Board placing it under constant review the writing was clearly on the wall.

Bridport Gundry bought back the whole of the issued equity for £110,000, and in December 1993 Bridport Gundry (Ireland) was sold for £559,000.

Bridport Gundry in Scotland

On its formation, Bridport Gundry already had a presence in Scotland with the Gundry operation at Campbeltown, while James Brighouse Ltd. of Aberdeen was added in 1964. During the next 30 years their Scottish involvement went through a series of changes as dictated by the needs of the fishing industry.

In June 1968 a new factory was opened in Aberdeen, to allow for the expansion of the James Brighouse operation and the closure of the Campbeltown factory, while a small depot, Craigwean Stores, was opened at Peterhead to manufacture nets and rigging, and was run by John Buchan. The difficult trading conditions, with the cramped conditions prior to the opening of the new factory, allied with the death of its Managing Director James Mowatt, resulted in a loss of £25,815 in that year. To help restore profitability Peter Cox was sent to Aberdeen, charged with exercising both general and administrative control.

The following year James Brighouse returned a small profit of £4,173 and, with the arrival of John de Freville, the business, which manufactured deep water trawl gear, was renamed Bridport Gundry (Scotland). 1970 was another difficult year producing only a small profit, but after some reorganisation sales increased significantly.

By 1975 however things were not looking good, with a loss again being reported. When this continued into the next financial year it was decided to withdraw from Aberdeen. The factory was closed and Bridport Gundry (Scotland) ceased trading at the end of July 1976.

To replace this operation a new company, Jackson Trawls of Peterhead, was formed in November 1975, in which Bridport Gundry held a 51% stake. This company was the result of a merger of Craigewan Stores with Seaquest Nets, run by Arthur Buchan who had a good record in the business of trawl-making for the inshore fleets of Scottish seiners. Aiming for quality, these products were not cheap but sold successfully. Craigewan Stores, opposite Seaquest's base, concentrated on fish cages, with

Above Arthur Buchan and Mrs Buchan. Buchan ran Seaquest Nets, joining with Bridport Gundry's Craigewen Stores to form Jackson Trawls in 1975.

Above right J. and W. Stuart's new factory at Musselburgh which opened in 1983. Bridport Gundry took a 51% holding in the company in 1978. In 1987, following the sale of its interest in Jackson Trawls, it became a wholly owned company within Bridport Gundry.

Alan Nute being sent up from Bridport to become depot manager. The new company was an immediate success, initially returning good profits to the Group. In 1980 a new rigging shed was opened in Peterhead to cope with the increased trade.

J. & W. Stuart of Esk Mills, Musselburgh had a long history, being founded in 1812 after taking over the business of Patterson, whose design of braiding looms were the first used in Bridport. The post-war period saw grants being made by the Government to renew cotton mill machinery, in order to stimulate sales in cotton goods. However the introduction of cheap imports soon saw this part of the business decline. In addition, the net making machinery was becoming rather outdated, not having been renewed in the post war period. In 1978 finding trading increasingly difficult the firm turned for help to Bridport Gundry, who took a 51% share in the business, with Walter Hay, who had joined in 1972, being made general manager.

In 1982 Bridport Gundry took over the whole shareholding of J. & W. Stuart, financed by selling its Lowestoft depot. Shortly afterwards a reorganisation saw the J. & W. Stuart operation merge with Jackson Trawls, in whom Bridport Gundry had a 51% stake. This allowed the designation of distinct trading areas, with Jackson Trawls dealing with the northern Scottish ports and J. & W. Stuart with those as far south as Hull.

The following year Jackson Trawls made an agreement to manufacture John West's oil slick recovery system and a new company, Jackson (PD) Ltd., was formed to do this, wholly owned by Jackson Trawls Ltd.

In the same year J. & W. Stuart opened a factory at Musselburgh, the result of the Scottish Development Agency (SDA) providing grants for new factories. Opening in July 1983, the building was initially rented from the

SDA but J. & W. Stuart later purchased the freehold for around £100,000, while the old Eskmills Factory was sold for development.

New trawl makers, comprising some ex-fishermen who had decided to come out of the increasingly difficult fishing market, were causing increased competition, producing problems for the joint concern. This was such that in September 1984 Professor Neil Hood was authorised to compile a report on the Jackson Trawls operation. He concluded that Arthur Buchan's involvement in the oil slick business had led him to lose focus on the trawl making market. This had allowed other trawl makers to take a significant slice of the business in Peterhead, while the more aggressive stance of Walter Hay in Musselburgh had seen Stuart's share maintained. The decision was made to introduce a new post of commercial manager, thus allowing Arthur Buchan to use his expertise for innovations in the market, a minor reorganisation which had an immediate effect on improving profits.

This arrangement lasted until 1987 during which time Bridport Gundry had found it increasingly difficult to work with Arthur Buchan. With J. & W. Stuart now being the stronger of the two companies, Bridport Gundry sold its interest in Jackson Trawls in exchange for gaining full control of J. & W. Stuart, who now became part Bridport Gundry Marine Ltd. Two years later the firm had increased

Walter Hay and Mrs Hay. Walter Hay joined J. and W. Stuart in 1972, becoming general manager in 1978. He became its managing director when Bridport Gundry disposed of the concern.

its net production facility by 50% and had opened a depot in Eyemouth.

With Peterhead now landing 60% of the Scottish fishing catch, some 24% of the UK total, the Fishermen's Mutual Associations of Eyemouth and Pittenweem sought to redress the balance. Accordingly they approached J. & W. Stuart with an offer to share the cost of a new factory at Eyemouth. In the event Stuart's went ahead on their own, renting a facility which opened in 1987.

With Walter Hay still at the helm, J. & W. Stuart continued to trade as part of Bridport Gundry Marine for a number of years. However, a review into their operations led Bridport Gundry to demand an increased return on their investment. With the trawl makers such as J. & W. Stuart absorbing significant amounts of management time, but yielding little financial return, this was unlikely in the current market. As a result was it was proposed that J. & W. Stuart should be closed. However in conjunction with Ed Greenslade, Bridport Gundry's accountant, an alternative plan was developed which led to the sale of the business

Fishkey Marketing Co.

Formed in 1982, this was an attempt to provide fully equipped fishing boats, especially to those countries which were in receipt of World Bank aid. Bridport Gundry Marine was to provide the fishing equipment, Cygnus Marine the boats and Hawker Siddley the engines. With the issuing of 99 shares of £1, each company had an equal shareholding in the concern

A slow start saw John Gundry take over responsibility in November 1983, bringing his experience to try and kick start the project. This failed to stimulate sales and in 1985 it was reported that no progress was being made, and that no further funds would be put into the venture. The following year some business was done in West Africa but then Fishkey was allowed to become dormant and did no further business.

NORTH AMERICAN OPERATIONS

Gundry Pacific and Gundry Bilmac

In 1969 Gundry Pacific, of Vancouver, acquired Bilmac of Montreal, a marine hardware company. The new company was renamed Gundry Bilmac, and reported an immediate 40% improvement in sales.

The following year, despite a communications strike at the height of the trading season, the company still reported a trading profit. In 1971, after three years of expansion, it finally broke even, with better returns being expected in the following years. This was seen in 1972, despite high inflation in Canada, and continued into the following year. However by 1975, with difficulties in the industry it served, wage inflation and increased charges, together with a series of strikes, its position had declined.

A review of the operation was subsequently taken and

the decision was made to close the business, which was sold in April 1976 for Can$100,000. The freehold in Vancouver was retained until the following year when it was sold, realising Can$ 415,000.

Gundry-Pymore

In 1971 Gundry Pymore, of New Brunswick, merged with the Gourock-Bridport Industries Company, following which Gundry Pymore served as an investment company, until finally wound up in 1981/2.

Gourock Bridport Gundry and
Gourock Industries

Gourock Bridport Gundry was formed with the merger of Gourock Bridport Industries Company with Gundry Pymore in 1971. Following a realignment of shares Bridport Gundry had a 49% stake in the company and in the short term it was profitable (see Table 21).

In 1972 new trawl-making premises were opened at

Year	Bridport Gundry share of profit/(loss) (£)	
1971	28,694	
1972	23,367	
1973	42,320	
1974	125,190	renamed Gourock Industries
1975	29,263	
1976	(-76,034)	

Table 21. Bridport Gundry's share of the profits received from Gourock Bridport Gundry between 1971 and 1976.

Halifax, Nova Scotia, resulting in an expansion of sales and providing a good return, even in a time of inflation. This upward growth continued for two years, with spectacular results in 1973/4 during which time the company was renamed **Gourock Industries**. However the following year a rapid decline set in.

The issue of a rights issue of £103,000, in 1975, allowed the company to open a new factory in Boucherville, some 18 miles south of Montreal. However an unsettled market and problems at the new factory resulted in a loss being reported in 1976. This was caused in part by the fact that Quebec law only allowed French Canadians to be employed and, as there were no experts in rope making amongst them, this made life difficult if not impossible. Fearful of further losses, and wanting a foothold in the USA, Bridport Gundry exercised their option to sell the company at asset value, which was done in January 1977, for Can$450,000, with the money realised used to buy Brownell and Co. Inc.

The distribution rights for Edwards Sports Nets, formerly held by Gourock Industries were taken back in-

Aerial view of Brownell's factory at Moodus, Connecticut, the last of 13 mills that once graced this town. It became part of Bridport Gundry in 1977, enabling the company to enter the US market.

house at a cost of four years royalty payments.

Like Gundry Pymore, the company remained as an investment company until it went in to voluntary liquidation in 1982, finally being wound up in June 1985

Bridport Gundry (Overseas) Limited

Following the purchase of Brownell Inc. and the Brownell Net Co. Inc. in 1977, Bridport Gundry (Overseas) Limited was set up as an investment company to service operations in the USA.

Bridport Gundry Inc.

Bridport Gundry Inc. was a wholly owned subsidiary of Bridport Gundry (Overseas) Limited. Incorporated in the USA in 1977, it held 90% of the shares in Brownell and Co. Inc., which was subsequently increased to 100% in 1982.

Brownell and Co. Inc.

In 1975 Bridport Gundry secured an order to supply the United States Forces with camouflage netting but this was subsequently cancelled by the US Government's 'Buy American' policy. As result Bridport Gundry decided to seek entry into the American market, which could only be done by acquiring a company registered in the USA. By December 1976, negotiations were taking place with Brownell and Company Inc. of Moodus, Connecticut, which was the last of 13 mills producing twines, lines and light ropes once found in the town.

The purchase took place in June 1977 and cost the company US$ 1.3m (£872,330), for a 90% share. President Howard Losea became a member of the Group Board, retaining the remaining 10% until he terminated his contract with Bridport Gundry. Also included in the deal

was the Brownell Net Company, a subsidiary which had been set up five years earlier and which was merged with its parent Company in 1978. The opportunity was also taken to place the Edwards' agency, previously held by Gourock Industries, with Brownell.

The financial performance of the new business was marred by poor deliveries of Edward's products to the USA. The reason for this was the simple misunderstanding by Edwards of the US date system. They took 4/8/78 as the 4th of August not the 8th of April! This was rectified the following year with results above target, helped by the sale of Brownell's Angler's Lines subsidiary, where margins were low. The space realised was set aside for the introduction of underslung air cargo nets and Edward's products.

While the results for 1980 were good, a recession in the following year caused a downturn in trade. However the new mix of products, including the recently introduced aviation nets, allowed the company to produce satisfactory results. In later years this was further helped by the annual US Government order for helinets.

In October 1981 an agreement was made by Bridport Gundry to take a 50% share in the Marinovitch Trawl Company of Biloxi. Designers and producers of warm water trawls, they used the type of netting produced by Brownell, however the US$875,000 deal was cancelled shortly afterwards (see Table 22).

In November 1982 Howard Losea resigned as President of Brownell to be replaced by Raymond E. Browne, who was already a director. At the same time Bridport Gundry took up the option of buying Losea's 10% shareholding, bringing Brownell under complete control of the parent firm.

Prior to this change, Pat Darley visited Brownell and produced a report on the future of the business. It was clear that there were problems, as sales had increased by a figure less than inflation and, without the helinet contracts, losses would have been made every year from 1979. The report suggested that changes to the distribution network should be undertaken. Likewise new product lines needed to be introduced more quickly, and should include new air cargo nets, camouflage netting and strong industrial threads.

It was recommended that it might be better to set up a sales and distribution system similar to that of Western Trawl. Here Tom McCarley, an ex-Brownell sales manager, took 21% of Brownell's production, which he sold on to trawl makers and other distributors. A report was also to be prepared by the University of Oregon on the possibility of a Pacific Coast centre in Seattle. However general trade had fallen to the extent that a four day week was in operation,

Table 22. Brownell's turnover from 1977 to 1983, after they became part of Bridport Gundry.

Brownell Turnover	1977	1978	1979	1980	1981	1982	1983
Sales US$ (000)	2,147	2,818	2,815	3,029	3,996	4,615	5,310

which was causing serious problems with sequencing the manufacture and delivery of the helinets and air-cargo netting

1982 saw an improvement in the sales of the traditional business of twines and lines, as well as in the newer area of air cargo netting, helped by yet another significant Government order. However the following year saw disappointing returns, caused in part by selling at low profit margins. Ray Browne took control of the situation and sought to raise the standard of equipment and productivity to that seen in the English factories, while trade was boosted by the awarding of the first US Army contract for camouflage nets.

In March 1984 it was announced that Brownell was to take an 80% shareholding in Western Trawl at a cost of US$560,000, with an option on the remainder when McCarley retired. The significance to Brownell was that sales to Western Trawl accounted for some 75% of the netting they produced. A loan of US$490,000 was arranged to finance the acquisition. McCarley was to enter into a service agreement to set up trawl centres in California, the Gulf and Florida, with Ted Blackburn of Tennessee taking on the Carolinas' agency.

Discussions continued for some months with an agreement in principal being made. However this was suddenly terminated, partly on misunderstandings over the value of the freehold land, which was to have been included as an option costing US$180,000.

Meanwhile Brownell's performance was improving, although there was still some way to go before productivity matched that seen in the UK. The annual order for helinets suffered a delay when the failure some of the fixing hooks made it necessary to find another certified manufacturer. As a result steps were taken to improve the stock control and recording within the Company.

Another factor to affect them was the actions of Tom McCarley, who still had the distribution agency in the Gulf. Brownell, concerned at their vulnerability to one person who now took 90% of their netting production, opened a depot in New Orleans, which operated in parallel with McCarley's from early 1985.

Around the same time McCarley purchased 12 Zang braiders, sufficient to make all his netting requirements, and offered to lease them to Brownell. When this was declined he threatened to set up in competition. At this point the agency agreement was terminated and the New Orleans depot took over completely, with McCarley releasing 80% of the stock kept at Western Trawl.

While the results for 1985/6 saw an improvement, the dependence on military orders, with their uncertain timing, caused problems in forecasting production needs. The business was reorganised into divisions, mirroring that of the parent UK Company. These were:
1. Brownell Marine, which included the New Orleans operation.
2. Defence and Aviation Products, covering air-cargo and camouflage netting.

Brownell	1983	1984	1985	1986	1987
Sales US$(000)	8,071	8,723	8,862	12,822	11,263
net profit US$(000)	180	153	177*	472	407
* excludes a stock write off of US$304,000					

Table 23. Brownell's sales and profit figures from 1983 to 1987.

3. Industrial Sewing Threads.

Following the success at New Orleans, a Pacific Coast depot was opened in Seattle in January 1987. Both were part of Brownell Marine and were managed in close collaboration with Bridport Gundry Marine. Around this time the New Orleans depot added Bridport Gundry wire rope and slings to their operation, partly the result of the parent company's acquisition of Halls.

In November 1986 a similar operation was set up in Dartmouth, Nova Scotia, with the formation of Bridport Brownell Limited, a Canadian company retailing and distributing nets, ropes and ancillary equipment, and whose shares were held by Bridport Gundry Inc.

1986/7 was a mixed year with problem with delays to the Aviation and Defence contracts and the loss of an important helinet contract, although the other two divisions performed well. During the year the Thread Division was incorporated into the Seattle business (see Table 23).

The next year was to be a critical one in the history of the company. Until then Brownell had been classified as a 'small company' and was able to be awarded contracts without the 'set aside rules', the lobbying and legal submissions needed by the larger concerns. Their competitors, however, had managed to get them reclassified, using their ownership by Bridport Gundry as the reason. No longer being a 'small company' meant that, on volume and cost grounds, the aviation and defence work was now beyond them. The only solution was to sell off the business thus enabling these orders to be available to the 'new' Brownell. Their cause was not helped by the firm, in an area of full employment, being unable to recruit the additional staff needed to fulfil a camouflage order gained in January 1988. The sub-contracting of the order meant that significant losses for that year were expected.

The decision was made to sell the business to a management buy-out team for US$3.03m, which would include the depots at New Orleans and Houma but not those in Nova Scotia or Seattle, which were growing outlets for Bridport Gundry's manufactured products, especially those from Bridport Gundry (Ireland). It was hoped that this would reduce the parent company's borrowings and allow them to pursue the profitable areas of the business.

When the management buy-out team failed to raise the necessary funds, Bridport Gundry decided to re-organise their US operation, rather than close it. The Gulf distribution centres were closed, along with the netmaking factory at Moodus, while the wire and rope rigging operation at Huoma was sold a short time later.

The core business of Brownell and Co. was now focusing on specialist textiles and sports products. Turnover was reduced by half and its workforce reduced by two-thirds. In the second half of the year ending July 1989 it returned a small operating profit.

In the meantime the Bridport Brownell marine distribution business based in Canada had gone from strength to strength. New depots had opened in Shelburn and Yarmouth, Nova Scotia. The firm also took on the sales agency of J. Boyd Butler and Son of St. Johns, Newfoundland in September 1987.

This state of affairs was not to last for, in the next financial year, poor results in the North American market led to the closure of the Seattle operation and the complete withdrawal from the Canadian fishing market soon after. The cost of this to Bridport Gundry was £1.789m and led to the sale of Brownell being actively sought.

At Brownell and Co. the greater attention to costs, allied to changes in manufacturing control, led to their return to profit. New products and better market penetration resulted in an improvement in archery, twine and cordage sales, which were able to offset the shortfall in government orders for helicopter nets. The company also acted as an agency for Edwards, bringing the latter closer to the US market.

Brownell's improvements were short-lived and it remained a fragile business with performance varying from year to year. Following the strategic review of the Bridport Gundry Group operations it was sold in July 1997 to A. A. Ferraz, its former President, for £0.8m.

Meanwhile, following the withdrawal from the fishing market, Dartmouth-based Bridport Brownell was limited to supplying industrial nets and ropes. However a change of name to Bridport Industries Canada brought a new focus. In the year ending July 1991 it returned a good profit and received an order for camouflage systems from the Canadian Armed Forces, which was worth Can$16m over the four years from 1992.

This was originally a Bridport Aviation Products contract but, as the Canadians demanded significant local input, it was decided to use the Bridport Industries factory at Dartmouth, Nova Scotia. Operatives and inspection teams were sent out from Bridport, in order to ensure that production standards and efficiency were met. After the first six months supervision became at arm's length from Bridport. With the first camouflage nets being delivered in July 1992, Bridport Industries Canada now had a regular production load, helped by the frigate construction programme.

The Canadian business managed to extend its stock distribution activities when the camouflage line was closed after the completion of the four year contract. In 1995 it acquired Creative Manufacturing Inc. of Bedford, Nova Scotia, which specialised in assembling textile products for a variety of industrial applications, such as parachute drogues. Operations were moved to their premises and sales growth continued in the following year, but with reduced margins. The Strategic Review carried out by the Group resulted in its sale, at the same time as Brownell.

SIX

Life after Bridport Gundry

THE DIVISIONS OF BRIDPORT GUNDRY

Bridport plc/Marmon/AmSafe Bridport

In February 1998 **Bridport plc** became the trading name of the company. It reflected the new direction in which the business was going, with its heightened market focus on aviation and separation from its roots in traditional netmaking. The figures for the year to 1998 showed a pre-tax profit of £4.2m on a turnover of £27.4m, a marked improvement which fully justified the new arrangements. During the year Bridport plc had taken over Air Carrier Interiors Inc. of Seattle, for £2.14m. Manufacturers of air cargo restraints, the business was complementary to the new UK owner. With Boeing initially as the dominant customer, this was to become Bridport plc's main US base.

In February 1999 Bridport Aviation Products was re-organised into three divisions: Airframe Systems, Cargo Restraint and Defence, while Robert McIlwraith had become Managing Director on the retirement of John Bowden.

At the same time the unresponsive nature of the Stock Market to relatively small companies, such as Bridport plc, together with a general weakening in the share price, led the Board to commence upon a review of its options for the future. However this was overtaken by a bid of £30.2m from the American firm Marmon, leading to wholesale changes in the Board shortly thereafter.

Since its formation by Robert Pritzker in 1953, the Marmon Group had grown to become one of the leading privately owned groups in the USA. In 1977 it had taken over the **Am**erican **Saf**ety **E**quipment Corporation of Phoenix Arizona, manufacturers of seat belts, for US $27m.

Bridport plc, now taken back into private status as **Bridport Limited**, remained part of the Marmon group until September 2004. As part of a restructuring of the US giant, both Bridport Limited and AmSafe Inc. were sold to AmSafe Partners Inc., a company formed by affiliates of

The Court, headquarters of AmSafe Bridport, continues to manufacture nets for the aviation industry. The former warehouse seen here now houses offices.

AmSafe have developed the cargo restraint net to withstand a force of 9g.

Quarterdeck Equity Partners Inc. and the Pritzker Group. The following year Bridport Limited's principal UK trading subsidiary was renamed **AmSafe Bridport**.

During this time the Bridport based company had expanded to have a world-wide capability. In 2001 a base was acquired in Sri Lanka as the company positioned itself for the future, allowing the low cost manufacture of high volume products. This was followed three years later by the opening of their operation at Kunshun, China. In addition AmSafe Bridport operates from Seattle, with a manufacturing base at the former Air Carrier Interiors Inc. site, and it also has a repair facility for barrier and bellyhold nets at Erie, Pennsylvania.

In the UK, as well as Bridport, it operates from Heathrow and has its military aftermarket at Ringwood, on the former Militair site, and its commercial aftermarket base at Gatwick, developed from the former Britannic Aviation site and now directly linked to another similar sized AmSafe operation in Portsmouth, New Hampshire.

The company has continued to develop its world leading status in cargo restraint systems over the years. In recent times new product developments have gathered pace and have included a 9g cargo restraint net for military cargo planes and a thermal pallet cover. This last named can provide temperature stabilisation for perishable cargoes.

Arthur Hart & Son Ltd.

Its continued success and diversification of products saw Arthur Hart and Sons become one of the core businesses in the reorganisation of 1997, continuing to work from the Crewkerne factory. In 2005 it became **AmSafe Bridport Technical Fabrics** and was relocated to The Court the following year, with the consequent closure of the Viney Bridge Mill after 216 years.

James Pearsall and Co. Ltd.

Pearsalls became one of the core activities of the Group following the strategic review, becoming part of the Marmon Group in 1999 when they took over **Bridport plc**. Here it joined American Medical Instruments, who

had entered the Marmon group in 1994. In 2003 a private equity firm, trading as American Medical Instruments (Holdings) Inc., acquired AMI and Pearsalls for £0.4m. In 2006 they were purchased by Angiotech Pharmaceuticals, along with its Pearsalls subsidiary, which now trades from Tancred Street, Taunton, producing medical sutures and embroidery threads.

Gundry Netting (Bridport) Limited

Bridport Gundry Netting Ltd. made a pre-tax loss of £126,000 in 1996, down from a profit of £2,000 the pervious year. This followed the withdrawal from its traditional fishing market and the reduction in staff numbers by 30%. The Bridport Gundry board felt that this was a good time to dispose of Bridport Gundry Netting Ltd. and at the same time generate cash which could be injected into other areas of the business. Consequently this part of the business was offered to John Clegg and Chris Louden, who were directors of Bridport Gundry Netting Ltd., for £550,000.

Clegg and Louden formed Spider Holdings, who would own the assets, primarily the weaving looms, of Gundry Netting (Bridport) Ltd. Spider Holdings also paid the salaries of the management, clerical and administrative staff, charging Gundry Netting (Bridport) Ltd. a management fee. Gundry Netting (Bridport) Ltd. took out a five year lease on 60,000 sq ft of space at The Court, at £75,000 p.a.

Gundry Netting (Bridport) Ltd. started trading in July 1997, with Chris Louden as chairman, John Clegg as managing director and Toby Eeles, a minority shareholder, as production manager. Their main business areas were seen as:

1. Base netting for Edward Sports and Bridport Aviation Products, who were their core customers.
2. Safety Netting, which included all the safety netting for the Millennium Stadium in Cardiff, a contract worth around £110k
3. Anti-litter systems, which Bridport Gundry had started to develop in conjunction with Somerset County Council.
4. Pest control netting for roofs, on which they sought to make a good profit.
5. Netting for Bridport Gundry Marine Ltd.

The raw material was to be sourced from Portugal, although not from Sicor, and made into netting on the machines bought from Bridport Gundry.

Despite making a profit its first year problems soon started to emerge. The large anti-litter nets were worth up to £0.75m each, the netting content alone coming to £80,000, thus demanding significant cash investment. While a number were sold, one customer kept on putting off the delivery of their order with resultant problems in cash flow.

Finally running out of money, Gundry Netting (Bridport) Ltd. went into voluntary liquidation in August 2000, with the workforce of 63 being made redundant. The factory space reverted to Bridport Aviation Products, with the liquidator selling the braiding machines to Sicornete.

Edwards Sports Products

While Edwards had returned a pre-tax profit for the year ending July 1996 of just £1,000, on net assets of £681,000, it was clear that it had no place in the new Group structure. It was offered for sale in September 1996 and Archie Barclay, who had been appointed General Manager in August, spent several months trying to sell the business as a going concern. Ultimately he headed a management buyout, along with Russell Raybould, Edward Gall and Sharon Hill.

The sale was formally announced in March 1997, with completion in July of the same year at a price of £270,000. The business immediately moved to new accommodation at North Mills, completely severing links with The Court. The removal of the management charge, levied by the Bridport Gundry Group on its subsidiaries, saw an immediate improvement in its fortunes, which were further enhanced by new management's strategies.

The new company was run as a sports equipment company providing whole solutions, rather than just netting, thus giving a greater added value to the sales. Some previous business, which was carried out between the various elements of the old Bridport Gundry, was deliberately lost, resulting in a temporarily reduced turnover, but as this was low margin work the effect on the overall profits was not great.

At the same time attempts were made to recover trade lost by Bridport Gundry over the previous years, as well as setting about understanding the new focus of the business. The success of the business is such that turnover has now reached £3million. The firm supplied all of the tennis equipment for the Beijing Olympics, which, for an industry that was ravaged by Far Eastern imports, gave all those in Edwards Sports Products no end of satisfaction.

In recent times an e-commerce facility for horticultural products has been set up trading under the William James and Co. name.

A practice soccer goal from Edwards Sports Products, continuing a tradition dating back to the 19th century. It was W. Edwards and Son, as part of Bridport Gundry that supplied the goal nets for the 1966 World Cup final.

Above Andy Murray at the net at Wimbledon's Centre Court. Wimbledon's nets are provided by Edwards Sports Products, carrying on a tradition started by W. Edwards and Son.

Below Edwards Sports Products also produces cricket nets for the Indoor Cricket School at Lords.

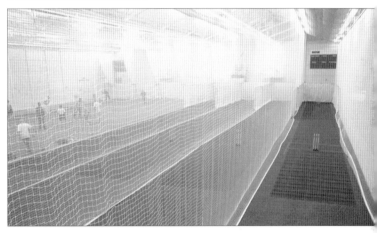

Redport Nets Ltd.

Redport was making a very high return for Bridport Gundry, producing pre-tax profits of £92,000 on assets worth just £146,000 in 1996. However it was a traditional textile business, with limited growth opportunities, and did not fit into the new plans for the company. Neither was it thought that it could operate as a stand-alone company within Bridport Gundry and consequently it was offered for sale for a £164,000.

It was purchased by Makejust Ltd., a company set up and run by Mary Newman, whose husband was employed by Bridport Aviation Products. The new company continued to manufacture the angling nets and billiard/snooker pockets which had been its product base for many years. It was the last of the Bridport companies to employ hand braiders.

In January 2005 it was sold to P. T. Winchester Ltd., of Bishop's Lydeard, and has now been integrated into its textile distribution organisation. Hand-made nets are still produced, with the company retaining one braider in Bridport to do this.

Gundry's Ireland Limited

It was no surprise when Bridport Gundry bought back the whole of the issued equity, now rated at 20%, for £110,000. The result was the sale in December 1993, for £559,000, of Bridport Gundry (Ireland) to a management team, together with a number of fishermen, forming **Gundry's Ireland Limited**. Pat Darley did not want Bob Holder to be involved in the buy-out. Consequently, although he did take a place on the Board of the new Company, he did not become chairman until later.

The new company moved into the production of fish cages, which compensated for the loss of fishing turnover seen in recent years, and which allowed the business to prosper.

The excellent relations between staff and management continued into the new operation. New employees were given a two week course of instruction before being put on the working floor, thus ensuring that the high standards for which the business was known were maintained. While a dividend was only given in one year, qualified staff were given shares in the company

In 1996 a branch was opened in Portland, Maine, which both manufactures and services nets for the east coast fisheries of the USA.

It was in the next year that a significant expansion took place when Gundry's Ireland Ltd. took over Strachan Nets of Fraserburgh, forming **Gundry's Scotland Ltd.**, allowing them to supply the Scottish pelagic and whitefish fleets.

During the same year Bridport Gundry were finally withdrawing from their traditional fishing base and sold off Bridport Gundry Marine. A team from Gundry's Ireland, together with three senior managers from Bridport Gundry Marine, purchased the company and so set up the third key operation, **Gundry Marine**, allowing Gundry's Ireland to service fishing fleets throughout the UK and Ireland.

For the next stage of the story we have to turn back the clock to Killybegs in 1974, when Albert Swan, the cousin of Tom Swan, started **Syversen** Sails. After trading for 27 years the company, now called **Swan Nets**, was taken over by the **Hamidjan Group** of Iceland. In 2002 Swan Nets merged with Gundry's Ireland Ltd., forming **Swan Net Gundry**.

Swan Net Gundry has taken over the mantle once served by Bridport Gundry and Bridport Gundry (Ireland) servicing the fishing fleets of the UK, Ireland and the US.

Gundry Bridport Ltd.

From 1997 Gundry Marine was part of the Bridport Gundry (Ireland) group. However, following a review of operations in 2000, the store at Bridport was sold off and is now trading as **Gundry Bridport Ltd.**, run by David George from a unit in Gundry Lane, Bridport.

J. & W. Stuart

When it was clear that J. & W. Stuart had no future in the Group, it was proposed that it should be closed.

However, with the parent company needing money to pay its shareholders, an alternative plan was developed, in conjunction with Ed Greenslade, Bridport Gundry Marine's accountant. Walter Hay was summoned to a meeting with Pat Darley in Bridport, where he was offered the chance to purchase Stuart's business. The money was raised by himself and a colleague, Ivan Stephenson, together with grants from the SDA and an Edinburgh concern. Walter Hay remained as the managing director of the new business, later trading as **Stuart's Nets**.

Around the same time, Eyemouth was announced as one of the head preferential fishing ports and this, together with the move into fish cages, led the new firm to build its own factory in Eyemouth and sell its Musselburgh operation, which had become increasingly difficult to staff.

Since 1993 the company has developed a niche market. It is too small to produce large volumes of products and instead relies on the sale of 6-8 nets for each order. This, together with the move into the export market, where trade is done with the Mediterranean countries of Malta, Turkey and Italy along with Libya, has ensured the survival of a firm which can trace its ancestry back almost 200 years.

After some thirty years in charge Walter Hay has semi-retired, passing his shares onto his two daughters and son. The last named has no involvement in the daily running of the business, which is the domain of Rhonna Bannaman, who is in charge of the production of fish cages, and Fiona Drewry, who is the designer and runs the office. The remaining shares are held by Ivan Stephenson and the Fishermen's Mutual Association of Eyemouth.

Brownell

1997 also saw the sale of Brownell, after it had made a pre-tax loss of £47,200 in 1996 on sales worth £3.19m. With assets worth £1.23m, the company was sold to A A Ferraz, the general manager and a director of Brownell, for £0.8m.

Soulet

Disposal of Soulet also took place in 1997 for £184,000.

OTHER BRIDPORT NET MANUFACTURERS

Bridport has a number of net manufacturers still operating from the town. All now buy in netting from abroad and assemble it at their factories. While fishing nets are still made, most firms have diversified into other types of netting, such as sports nets, field sports, garden nets, pest control and safety netting.

Huck (UK) Ltd

By 1993, following the withdrawal from the N. American market and the sale of its Scottish and Irish subsidiaries, Bridport Gundry's traditional fishing market was at risk because the new 'private' companies were no longer tied to

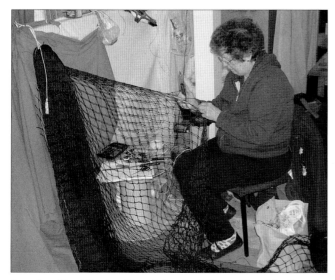

Some hand braiding is still carried on in Bridport. Here Mrs Dorothy Lovelace is working at the Sicor International factory at Gore Cross in 2009.

Above While not being as important as in past times, fishing nets still form part of the output of various Bridport firms. Here one of Sicor's nets is being raised ready to release its catch.

Below Litter control has become an increasingly important part of the portfolios of Bridport firms. Sicor International has produced portable litter control nets which run on rollers, enabling them to be moved to where they are needed.

Below Netting provided by Sicornete is being made up at Sicor's factory at Gore Cross. The shelving in the background is used to store the netting imported from Portugal prior to being made into nets.

the old parent firm for netting.

One result of this was the formation of Pelacon Nets, in which Richard Connolly had an involvement. At the same time Connolly was on the steering committee dealing with the change of safety netting from British to European standards. It was here that he met Stefan Huck, whose father Manfred had started Huck Nets in the 1960s.

Following discussions a joint company was formed to trade in the UK - Huck Pelacon, which opened its first factory at the old Ewen's Mill in Foundry Lane in 1996. The following year accommodation was taken on the new Gore Cross Industrial Estate.

Now trading as Huck Nets (UK) Ltd., it occupies some 48,000 sq. ft. of factory space, which has resulted from six phases of expansion over a ten year period, during which turnover has risen to some £6m. The firm gets its nets from the Dresden factory, built by the parent company after the fall of the Berlin Wall. The netting is then transported to Bridport for assembly into the various products which include sports nets, children's play areas and safety netting.

Sicor International UK

After the failed attempt by Bridport Gundry to forge a link with the Portuguese company Sicor, the latter set up Sicornete, the net making facility, in 1992. Alan Nute had been involved with Sicor and Gundry and following the decision not to collaborate further he went to work for Sicor.

Sicor International, with Alan Nute as Managing Director, was formed in 1994 when a new factory was opened in Aberdeen to serve the Scottish fishing fleet. By 1997 a warehouse had been opened at Beaminster, so that the netmaking skills of the Bridport workers could be utilised. In 2003 the company moved to a purpose built factory on the Gore Cross Industrial Estate. Since then it has grown to occupy 20,000 sq. ft. of floor space and employs some 30 people.

Knowle Nets carry on the netmaking tradition at the former Asker Mill site.

Netting from Sicornete is imported to the Bridport factory where it is made up into the various product lines, which include fishing nets, sports and leisure nets, industrial netting and litter control nets.

Bridport Nets Ltd.
This firm started as Barry Law (Bridport Nets) in the 1970s. When Law left the concern was operated by Patrick Pearce, who took on Mr Lillee as a partner in the early 1990s. A few years later Bridport Nets was formed, with Patrick Pearce and Mrs Lillee as partners, and today they trade as Bridport Nets Ltd. Based in West Bay their core business lies in field sports nets but their portfolio extends to fishing, sports and safety nets.

Coastal Nets, including Protec Nets
Coastal Nets was formed in 1987 by Rod and Georgina Barr. They make fishing nets, and construction safety netting, as well as sports perimeter nets, and are based in Unit 61, St Michael's Lane Trading Estate.

Knowle Nets
The firm of Knowle nets was started by M. Langran in 1965, but was taken over by the current owners, Susan and Jeremy Tweed in 1996. Operating from the East Road Business Park, on the former Asker Mill site, they make nets for gardens, game and poultry as well as sports and safety netting.

Collins Nets
Started by Nigel and Nick Collins in 1982 the firm concentrates on nets for fishing and for the Environment Agency. They have more recently moved on to sell nets for gardens, game birds and sports netting.

Game Fayre
Game Fayre was started in the mid-1980s by Stephen Thomas, who had previously worked for Bridport Gundry. The firm concentrates on netting for game birds and for thatchers. It operates from the North Mills Industrial Estate, with Stephen Thomas as managing director and Nicola Lick running the netting side.

Bridport Leisure and Industrial Products
Making sports nets, BLIP was started in the mid-1980s by former Bridport Gundry Netting managers. However in 2000, when based at the North Mills Industrial Estate, it went into voluntary liquidation and its assets were bought by Rombull UK.

West Dorset Nets/Deben Group
West Dorset Nets was founded by Geoff Pearce in 1976 and made nets for field sports and pest control. In 1985 it was taken over by the Deben Group of Woodbridge in Suffolk. The firm relocated to the Gore Cross Business Park and the pest control business was sold to Huck Nets in 2005. Deben continues to manufacture shooting and game nets, which are supplied at cost to the parent company in Suffolk. In addition Deben also have their own customer base at Gore Cross.

PART THREE

The Bridport Textile Manufacturers

An aerial view of Pymore Mill, showing the linewalk running up towards the mill.
The original mill and its eastward extension can be seen next to the linewalk.

(see chapter 9, page 96)

SEVEN

Joseph Gundry & Company

THE EARLY DAYS

The story of the Gundry family starts with the arrival of John Gundry I, a felt maker, who leased 48-50, West Street around 1620. It was from here that the family business, which eventually led to the twine firm of Joseph Gundry and Sons and the brewing concern of Samuel Gundry and Company, started.

John I had two sons, John II, who followed his father as a felt maker, and Samuel I, who was described as a maltster in his will of 1708. Around this time we also find two more Gundry brothers, but where they belong in the family business is uncertain; Daniel I is described as a merchant in his will of 1716 and John as a mariner in his will of 1707. This line however leads to a dead end and plays no further part in the story.

Thus it is not clear as to which Gundry started the family business, whether it was John II, Samuel I or Daniel I; neither is it clear if the initial trade was in twine, rope and net making. Tradition has it that the firm was founded by Samuel I in 1660, around the time he married Catharine Alford, whose father owned significant property in East Street. However the main occupation of the Gundry family was as maltsters and this continued down to the fourth generation. However in the contemporary period it is likely that more than one trade was carried on, and that of a maltster was either the main one, or the more socially acceptable one.

The polarisation of the textile and brewing interests started in the mid-18th century, helped by Samuel II passing on his estate to his wife. When she died in 1733, all her interests passed to Joseph II, while his brother Samuel III concentrated on the trades of a tallow chandler, maltster and brewer. Joseph II was described as a maltster in the 1750s but by 1766 he has also developed his textile interest, being described as a twine spinner and sailcloth maker, as well as a brewer. He had a considerable investment tied up in these concerns; an insurance valuation for that year is for £4,600.

The first mention of twine spinning was in 1736, when John IV was so described on being given the lease of The Court from his uncle, John III. Two years later he was given the houses owned by his late uncle in trust to provide his cousin, William Hounsell, with a weekly income. From this time John IV described himself as a maltster, although it is clear that he was also building up his twine business. In 1742 he was in partnership with his brother, Samuel III, in a brewing business, owning a number of public houses.

He was also a member of a brewing partnership that leased the Town Brewhouse.

John IV took on the role of producing the twine and nets that, following the development of the Newfoundland fishery, were increasingly needed by fishing industry. At his death in 1763 he passed the net making side onto his nephew Joseph Gundry III, while his brewing interests passed onto Samuel IV. It is this multiplicity of interests that makes it difficult to ascertain the precise details of the history of the family businesses.

After the death of Joseph II in 1772, the two sides of the business were merged. While Joseph III was free to continue the netting business on his own account, his father's will made it a condition of the inheritance that Joseph should take his brother Daniel III into partnership in the twine and sailcloth side. The late Joseph II recognised the shortcoming of Daniel as a businessman but thought that the two should work together for a period of at least seven years. If Daniel chose not to follow his father's

Hutchin's map of 1777 shows the yarn barton and warehouses of Joseph Gundry. They can be seen in the field by the words 'St. Michael's Lane'. It was here that the yarn was bleached and dried prior to being woven into sailcloth.

LOCATION OF MILLS AND FACTORIES

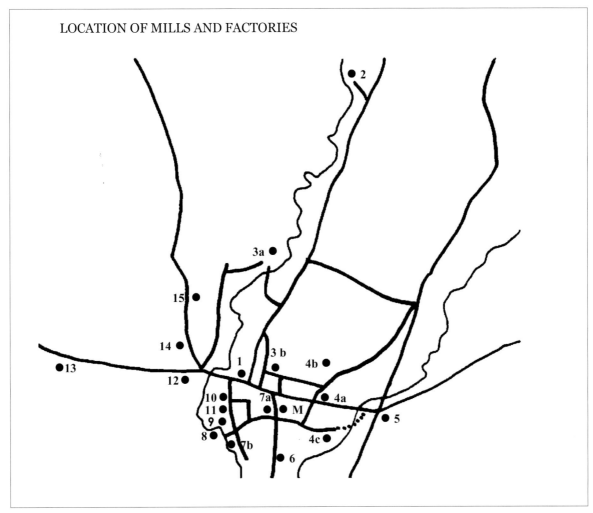

1. Gundry's The Court	4c Pelican Works	10. Ewens & Turner
2. Pymore Mill	5. Asker Mill	11. William Gale & Sons
3. W. Hounsell	6. Thomas Tucker	12. Rendall & Coombs
3a. North Mills	7. S. Whetham & Sons	13. Ewens/William James
3b. Wykes Court	7a. Gundry Lane, Warehouse	14. Robert Hounsell
4. Herbert E. Hounsell	7b. Priory Mill	15. Richard Tucker & Sons
4a. East Street	8. Ewens & Golding's Mill	M Museum
4b. Sparacre	9. William Edwards & Son	

wishes, or break off the partnership in under that period, he was to get £1,500.

The work was being carried on at two locations - The Court, where the netting side was concentrated, and at the yarn barton in St. Michael's Lane, which was centre of the sailcloth making venture. This can clearly be seen in Hutchins' map of 1777, and consisted of three warehouses, workhouses, a bucking or bleaching house as well as a bleaching and drying ground.

The will of Joseph II gives some insight into the structure of the business. While all his sailcloth weavers were given 5/-, it is uncertain as to the number involved. However he was employing five line makers and five warping boys. Mary Stone of Burton Bradstock and a woman assistant were employed to fit his nets and make his seines. Two twine spinners are mentioned by name, John Gardiner of Allington and John Ackerman of Bridport. This suggests that he was directly employing these workers, rather than simply using them as outworkers.

Joseph III and Daniel III worked together until Daniel moved to live near Exeter, around 1790. During the partnership the brothers had moved away from the sailcloth business to focus on twine spinning, line making and net making. The yarn barton and warehousing at St. Michael's Lane were closed and were replaced by additional warehousing at The Court.

JOSEPH GUNDRY AND COMPANY 1795 - 1859

In Daniel's place, Joseph III took his nephew Joseph Gundry Downe into partnership, probably forming Joseph Gundry and Company at the same time. This partnership lasted until 1811 when Joseph's son, Joseph IV, was taken on as a partner.

In 1803, they owned two houses on the south side of

83

West Street, as well as The Court and its warehouse on the north side. There were three plots with spinning ways and a spinning loft in St. Michael's Lane. Finally there were two more houses, one in East Street and another in Weeks (Wykes) Court Lane. An inventory of 1812 shows how little capital equipment the firm needed for the production of twines, lines and nets; they owned just 36 line waggles, 15 hackles at home and four with Caleb Crabb. There was also the drying room furniture and a large copper used for tanning the nets.

Most of the spinning was carried out by a handful of people, many of whom lived in St. Michael's Lane. Caleb Crabb lived at No. 20, along with John Thompson, while Matthew Powell was to be found at No. 36. At this time these workers would carry out all the tasks, from hackling to the finished twine, which was then given to the braiders and line makers, such as Andrew Crabb, to produce the finished goods.

The 1780s saw an upsurge in business, as the firm expanded its Newfoundland connection. They were also trading with the eastern seaboard towns of the United States ten years later. In 1797 they took over the warehouse at Bridport Harbour from Kenway and Downe, which they used to store the raw and finished material. The same period saw the firm invest in their own ships, usually in

Samuel Gundry and partners opened the Old Brewery in about 1796, a time when it was common for merchants to have more than one business. 200 years later the main building has changed little.

partnership with other traders. This allowed them to trade direct with North America, which could be hazardous as the French wars were raging at this time; on one voyage in 1807 a ship was captured by the French.

In 1809 the firm was trying to get a trader in Liverpool to take on the transatlantic trade. However Joseph Gundry was to bemoan the fact that there seemed to be a prejudice against Bridport twine in that port and it is unclear whether he was successful in getting someone.

Meanwhile, Samuel Gundry IV re-entered the textile trade in the 1770s, as a twine spinner and hemp and flax merchant. This was carried forward by his son Samuel V, who also opened the Old Brewery in 1796. During the next few years Joseph III and Joseph Gundry Downe, the partners of J. Gundry and Co., and Samuel V entered into a series of partnerships. The first of these happened with William Fowler in 1799, leading to the formation of the Pymore Mill Company.

In 1808 further expansion took place with an agreement with Thomas Fox, to whom they were related by marriage, and Henry Saunders to work Slape Mill, Netherbury as a swingling mill. The partnership was carried on until the mill burnt down in 1814, although it was some years later before it was formally dissolved.

In 1811 they joined forces with Samuel Gundry V's son, Samuel Bowden Gundry, to run the shoe thread manufactory of Bowden Gundry and Company. The partnership lasted until 1823, after which it was carried on by S. B. Gundry alone, by now twine, lines and nets had been added to the portfolio.

In 1811 Joseph Gundry IV was admitted as a partner in the firm of Joseph Gundry and Co., with Joseph Gundry Downe taking out £3,264 from the business, being his share over and above the one-third he was leaving in. This values the concern at £19,584, which was confirmed by Joseph Gundry putting in £1,190 to cover the increased share of father and son. A few years later, Joseph Gundry Downe left to live in Wellington, Somerset; dying there in 1818, after which the partnership was carried on by the two Josephs.

At the death of Joseph Gundry III in 1823, the business was worth £23,066, including £15,970 owed by creditors, long credit terms being common at this time. Joseph Gundry IV continued running the business in the traditional manner until 1835, during which annual sales were around £14,000. Likewise assumed profits were stable at around £2,000 per year, with the money being owed by creditors averaging £12,000.

Then suddenly credit seems to have been called in, falling from £11,604 in 1833 to just £2,032 the following year. The money realised was converted into the capital value of the business, which increased by £7,000 to £20,931. It was during this period that Joseph Gundry and Co. was investing in the capital expenditure required by the introduction of steam power at Pymore Mill. Additionally, they were rebuilding Slape Mill as a spinning mill in, conjunction with Samuel Gundry and William Hounsell and Co. It is likely that some of the money was being directed towards these projects, especially as there is no visible investment in machinery at The Court. Following this, there is evidence that sales increased, probably as the bottleneck on production had been overcome.

Even now the working methods of the firm do not seem to have changed significantly. The hemp twine was still made by hand, usually by a select group of workers. At 20, St. Michael's Lane, the Powell family were now making the firm's hemp twine, while John Crabb worked as Gundry's line and rope maker at 84, East Street. By the 1840s John had been replaced by his son Edward, while, in St. Michael's Lane, the spinning was being carried out by Robert and George Powell, who were later joined by John Vivian.

After Joseph Gundry IV died in 1841, the firm was run by his son, Joseph Gundry V, who had been admitted as a partner in 1836. Benjamin Pearkes Fox Gundry, his younger brother, joined the business in 1842. Under the direction of these two the capital value of the company rose significantly, reaching £104,229 at the death of Joseph V in 1877.

One feature of this period was the variability in the company's profits, which seemed to follow a six year cycle. The business was not helped by the series of trade recessions that occurred during these years and losses were recorded on a number of occasions. One important factor was the increased use of cotton in lines and nets. The cotton, which came ready-spun, reduced the added value that could be placed on the final goods.

The development of trade in the late 18th century had seen many county banks springing up. Bridport's first bank was opened in October 1791, by Joseph Gundry III, Samuel Downe, Joseph Pike and Samuel Farwell. Following a minor crisis in 1797, caused by one of the partners absconding, the bank reopened with Joseph Gundry III and William Downe as partners. From 1814, after a series of partnership changes, the bank was run by Joseph Gundry III and Samuel Gundry V. Following the death of his Uncle in 1823, Samuel V continued alone until his son Walter Eustace Gundry was taken on as partner in 1825. The two worked together until the concern failed in 1847.

JOSEPH GUNDRY AND COMPANY 1859 - 1915

The late 1850s saw the introduction of machinery into The Court, with a £300 invoice for braiding machines and iron work carrying a date of 1859. A new line and twine shed was built at The Court in 1861, with Edward Crabb leaving his line walks at East Street to work there. By 1864 its machinery was being powered by steam. Much of the design and installation of the machinery seems to have been the work of J. B. Payne, working from his factory at Perry Street, near Chard. He involved Edward Crabb in the detail of the design, asking him to go to Chard on a number of occasions, to give his opinions on the work in progress.

Payne was producing machine-made nets at his Perry

Joseph Gundry in his Grand Masters uniform, in about 1866. He was responsible for bringing The Court into the machine age, with the building of the linewalk and introduction of braiding machines.

Street works using Gundrys' own workforce, who lodged locally. Gundrys were charged for the length of net being supplied and it would seem that Payne was improving the braiding machines, which he described as producing broad or narrow nets, to his own specification.

In 1867 a new laying and finishing shed, to be built by Cornick, was being planned, although Payne was expressing concern over the design of the roof. The next addition seems to be the braiding shop, which was likely to have been built around the same time, for a number of braiding machines were supplied in January 1869.

By 1875 The Court was being used as an office and warehouse. The extensions of 1838 and 1844 had been added to cope with the additional demand. Behind was to be found the braiding shop, together with the adjoining line

J. B. Payne, of the Perry Street Works, Chard, provided the early braiding looms for J. Gundry and Co. in the 1860s. While the looms were being developed, workers from Bridport lodged at Chard, producing the netting at Payne's works. The dial on the left records the rows of knots being made.

A group of Gundry's mill workers taken around 1900. Behind them is strung a fishing net probably being dried after tanning.

and twine sheds. Between them and The Court was the net stretching path.

The swings in profits show the difficulty of the trading position. The losses recorded in 1861/2 were rescued by the American Civil War, but recession again returned, with the firm losing £6,911 during the years 1868-1870. A brief period of prosperity followed until the recession of 1873/4 caused losses of over £3,000.

The death of Joseph Gundry V in 1877 marked the start of a difficult period for the firm. The new partnership started with Joseph Pearkes Fox Gundry at the helm. Initially his other partners were Joseph's executors, Joseph's widow Margaret and James Williams. Their share later passed to the parents of Charles John Gundry Still, who were to look after his interests until he became a partner at the age of 24. The Still family's active involvement lasted only until

Tan house at The Court around 1910, the tanning of nets increased their useful life.

1886. The declining profit levels resulted in them taking out £7,000 from his share of the business, to be followed by relinquishing the remainder of his interest in the partnership in exchange for an annuity of £500.

The day-to-day running of the concern was undertaken by John Hookins Gundry who, while he had no capital in the firm, was to get a salary of £150 and a quarter share of the profits earned by J. P. F. Gundry. The latter had only to attend the business when he so desired, whilst the other partners took no active interest at all.

In 1881 John Hookins Gundry was replaced by John Pickard Suttill, the managing partner of the Pymore Mill Company. He took daily control of J. Gundry and Co. in return for the use of Benjamin Pearkes Gundry's house in West Street, a salary of £200 and a half share of the profits accruing to J. P. F. Gundry. In 1885 a new 10 year agreement was reached giving him an increased salary, while his share of profits was reduced to 13/32nds of those of J. P. F. Gundry.

The mid-1880s saw the onset of a deep and continuing depression, which hit Joseph Gundry and Co. hard. Losses were recorded every year for the ten years from 1886. Ranging between one and eight thousand pounds annually, they totalled over £39,000 for the period. Between 1878 and 1894 the capital value of the business was slashed by nearly £60,000, to just £32,000.

Following the death of their father in 1891, Joseph and Edward Pearkes Gundry took control of the family business. The precarious position of the firm soon became clear, but it was not until after the Newfoundland crisis of 1894 that action was taken. Ball, Baker, Deed and Cornish, a London firm of accountants, was called in to advise them on the best way forward, duly reporting their findings in October 1895. Gundrys' accounts were described as chaotic, no revenue account had been kept, nor were nominal and

expenditure accounts being recorded. The accountants had to analyse **every** item in the cash book for the three years ending May 1895, and for the year 1884. The figures were appalling, between 1884 and 1895 sales had fallen from £60,000 to just £25,000. Around ten percent of this loss was due to the crisis in Newfoundland. While other Bridport firms were also affected, the effect on Gundrys, being largely dependent on the fishing and Newfoundland trade, may have been greater than most.

It was reported that these heavy losses were the result of extravagances in wages and the high price of raw materials. In 1884 purchases had been 41½% of sales, now they accounted for 60%; while wages were now running

J. Gundry's workforce at The Court, photographed c1907 in front of the engine and boiler houses.

at 20% of sales income, meaning that some 80% of sales income was being eaten up by these two items. It was advised that wages should be cut by some £500, removing ten employees, including two clerks, and reducing the pay of the manager. To improve efficiency, reorganisation of the staff was to be undertaken and they were to be paid at

The accounts of Joseph Gundry and Co. from 1823 to 1887. It shows the increase in capital and asset value peaking in the 1870s before declining with the onset of the recession that hit Bridport. Note that even this business made losses on a number of occasions.

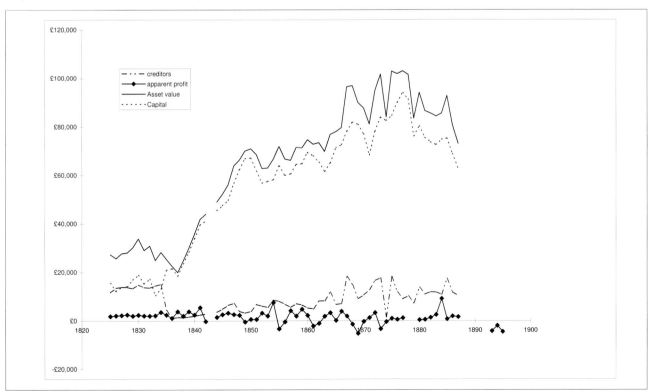

Striking braiders outside The Court in 1912. In 1910 their wages had been reduced during a brief recession. At the end of this recession their request for a return to their previous wage was refused.

piece rates. It was also noted that the use of coal was too great for the size of the business. It is assumed that these recommendations were approved by the partners.

It was around this time that the old jumper braiding looms started to be replaced by the new 'Mons' machines. These multi-shuttle machines, from M. Zang of Paris, were capable of tying up to 1,000 knots at a time, resulting in improved efficiency. The Boer War of 1899-1902 also came to the firm's rescue, with increased orders for the military, a trend which would happen in other conflicts. However, as no accounts survive from the period, little can be said about the firm's position over the next few years. One significant event however was the employment of James Oliver MacDonald as general manager from 1908.

A couple of years later came another brief recession, resulting in Gundrys reducing the wages of the French machine braiders, who asked to return to the old remuneration in 1912 when times were better. Following a refusal by the management they went on strike, the outcome of which is not known. This, and the lack of young people wanting to go into the local industry, was probably the reason for the firm buying land in Newcastle

Street, Swindon in 1914, where a netmaking factory was opened the following year. Accommodation comprised of a machine room, housing seven Zang braiding machines, a net repair room and facilities for reeling, spooling and packing the nets. Thirty women were employed under the supervision of Edward Welch, who had been sent up from Bridport. As well as war work, the factory made nets for export, especially to Norway and Portugal.

JOSEPH GUNDRY AND CO. LTD. 1915 - 1947

In common with other manufacturers, the First World War saw the firm produce materials for the war effort. The usual twines, lines and nets for the fishing industry took a back seat for the duration of the war. Shortly after the war began it was decided to convert to a private limited company. This took effect in March 1915, although the conveyance of the freehold did not take place until October. J. O. MacDonald was appointed as managing director at a salary of £700 and 15% of the profit. In 1919 the appointment of M. W. Burrough as company secretary completed the management team, which was to serve the company for many years.

The new company had a share issue of £30,000 and a debenture issue of £32,000. By 1920 the share issue had been increased to £50,000 and was split between Edward Pearkes Gundry (£30,000), Capt. Joseph Gundry (£10,000)

J. Gundry and Co. advertising card of 1900. The firm had just provided nets for the Royal Yacht 'Victoria and Albert'. While fishing nets and lines were their main products, the card shows that they were also producing sports and game nets.

Sorting the flax coming off the dressing machines into different grades, at The Court in the late 1940s.

Above A view of the Court Works factory taken from the Court around 1890. Compare this with the plan.

Below A plan of the Court Works during the twentieth century showing the location of the buildings and their uses.

and James Oliver MacDonald who had the balance, which had replaced his percentage of profits. The debentures were split into three units, one, of £12,000, was intended to provide an annuity of £500 for Mrs Gundry. Two other units of £10,000 were issued; one to Major Joseph Gundry and the other to Edward Gundry and H. Medlycott.

The company's annual reports give a picture of Joseph Gundry and Co. just after the end of the World War, when the company had assets of £38,545, with sales reaching £181,406 in the year ending June 1920. This has to be compared with the last available results in 1894 where sales were a mere £25,000 (£111,000 at 1920 prices) on an asset value of £41,500 (£67,000 at 1920 prices). Whereas sales had more than kept up with inflation, the actual value of the business had fallen away significantly, indeed the freehold assets were only rated at £12,000, which included £800 in respect of Swindon.

The accounts of 1921 provide the first modern description of The Court Works, which included a line shed with a Haskell Dawe ropemaker and a twine shed with a Bywater twine layer. There was also a tanning house, combing shop, yarn store, slipper shop and a warehouse. The Lancashire boiler, which no longer powered a steam engine, was linked to a generator which provided electricity for the factory. The braiding shop housed nine 'Mons' machines and six 'Zang' machines, two of which were new. There was also a weaving shop, housing nine canvas looms, probably those of S. Whetham and Sons' Priory works which Gundrys had just taken over

Shortly after the end of the War, it was decided to close the Swindon factory, sell the site and move the equipment back to Bridport. This took place in 1920, producing

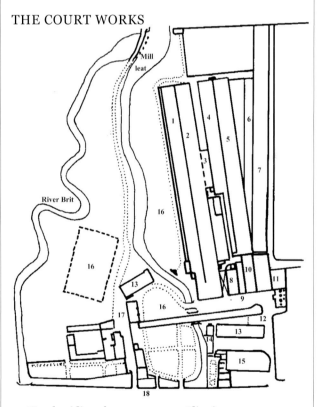

THE COURT WORKS

1. New braiding shop
2. Old braiding shop
3. Fitting room
4. Mending room
5. Twine shed
6. Striking shed
7. Line Shed
8. Boiler house
9. Engine house
10. Slipping room
11. Tan house
12. Stretching path
13. Stores
14. Tar House
15. The Court - warehouse
16. Drying ground
17. Coal Store
18. West Mill

'Mons' braiding machines at The Court c1910. Capable of tying 1,000 knots at a time they were much more efficient that the older 'jumper' looms.

£15,000 and realising a £6,889 profit, although the company rented back some space until the site could be cleared.

At the same time, it was decided to open a netmaking factory in Great Yarmouth, to service the East Coast herring fleets. The factory was built during 1920, at a cost of nearly £16,000. It included the braiding shop, a warehouse, tan house and net fitting shop. The plant, which included four 'Mons' braiding machines, cost £2,000. Additional 'Mons' machines were added in 1922 and 1924. All were powered by electric motors by 1925

B. F. H. Dammers, who was appointed to manage the new factory, had been the principal of W. Hounsell and Co., until 1914. Joined by J. P. MacMillan in 1922, he ran the Great Yarmouth branch until 1925, when he left and was replaced by Woodhead.

The venture did not prove as successful as the company hoped. As early as 1922 they considered closing the works, if the herring fishing industry did not emerge from stagnation. While annual sales were running at around £13,000, they reported annual net losses of over £2,000. Nevertheless the operation there continued until 1932, when the plant was sold, entailing a further loss of £2,872. The site was not sold until 1938, with Miller Ltd. buying it for £9,200, of which £6,950 was mortgaged to J. Gundry and Co.

In 1920, the purchase of Stephen Whetham and Sons for £23,500, marked the start of an expansionist phase. Whetham's continued to trade separately for a number of years before being liquidated in 1932; the Priory Mill site having been sold to W. Edwards and Sons some four years previously.

In 1924 it was decided to buy the Pymore Mill Company, in which Gundrys held the majority of the shares, for £30,000. The merger consolidated Gundrys' control over its spinning mill but at a cost to its profits, as Pymore lost money for five of the next ten years. It also meant that there were now 12 shareholders in the parent company not three.

The next acquisition was Thomas Brown and Co. of Campbeltown, Scotland, for £4,300. The deal was triggered by three seasons of poor fishing, with the local Sheriff's office employing a debt collector for the first time in memory. Whilst making a profit up to 1930, the subsequent years saw annual losses of between £200 and £400. However it provided a supply base for the Scottish fishing fleet and was to remain open for many years.

By 1923 the firm had a Canadian agent, W. H. Stewart, who was to oversee the forthcoming developments there. In 1924 J. Gundry and Co. bought land in Monkton, New Brunswick, which was used to launch a new company, Gundry-Pymore; with the freehold being transferred to the new company in exchange for shares in 1926. In 1933 Edward Fox Gundry was working in Canada and two years later he was responsible for setting up the branch at Toronto.

The last inter-war acquisition was that of the cotton spinning and doubling mill of Mitchell and Marsden of Rochdale, which had been supplying Gundrys for many years. When they were declared bankrupt in 1930, Gundrys bought the mill for £4,300, in order to safeguard their cotton twine supply. Shortly afterwards the mill's steam engine failed, necessitating a replacement costing £3,300. In 1935 a generator plant was added to the mill, bringing them into line with Gundrys' other factories. Providing sales of between £18,000 and £30,000, it provided a significant income to the parent company although during the mid-1930s, as the national recession tightened its grip, it was making a net loss.

The final extension of the business was at St. Ives, Cornwall. However this venture seems short lived, only appearing in the accounts for 1928 and 1929. Likewise an acquisition, of which little is known, was that of Becos Traders Ltd, first mentioned in 1926 it was written off by 1930.

Joseph Gundry and Co. also entered trading arrangements with other Bridport firms. In 1928 an agreement was made with William Edwards and Son, which was to reduce unnecessary competition. Running for 10 years, it stipulated that Gundrys were not to enter the sports nets arena or to work with other netmakers, while Edwards were to limit their interest in fish nets to the development of the multishuttle slip knot braiding loom. Edwards also agreed to buy a set amount of twine from the Pymore Mill Company.

In 1931 an agreement was reached with the other major manufacturer, Hounsell's (Bridport) Ltd., who were to use Gundry-Pymore as their Canadian agent for the sales of their fishing products. The agreement was renewed in 1935, being extended to include the USA.

During the period prior to World War Two, The Court also saw significant developments. In 1920 they had nine 'Mons' and four old Zang machine braiders. The following year two new Zangs were added, at a cost of nearly £1,000.

It was decided to build an extension to the braiding shop, at a cost of £2,036. This became the new or Zang braiding shop, with the original shop housing the 'Mons' machines. The transfer of the Zangs from Swindon, along with further purchases, saw the need to extend the new shop in 1923, at a cost of £900. By 1926 they owned some 50 Zang machines, and had refurbished the older ones bought in the early 1910s. In 1928 a heavy duty Zang was purchased, along with a Genesse netting machine. Gradually electric motors were added to operate the Zangs, the first record of this being in 1924, the work being done by the firm of Ackerman based at Folly Mill, Bridport. While in 1927 the firm acquired their first double knot braiding machine, to be followed by two more the following year.

During the inter-war years, the performance of the company followed the national economy. Sales fell sharply following the end of World War One, reaching a low in 1923. After a recovery during the later 1920s, the recession of the next decade started to bite. Sales fell, bottoming out in 1932. Net losses were made in four years between 1921 and 1932 and, even in the better times, net profit was only around 4% of sales. The recovery from this recession started in 1936.

Joseph Gundry and Co. was fortunate to have a stable management during this time, for in 1926 Edward Pearkes Gundry died. His son, Edward Fox Gundry, did not join the firm until 1928. He had spent some time at John Holden and Sons of Bolton, to gain experience of cotton spinning and doubling, before returning in 1932 to work in the sales department.

During this period, the business was controlled by managing director J. O. MacDonald, who was ably helped by M. W. Burrough, who had been promoted to the board in 1927. The Court itself was the province of the works manager, E. J. Weadon. By 1921 they had a London office, which was run for many years by Thomas Male. A Manchester office, run by W. H. Thacker, was also opened

Above In 1930 Mitchell and Marsden's Rochdale spinning and doubling mill was bought by J. Gundry and Co., providing them with their own source of cotton yarn. Shortly after its acquisition Gundrys had to buy a new steam engine when the old one failed

Above Gundry Pymore, of Monkton, New Brunswick, was a joint venture between J. Gundry and Co. and the Pymore Mill Company. Formed in 1924, it marketed their products in the eastern coast of Canada.

Below Gundry Pacific was started by Edward Gundry in 1944 at Vancouver. It provided an outlet for Gundry's products on Canada's western seaboard.

Above Polishing freshly spun twine at The Court in the late1940s. The twine passes through a bath of size before being polished by the rollers. It was wound onto the bobbins on the left. Note the fine collection of 1940s 'pin-ups'!

Below Camouflage nets at The Court following the outbreak of war in 1939. The two lorries on the left belong to the GWR and will take the nets to Bridport railway station.

in the early 1920s, probably in response to that opened by W Edwards and Son, but closed in 1938.

The 1930s saw the first of the merger proposals appear, the details of which are dealt with separately. In 1932 Joseph Gundry and Co. put in an offer to purchase the firm of William Edwards for £36,000, while another approach occurred in 1939.

Fitting anti-torpedo nets at The Court following the outbreak of the Second World War.

1939 saw two significant events, while the onset of the Second World War was one, the other was the death of Capt. Joseph Gundry and, with Edward Fox Gundry in Canada where he was to set up Gundry Pacific in 1944, it fell to Joseph Charles Fitzgerald Gundry to take his place as chairman. The daily running of the business however remained in the hands of J. O. MacDonald, M. W. Burrough and the works manager

In April 1939 preparations were being made by the Bridport manufacturers to cope with production in the event of war. The Bridport Manufacturers Association co-ordinated the contracts and Gundrys produced camouflage nets, a speciality of theirs, as well as having a share in the other nets required by the military. While this provided full employment, it necessitated the declining of other orders. As a number of clients sought orders elsewhere, this was to have an effect on post-war trade. The wartime upsurge in orders had a positive effect on the firm's finances, with pre-tax profits rising from around £6,000 in 1938 to a maximum of £130,000 in 1943, before falling away as the war ended.

As it was thought that Bridport would be a strategic German target, in 1940 the decision was made to set up the Pioneer works at Beer caves in Devon, to ensure continuation of supply in the event of the Bridport factories being bombed. 14 Zang machines were moved there, under the supervision of David Hyde. The machines returned to Bridport after the war, when a possible purchase bid for them failed to materialise. In the event only two bombing raids occurred, neither of which was targeted on the factories.

Like all other manufacturers, Gundrys was finding it hard to find the necessary workforce and, when asked to consider working double shifts, they replied saying it was unlikely that could get enough workers. It was easier to seek permission to work 10 hours of overtime per week, which necessitated a 6am start. Bridport was fortunate that, by making use of its outworkers, the firm was able to make up for the restrictions on the factory workforce. Some 1,000 outworkers were being employed to produce part of the camouflage net order; making up to one ton per day and completing the order in three weeks.

By 1945 it was hoped that the post-war period would see the merger of all Bridport firms into one organisation, of which Gundrys would be part. However this was not to be as they pulled out at the last minute and carried on alone now competing against increased competition from both foreign and local quarters.

EIGHT
William Fowler

William Fowler (c. 1741-1824) was a twine spinner and sailcloth maker, who married Mary Symes in 1770. He was to play a major role in the establishment of one of the important manufactories in Bridport.

In 1776 his home, together with a warehouse, shop and tan house, was in Bridport's South Street. In addition, he also had a weaving shop and another warehouse near South Bridge. During this time he was in partnership with William Davie, who was the miller at South Mills. By 1785 he was trading alone, still from the same property.

However, things were about to change, when, in the following year, he bought Wykes Court from Samuel Glyde. Previously a farm, Fowler began converting it to a sailcloth manufactory, with the provision of warehousing and a weaving shop, the twine for which was produced in the local spinning ways.

By 1789 he was leasing Pymore Mill, a flour and bolling mill, from J. T. Bull. Ten years later, he was operating it as a flax spinning mill in partnership with Samuel Gundry, Joseph Gundry and Joseph Gundry Downe.

By the end of the century he was a successful businessman. One of his daughters, **Elizabeth** (b.1775) had just married **William Good**, who was involved in running the shipbuilding business at Bridport Harbour with **Nicholas Bools**. In 1810 his other daughter, **Mary**, by marrying **Thomas Collins Hounsell**, formed a link with one of the fast rising merchant families in Bridport.

In the early years of the 19th century he was in partnership with his son **George** (b.1778) as W. & G.

Portrait of William Fowler, the sailcloth manufacturer who was instrumental in forming the Pymore Mill Company. He was also a partner in the Dorsetshire General Bank which failed in 1812.

Fowler. His out letter book of that period survives and shows a thriving business in twines, lines, nets and sailcloth. He was supplying goods from Cornwall to Essex and further around the coast. However much of his business was tied up with the export trade. The link with Newfoundland was already well established and goods were also being sent to the east coast of the United States, with Boston providing a regular market. Additionally he was sending goods to Jersey via Lyme Regis. While most of his goods were taken from Bridport by sea to their destination, use was also made of Russell's waggons.

Around this time Fowler and Son produced four bolts of canvas for Lord Dundonald, who was concerned by the poor quality of Navy sailcloth canvas. Experiments on these showed that, although they cost more than those used by the Navy, they lasted twice as long, resulting in a saving in the long term. It may be that, following these experiments, William Fowler was instrumental in getting sailcloth orders for the Bridport manufacturers.

Another son, **Daniel (b1780)**, was in partnership as a tea broker in London, trading as Fowler and White. At the same time, he acted as the London agent for his father, who

Wykes Court, the home of William Fowler and then T. C. Hounsell. The warehousing occupied the space behind the photographer. It is now in use as a car park.

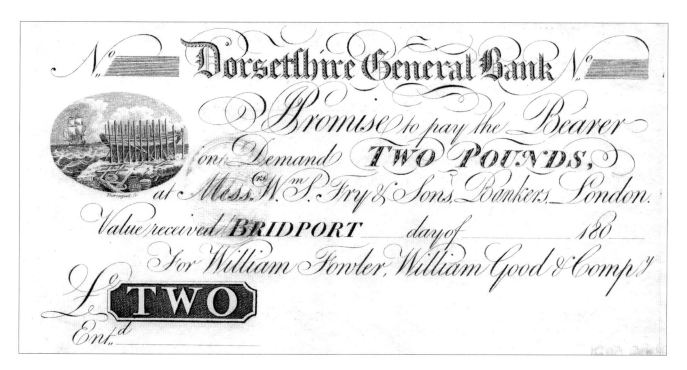

reciprocated by recommending him to other clients. Around 1805 Fowler and White opened a London bank, to which William transferred his allegiance and his money. Following Daniel's lead, William opened the Dorsetshire General Bank in Bridport, with his son and **William Good** as partners. While commendable, it proved to be the beginning of the end for William Fowler. He became bankrupt in 1812, a result of some poor investment decisions by Daniel or, more likely, through the involvement of William Good with Matthew Yeates of Exmouth, in a banking venture which failed in January that year. In January 1813 his sailcloth, weaving looms and other machinery were sold at Wykes Court.

However this was not the end, for it would seem that his friends rallied round to help him, either by buying the items offered for sale or in other ways. One possibility is that William Battiscombe, who was described as a sailcloth maker in 1824, took over the sailcloth business, with Fowler continuing to run it. The upshot was that Fowler

A bank note of the Dorsetshire General Bank. It was run by Fowler, Good and Co. until it became bankrupt in 1812. The lack of a date suggests that this note was never used.

continued to live at Wykes Court and retained his interest in the Pymore Mill Company.

After William died in 1824, having been nursed by his daughter Elizabeth Good for two years, Wykes Court was bought by his son-in-law, Thomas Collins Hounsell. In 1825 T. C. Hounsell let one of his houses in Barrack Street to Mrs William Fowler, the widow of William Fowler jnr. (1771-1825). As Jane Gummer before her marriage, she was the daughter of Robert Gummer, another Bridport merchant. After Jane's death her daughters, Jane (b1808) and Matilda (b1809), carried on living there until immigrating to Newfoundland in 1837, where they met up with their brother **Daniel Fowler** (1805-1844), a shipping agent at St. Johns. After his death in Bridport the shipping agency was taken over by Hounsell, Schenk and Hounsell.

NINE

The Pymore Mill Company

The textile mill complex at Pymore, with its industrial buildings and integrated social housing, represents one of the few examples of a relatively well preserved industrial site in Dorset. It is an important site, which has been sympathetically re-developed in recent years. (See also the aerial photograph on page 81.)

The first mention of a mill at Pymore was in 1707, when Samuel Bull purchased it from Ichabod Hearne; by 1737 the miller was Thomas Fisher. It is a character of the Bridport mills that they were usually multiple mills and Pymore was no exception. In 1785 Samuel Gundry IV was using it as grist and oil mill, the latter involved the pressing of flax seeds to remove the linseed oil. By 1789, when the lessee was William Fowler, the stone built and thatched mill was being used as a flour and bolling mill.

In 1790 Fowler purchased the freehold from John Thompson Bull for £543. Little probably changed until 1799, when Fowler sold shares in Pymore Mill, which was now valued at £1,000, to two other Bridport textile manufacturers. A one third share was taken by Samuel Gundry V, who had business interests in the textile industry and the newly opened Old Brewery. The other one-third share was taken by the partners of Joseph Gundry and Company, Joseph Gundry III and Joseph Gundry Downe.

Once a double mill, Mangerton Mill has the waterwheel for the corn mill on the left, while that for the bolling mill was on the right. The corn mill has been restored to use and the mill house is now a tearoom.

THE PARTNERSHIPS

The partners financed the conversion of Pymore Mill to a flax spinning mill, which began operation in April 1800. At this time the business was a loose association between the partners, for whom the mill provided their flax twine. However, when it became clear that a wider market existed for their products, they gradually took on more customers.

It was in response to this expansion that The Pymore Mill Company was formed in October 1801. With this change, the partners felt that help was needed in running the new concern. As a result John Cole was appointed as the manager, to look after the day to day operation, at a salary of £52 10s. Two years later he became a partner, which was backdated to 1801. Cole was an enigmatic figure; his family came from Dawlish and was clearly of some import locally, having a family vault in the parish church. While his brothers were merchants, one in Bideford the other in Glasgow, little is known of John Cole himself. His partnership did not extend to the freehold of the land, which was retained by the original partners. This partnership was dissolved in late 1817 and, in the following year, Cole took over the New Brewery. However in 1820, Cole was still describing himself as a partner, thus it might be that the 1817 change saw an addition to the partnership. If so, it would seem that the major change in partners took place in 1821, with Cole leaving the concern.

Changes had taken place prior to this, for in 1812 Joseph Gundry IV was taken on as a partner in Joseph Gundry and Co., consequently taking a share in their interest in Pymore. When Joseph Gundry Downe died in 1818, it seems that his two-eighteenths share went to James Templer, a local solicitor, who had moved from his native Devon to settle in Bridport.

The separation of the freehold partnership from the machinery side continued for some time. Entries in a Pymore ledger between 1833 and 1851 indicate that the Old Pymore Company was renting the mill and, from 1843, the new warehouse to the New Pymore Mill Company. However one of the problems is that the style of each ledger differs and, although they cover the period from 1800 to 1851, this lack of consistent display makes for some difficulty in deciphering the actual sequence of events.

In 1821 William Fowler, whose earlier bankruptcy had no affect on his contribution to Pymore, sold his shareholding, with two-eighteenths going to each of the following: Samuel Bowden Gundry, son of Samuel; James

A view of Pymore Mill showing the drying lines on the site of the lower reservoir. The photograph dates from the early years of the 20th century, following the construction of the factory extension on the right.

	S.B. Gundry	J. Templer	J. Gundry & Co.	S. Gundry
1821	2/18	4/18	6/18	6/18
1826	2/18	5/18	5/18	6/18

Above Table 24. The distribution of shares in the Pymore Mill Company during the 1820s.

Below Table 25. The distribution of shares in the Pymore Mill Company in 1853.

	S.B. Gundry	W.E. Gundry	J. Templer	J. Gundry & Co.	J. Suttill
1853	1/18	1/18	4/18	9/18	3/18

1865	S.B. Gundry	W.E. Gundry	R.B. Templer	J. Gundry & Co.	J.P. Suttill
			W. C.Templer	(B.P. Gundry)	B. Templer
			J.T. Prior		S. Allport
					A. Jones
shares	1/18	1/18	4/18	9/18	3/18

Above Table 26. The distribution of shares in the Pymore Mill Company in 1865.

Templer; Joseph Gundry and Company. This was followed by Joseph Gundry and Co. selling one of their shares to James Templer in 1826 (see Table 24).

The partnership was renewed in 1836, continuing until 1843, when Samuel Bowden Gundry gave up one of his shares to his brother Walter Eustace Gundry.

In 1847 the Bridport Bank, run by Samuel Gundry and W. E. Gundry, failed, necessitating a realignment of shares.

A new partner entered the firm - John Suttill, whose family were to be involved with Pymore until it closed over a century later. The new partnership was formalised in 1853 and is thought to have consisted as shown in Table 25.

The deaths of James Templer in 1858, and John Suttill in the following year, complicated the partnership. In their wills, both had assigned shares to their children with the result that there were now 13 partners. Even so a new partnership agreement, which was to last for 14 years, was signed between 10 partners in 1865 (see Table 26).

This clearly made for difficulties and, from the late 1860s, Joseph Gundry and Co. sought to buy back the shares. Those of the late James Templer were purchased in 1867 and 1868 and those of the female members of the Suttill family, along with some or all of the allocation of the late S. B. Gundry, were bought in 1870. By 1881, when J. P. Suttill was given a partnership in Joseph Gundry and Co., that company effectively controlled The Pymore Mill Company.

When the Pymore Mill Company became a limited company in 1899, the shares were retained by the current partners. The Pymore Mill Company retained its nominal independence from Joseph Gundry and Co. until 1924, when it was purchased for £30,000. In 1928 its accounts were presented with those of its parent company for the first time, formalising a state of affairs which had really existed for many years previously.

THE INFRASTRUCTURE OF PYMORE MILL

The original mill was likely to have been similar to the early Bridport mills, such as East Mill. It is likely that the early alterations were not that expansive; simply replacing the older mechanisms with the spinning machinery, while retaining much of the original structure.

When the Pymore Mill Company was formed in October 1801, the value of the machinery was £2,157. With the development of the business, additional machinery was purchased, usually from J. & W. Drabble of Leeds, and included spinning frames as well as carding and winding engines.

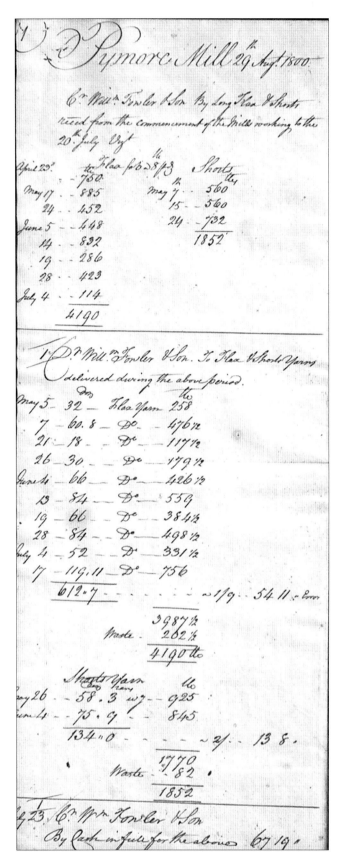

The first bill from Pymore Mill shows that the mill started work in April 1800.

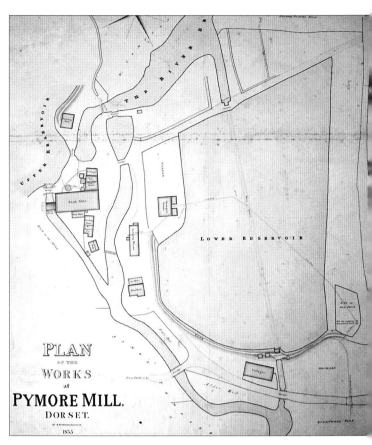

The 1835 plan of Pymore Mill, produced just after the installation of the steam engine, it shows the location of the lower reservoir and the first hostel. The mill was later extended across the leat. Although the mill burnt down in 1960 the ground floor walls remain.

In 1804, to cope with the alterations being planned for the mill, the partners purchased an extra 12½ acres of land. A new waterwheel was added in 1805, with the aim of increasing the power of the mill so that it could operate more machinery. The report of the same year, by the renowned engineer John Rennie, showed that the waterwheel was 6ft 3in wide, with a diameter of 12ft, and ran at 5rpm, developing 25hp. The following year alterations were made to the wheel race to improve the flow of water.

Although it seems certain that carding machinery was in operation from an early date, a new hackling shop was built in 1802. In 1817 The Pymore Mill Company paid £382 for some of the machinery from Slape Mill, which had been destroyed by fire. 1819 saw a further expansion of the mill, with the building of a new warehouse and counting house by Richard Galpin, while a new waterwheel was provided by William Geekie.

In 1829/30 the mill had four operating rooms, the first housing 10 carding machines and 18 roving spindles. The second room had nine tow spinning frames with 268 spindles, six flax spinning frames with 200 spindles, three spreading heads, three drawing frames and five roving frames. In the third room were three spreading heads, two drawing frames, five roving frames of 10 spindles each and 18 flax spinning frames with 616 spindles. The last room had two tow reels and 10 flax reels. This would fit the description of a typical spinning mill.

As early as 1806 it was being remarked that the water supply was sometimes not all it should be. In order to cope with this the mill was provided with two reservoirs, both being fed by the River Brit.

Eventually, in order to overcome this variability in power supply, it was decided to install steam power. In 1834 the Neath Abbey foundry provided a steam engine, which

The winding shop at Pymore Mill, where yarn was wound onto reels. It has recently been converted into housing.

The inside of the winding shop in the early 20th century, showing the arrangement of belt and pulleys that delivered the power from the engines to the machines.

Above The 1843 warehouse, which was originally connected to the mill by means of a footbridge leading from the door in the upper storey. This picture, taken in 2006, shows it being converted into housing.

Below The raw materials warehouse at Pymore. When this photograph was taken in 2006 it was in use as offices for the company 'And So to Bed'. The brick chimney to the left marks the position of an engine house.

was installed adjoining the north wall of the mill. A 20hp engine, it seems likely that it was the condensing engine replaced in 1859. The reason for the choice of Neath Abbey probably lies in the fact that Thomas Fox of Beaminster had a connection with both the Neath Abbey colliery and the Gundry family. By now the waterwheel was developing 30hp and was approximately 15ft wide, with a diameter of 12ft.

A plan of 1835 provides a description of the mill. The site was dominated by the water supply, with the River Brit feeding two reservoirs. The lower one, adjacent to the road from Bridport to Watford, had raised banks on its southern and western edges. The mill, which lay between the reservoirs, was 70ft long and 35½ft wide, with the waterwheel on the western wall. Adjoining the north wall of the mill, were the engine and boiler houses. The boiler was fed by pipes bringing water from both the river and upper reservoir. Joining the boiler house was a cottage. In the angle between these was the gas holder which, along with the gas plant, was built in 1834.

To the south of the mill were the workshop, counting house and blacksmith's shop. There were two hackling shops, one adjacent to the blacksmith's shop and the other next to the upper reservoir. Between the river and the lower reservoir was to be found the manager's house; to the south of this, and on the opposite side of the track, were the lodging house, the stable and cart house.

There was a set of cottages on the lane leading to the road to Bridport, near the bridge over the stream from the lower reservoir. On the south east corner of this reservoir was the 'old pond', which was then being used as a well supplying the houses with fresh water.

Further development took place in the following years. There was a change in the manufacturers from whom the machinery was ordered, with the Leeds firms of Fairburn & Taylor and Wordsworth & Company supplying much of that ordered up to 1851. In 1843 a new warehouse was built between the river and mill, linked to the latter by an iron bridge. This building was later used as the carpenters shop. That same year saw Gerard Samson, the Bridport

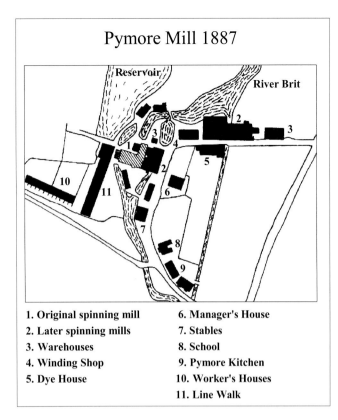

Pymore Mill 1887

Reservoir

River Brit

1. Original spinning mill
2. Later spinning mills
3. Warehouses
4. Winding Shop
5. Dye House
6. Manager's House
7. Stables
8. School
9. Pymore Kitchen
10. Worker's Houses
11. Line Walk

A plan of Pymore Mill, in 1887 showing the location of the buildings.

The 'new' spinning mill between the winding shop and the warehouse. This was built to house two ranges of spinning frames.

iron founder, rebuild the gas works.

The next period of development seems to have taken place in the early 1850s. In January 1852 the steam engine from the Burton Spinning Mill was erected at Pymore. This follows the advertisement in the previous year for new workshops and offices. Other reports suggest that the mill was greatly enlarged at this time. In 1857 tenders were issued for a 'building', in 1860 for a new warehouse and in 1863 for a 'new building'. However these do not give enough detail to place these buildings in the wider context of the mill. The expansion may relate to the introduction of the machine-spinning of hemp, which was being introduced to Bridport at this time. The 1860 warehouse replaced the one in Downe Street, Bridport, which had been rented since 1834.

This expansion can be followed indirectly through the partnerships; in 1836 the business was valued at £17,155. This had increased to around £40,000 by the 1860s, which confirms that a major expansion happened around this time. Although a new warehouse was added in 1872, there is no further record of tenders being issued for work until 1898.

The next description of Pymore Mill comes from the *British Mercantile Gazette* of 1876 and can clearly be related to the *First Edition of the Ordnance Survey*, published in 1887. The article is illustrated by a print of the mill, taken from the southern corner of the old lower reservoir. The first building on the northern access road was used as a storehouse for hemp and flax. Most of the machinery still came from Leeds manufacturers which included, in addition to those already mentioned, Lawson and Sons, Newton and Co. and J. Dockray. The hackling

machines were supplied by George Horner of Belfast, while the finishing of twines was carried out on a machine built by W. Bywater of Leeds.

Bleaching was carried out chemically, rather than by the traditional action of sunlight; in addition the use of aniline dyes had been introduced. The bleaching and dyeing house was at the north east corner of the old lower reservoir. The bleaching ground, on the site of the lower reservoir, was still in use for the drying of hanks of twine and thread.

In 1876, in addition to the waterwheel, there were three powerful steam engines in operation at Pymore, each to a different design. As well as that situated in the original mill, one had been built next to the storehouse on the northern drive, opposite the dye house. This was the site of a new spinning mill, the width of which gave space for two ranges of spinning frames. The third engine was closer to the original one and was probably linked to an extension of the original mill.

In addition a covered line walk had been built, where the lines and cordage were made, using a carriage that ran on rails. The last major expansion came in 1898, with the buildings erected to the north of the site. It cost £9,000 and was built by Sprackling of Netherbury.

With the increased control of the company by Joseph Gundry and Co., a telephone line was installed between The Court and Pymore in 1881. The work was carried out by the United Telephone Company of Bristol and was operating over a decade before Bridport had its own system.

THE CUSTOMERS

In its first year Pymore Mill only supplied its partners with twines. However, following re-organisation in October 1801, its products were made available to other customers. Until 1817 its customers, although centred on the Bridport area, extended to the South Somerset textile industry, located in the area between Crewkerne, Yeovil and Ilminster. However as more spinning mills opened this trade was much reduced, although Richard Hayward of West Chinnock and Templeman of Lopen were supplied

1801-03	1803/4	1804/5	1805/6	1806/7	1807/8	1808/9	1809/10	1810/11
£1,503	£1,064	£812	£968	£1,732	£2,400	£3,740	£2,540	£2,400

Above Table 27. The profits earned by the partners of the Pymore Mill Company during the early years of operating.

Below Table 28. The distribution of assets of the Pymore Mill Company in the 1820s.

	cash	stock	debts due	machinery	buildings	land
1822-3	£21	£874	£5,297	£4,239	£4,088	£1,550
1823-4	£35	£245	£3,542	£4,412	£4,248	£1,550

with yarn into the 1830s and 1850s respectively. From 1817, Pymore mainly supplied the businesses of its partners, as well as the smaller Bridport manufacturers.

The demand for twines led the Pymore Company to lease the Burton Spinning Mill in 1823, keeping a presence there until they introduced steam power at Pymore. Even so, in 1844 they bought the Burton Spinning Mill to provide an additional source of spun fibres. At times of peak demand they also sourced twines from small concerns, including Devenish at Puncknowle Mill and the Ilchester Flax Factory.

PYMORE MILL ACCOUNTS

Unfortunately only very brief glimpses of the accounts for Pymore Mill survive, the earliest of which date from 1801 to 1811 and show the profits earned by the partners (see Table 27).

The expansion in business following 1806 can clearly be seen. It was not all good news however as a loss of £2,637 in 1823/4 followed a profit of £944 the previous year.

While it is not until the 1920s that accounts for the mill survive, estimates of how well the firm was doing can be gauged from deeds relating to partnership changes. In 1822-24 the accounts show a period of poor trade, where debts were called in and the stock levels reduced in order to restrict the losses (see Table 28).

The figures given below in Table 29 relate to the exchange of shares and indicate a slow growth from 1823 to 1836, where the firm's value increased by about £36 p.a.

Share Purchase	Mills and land	machinery	total
1867	£12,150	£27,000	£39,150
1869	£13,744	£28,237	£41,958
1870	£15,582	£27,825	£43,407
1880	£17,010	£31,416	£48,426

Above Table 30. Valuations of the Pymore Mill Company based on the purchase of shares.

The partnership valuations, assuming that they are based on the same parameters, indicate that in the next thirty years average growth was nearly £300 p.a., and it is expected that most of this took place from the late 1850s, when it is known that the mill expanded in size.

The final set of figures (see Table 30) relate to the period 1867 to 1880 when the Gundry family was buying back the shares from the Suttill and Templer families.

The 1867 deeds show that the machinery was worth £39,150, with the total value of the mill being £51,300. As the original mortgage included both the freehold and the machinery, and since a fall of £10,000 in the value of the machinery is unlikely, the 1867 figures have been adjusted, bringing them into line with the others.

From the 1880s, little evidence is forthcoming about the financial condition of the company, until taken in house by Joseph Gundry and Company in the 1920s, when the Pymore accounts were included in the parent company's returns.

Below Table 29. Valuations of the Pymore Mill Company based on the exchange of shares.

Exchanges of Shares	1821	1823/4	1826	1836	1865
valuation at partnership				£17,155	£25,497
account value		£16,719			
buildings, machinery and land only		£10,210			
Total		£26,929			
sale of shares in mill and machinery	£8,550		£8,820		

EMPLOYMENT

The employment provided by the Company can be followed from a number of sources, providing another line of evidence for the dates of the expansion of the mill (see Table 31).

These figures confirm the expansion phases that happened in the early 1850s and again in the 1860s.

John Cole was appointed as the first mill manager in 1801. In 1817/18 Thomas Gould was working on a salary of £160, suggesting that he was now the manager. By 1823 an acting manager, John Hinde, was in place; the following year he was replaced by Thomas Gosels(Gould?). In 1834 Walter Stephens was the manager, remaining there until he moved to run the family flax spinning mill in Bristol, being replaced by John Suttill.

John Suttill was born in Pateley Bridge, near Halifax in 1796, arriving in the Bridport area in the early years of

Hackling hemp at Pymore in about 1925, note the flat caps and the fragments of hemp on the ground. The atmosphere here was always full of dust and most workers suffered in later years from respiratory diseases.

the 19th century. This move was probably the result of his father's involvement in the installation of new machinery at the new flax spinning mills. John Suttill was employed as a clerk in July 1817, at the salary of £80 p.a., although the family records suggest he started working here in 1812. His stay at Pymore was short, leaving at the end of December 1818, being presented with a £5 present on his departure. His place was taken by Samuel Rooker Champ at the reduced salary of £50.

It would seem that John Suttill left to join his father William, as, in 1819, the Pymore Company sold a double spinning frame to a W. and J. Suttill of Burton Bradstock. It is possible that the two were working for Richard Francis Roberts, running his Burton Spinning Mill. In 1823 the Pymore Company was operating this mill for Roberts and Darby, probably with John Suttill as the manager. However, following the death of Darby in 1838, John Suttill

Table 31. Employment figures for the Pymore Mill company from 1834 to 1882, derived from a variety of sources.

Date	men	boys	male	women	girls	female	total	Source
1834	8	10	18	44	19	63	81	PMC
1837							87	mill data
1851	36	12	48	80	22	102	150	census
1861	62	46	108					census
1871							c.340	census
1876							300	article
1881			146			100	246	census
1882							276	Bridport News

Above John Pickard Suttill, managing partner at Pymore from 1859. He later ran The Court for J. Gundry and Co. as well. The Suttill family were involved in running Pymore Mill until its closure in 1955.

Below The Pymore cart which delivered around the Bridport area until the 1950s. Here Tom Shear is in charge of 'Rock'.

Below Pymore Terrace, which was erected in two stages (1858 and 1865), provided accommodation for the workforce. There was also another terrace of workers housing opposite the Pymore Inn.

returned to work for the Pymore Mill Company.

Soon after returning and taking over the manager's position, John Suttill established himself as an important force at Pymore. In 1851 he was made a managing partner, and was the person charged with the day-to-day running of the mill. His position as manager was taken by Frederick Patten, who was promoted from foreman.

After the death of John Suttill in 1859, the managing partner's role fell to his son John Pickard Suttill. In 1881 he was made a partner in the parent firm of Joseph Gundry and Company and, although he now lived in Bridport's West Street, he was still charged with the overseeing of business at Pymore.

Following J. P. Suttill's move to The Court, his place at Pymore was taken by Henry Squire Suttill, who became the third member of the family to be the manager. Henry Suttill had been educated at Dorchester and Germany. This was followed by a spell at Leeds, where he gained a practical knowledge of the spinning machinery, before starting at Pymore in 1873. He married Ada Tucker, the daughter of Richard Tucker and another of Bridport's textile manufacturers, in 1882. In what was now becoming a family tradition, following his father's death in 1898, H. S. Suttill became the managing partner; becoming the managing director when the firm became a limited company the following year. His son, Kenneth, continued the tradition when he became managing director in 1934, and was still at the helm when the business closed in 1955.

Following the increase in the workforce, it was decided to provide accommodation closer to the mill itself. In 1858 a row of six cottages was built to the west of the mill, close to Lower Pymore Farm, and was followed by a second row of six in 1865. The Pymore Mill Company also had another eight cottages on Pymore Road available to them, which James Templer had built before 1838, His executors sold them to the company in 1862.

Accommodation for unmarried women was provided by a lodging house, which had been established on the bank of the river Brit near the manager's house by 1835. In 1841

Above Even from its early years Pymore Mill provided accommodation for single women who came from outside the Bridport area. The original hostel, which was opposite the mill manager's house, was replaced in 1863. The new one, known as Pymore Kitchen, is seen in this photograph.

Below Pymore School and Kitchen as seen today, they now part of the Pymore Village development. The school was built in as a memorial to Edward Gundry by his mother. Her son drowned when swept off the pier at the harbour during a storm in 1869.

Pymore Inn, which opened in the 1850s to quench the thirst of the workforce, also had a shop to supply them with provisions and save them the walk to Bridport.

Joseph Loveless and his wife were running the hostel, with four women lodging there. In 1863 a new hostel, known as Pymore Kitchen, was built on the drive leading from the mill to Pymore Road.

The educational welfare of the children at Pymore was catered for by the building of a school in the early 1870s. It was built as a memorial to Edward Gundry, who was drowned at Bridport Harbour in 1869, and was paid for by his mother.

In order to cater for the workers a beer house, the Pymore Inn, was opened in the early 1850s. Built opposite the Pymore Lane cottages and originally run by William Gibbs, it housed a shop enabling those who lived nearby to buy their provisions, saving them a trek to Bridport. By 1891 John Farnham was running it, now 60 he had retired from the mill were he had been a foreman.

The mill was a considerable walk to the nearest church, which was in Bradpole. In 1882 the Gundry family donated the land at Dottery, on which a chapel of Ease, made of corrugated iron, was built. The chapel remains in use today.

CLOSURE OF THE MILL

The changing fortunes of the textile trade after the Second World War led to the formation of Bridport Industries in 1947, resulting in Pymore losing the contract for supplying Edwards and Son with twines. This, allied to the increased foreign competition, left the mill working at less than full capacity. This was not helped by move toward the use of man-made fibres, for which the installed machinery was not suitable.

If this was not enough, there was the difficulty of the recruitment of new workers. In 1955 only 50% of the available posts were filled. It would seem that the school leavers of post-war Bridport had no wish to follow their parents into the town's staple industry.

The mill was closed in June 1955 and, the following year, the old line walk was sold for £5,000 to Aqua-Craft Ltd. In 1959, when orders for their high specification craft dropped off, some workers were laid off. It was taken over by a Liverpool Boat Agent, who re-launched the business as Aquacraft (1960) Ltd., with D. Bayley as manager.

In March 1959 another part of the mill was bought by the General Woodworkers of London. Part of the De Savery portfolio and trading as Duncan Tucker, it opened in 1960 making windows for property developers Laing and Wimpey. George Heaver was the manager and he later set up his own business, which still makes windows today. Shortly after the new business opened, the original mill caught fire and was badly damaged.

Between 1966 and 1968, the Charlton Concrete Company Ltd. was another business to be found at Pymore Mill.

In more recent times part of the spinning mill has been used as an outlet for a firm selling beds. Another part of the complex has been taken over by Morey's, the auctioneer who moved here after their auction house in St. Michael's Lane was destroyed by fire. The old warehouse by the northern entrance is also in industrial use.

Over the past few years the rest of the site has been redeveloped. The older buildings have been stabilised and some, like the line shed, have been demolished. The remaining area has been used for a housing development, resulting in a mix of industrial buildings and traditional style housing.

TEN
The Roberts Family & the Burton Textile Mills

Francis Roberts came to live at Bredy Farm in the mid-18th century, and it was here that he married Grace Travers. Born in 1748 their first son, Francis, was destined for a life at sea, although he retained a shore base at Mapperton Manor, near Powerstock.

Richard (1752-1820) carved out a very different career path. In 1778 he was a miller, having just taken over the manorial corn and grist mill in Burton Bradstock from John Lawrence, and a corn-factor, in partnership with his cousin Richard Travers of Loders, with a warehouse at Bridport Harbour. This dual business activity continued for some years, with Roberts still being described as a miller in 1785.

However things were about to change, in 1786 he married Martha, the widow of Samuel Best a local farmer, after which he was described as a gentleman. From this time he started to lease the grist mill, initially to Marsh and Stone.

Another indication of his advancement was the development of his partnership with Richard Travers. Following the American Wars, the textile industry in Bridport was developing and, with it, the need to import the raw materials through the harbour. Travers and Roberts seem to have taken full advantage of having the warehouse at the Harbour, with Richard Roberts being described as a merchant by 1789.

Following the development of the first reliable flax spinning machine in 1790, Richard Roberts bought some land near the parish church from John Lawrence and his daughter Ann. Here, in 1794, he built a small water-powered flax spinning mill, probably the first in Dorset, after which he withdrew from the venture with Richard Travers.

The original mill measured 37 feet square and seems to have been a typical three storey spinning mill. The waterwheel, which was on the southern wall, was covered by a building which spanned the leat bringing the water to the mill. Prior to 1822 a new mill, which was 24 feet square and had its own water wheel, was added to southern end of the old mill.

In 1800 he built a new warehouse by the church, just to the north of his mill and close to the cottage he had purchased in 1786. This cottage was transferred to his son Richard Francis Roberts in 1808, later becoming the home of the Mill Manager.

In 1803, near the grist mill in Grove Road, he built the first swingling mill to be found in the county. This consisted of a single storey building with six bays, which

Above The warehouse built in 1800 by Richard Roberts, shortly after he had built the nearby spinning mill. The warehouse has now been converted into housing.

Below In 1803 Richard Roberts built the first swingling mill to be found in the south West. Its working life was probably short, since most of the flax later came from Russia already scutched. The six vertical bays which once housed the machinery can still be recognised.

were probably covered by wooden louvers. The swingling mill probably operated until it became the norm to buy imported flax, which was already scutched (swingled).

Richard Roberts, like the other merchants of the time, placed out the spun yarn to be worked into the woven products in which he specialised. By 1813 he was making table linen, sailcloth, hammocks and sacks of various descriptions, employing almost 200 looms for the task.

Roberts mainly sold the finished products in the South West, although some customers were to be found in the southern and home counties. By 1814 he was employing John Dyson, of Penryn, to collect the monies from the customers living in Devon and Cornwall.

The Grove spinning mills date from 1811 and 1814 and were built by Richard Roberts. The later one was designed to produce very fine yarn. Both mills have been altered during the conversion into housing.

In 1811, with trade flourishing, he decided to build another mill and sent his foreman, Samuel Hoare, to Leeds to investigate the machinery he needed. Hoare had been employed by him since the opening of the original mill, and may have even have come to Burton from Leeds with the machinery for that mill.

The Grove Spinning Mill was built adjacent to the swingling mill and was being constructed in August 1811, when he wrote to the Pymore Mill Company asking them to lend him Joseph Grinstead to help set up the machines accurately. The new mill was working by the end of the year, when Hoare left to work in a rival's mill at Castle Cary. That was not the last the Roberts was to hear of him, for Hoare returned shortly afterwards and, gaining access to the Grove Spinning Mill, took some of its commercial secrets to his new employer. Having been caught out, he was forced to make a public apology. In his place, Roberts engaged Jesse Pittard as his new foreman.

About the same time Roberts ordered a supply of trade tokens from Landers and Astbury of Birmingham. With values of 6d, 12d and 2/-, they were intended for his mill workers and outworkers.

Richard Roberts had three sons; Richard Francis (b1787), Francis (b1788) and William (b1796). Richard Francis Roberts joined the Navy, serving with Nelson on board the Victory at Trafalgar, before returning to Dorset at the end of 1806. Francis served in the Navy from 1806 to 1811, returning as a half pay officer, while William lived in Burton all his life, working for his father until he died at the early age of 23.

On his return Richard Francis Roberts worked for his father, superintending the local flax crop. After learning the trade, he entered into partnership with his father in 1812, with the concern trading as Roberts and Son.

Later the same year, Richard Roberts again succumbed to poor health, having had a previous bout in 1803. Being concerned enough to consider giving up the greater part of his business, he decided to sell the original mill to Richard Francis Roberts. However, with slackening of trade, sufficient for Richard Roberts to call in his outstanding debts, this did not happen. Instead Richard Francis Roberts leased the Burton Spinning Mill, which was probably being run by William Suttill.

In 1814 Richard Roberts was enquiring about obtaining a licence to use James Lee's new carding machine, which allowed the spinning of a finer flax yarn than could be done at Burton. Construction of the new mill, probably the four storey mill attached on the east end of the Grove Spinning Mill, followed and was being fitted out with new machinery from Leeds in August. Trials in spinning the finer flax counts started in October, with the new mill being expected to produce 21,600 yards of yarn per pound of flax. Clearly a success, Roberts became Lee's agent for Dorset, Somerset and Devon

Thus, by late 1814, Burton had four water-powered mills; three spinning mills and the grist mill. While his main business was the production of woven goods, Roberts also traded to a certain extent in the sale of flax seed and would occasionally spin yarn for local merchants such as William Fowler.

It would seem that much of his flax was purchased from the London merchants, Atkinson and Yeates, who had a warehouse at Bridport Harbour. Between 1801 and 1804 he also had his own warehouse there. Whilst much of the raw material and finished textiles were transported through Bridport Harbour, he also relied on carriers, mostly using Russell and Co.

The parallel, but separate, businesses of Richard Roberts and Richard Francis Roberts carried on until the former's death in 1820, and his will clearly illustrated the divisions between the two by this time. He left the mills and factories at the Grove to his son, Francis, ensuring that they had priority over the water supply that was common to both sites.

More significantly he ordered that the Burton mills and factory be sold, with the profits to be divided as follows: a one seventh share was to be given to Richard Francis Roberts, with a three seventh's share going to each of his daughters, Sophia and Martha. He explained that he had already done more for his son than any other of his children.

The outcome of the terms of the will was to unsettle the textile business and each mill will be dealt with separately to follow the events during the Roberts family tenure.

BURTON SPINNING MILL

Finding he was likely to lose the mill he had run since 1813, Richard Francis Roberts had to find a partner to enable him to buy the freehold of the mill. That person was George Darby, a manufacturer of woven goods from Bridport. They made an informal alliance, on an equal footing, allowing Roberts to keep the spinning mill and giving Darby a source of flax yarn for his business.

Richard F. Roberts did not have the business acumen of his father, and seemed not to have any interest in running the mill at first hand. In 1823, Roberts and Darby leased the Burton Spinning Mill to the Pymore Mill Company, who paid £5,000 into an account for Richard F. Roberts and £4,000 into a separate one for George Darby. Their profits were paid into these accounts and, while Darby used his profits to purchase yarn for his Bridport business, Roberts used his as a bank account. Accordingly when the agreement came to an end in 1835/6, Roberts' share of the business remained at £5,000 while Darby had built his up to £7,000.

The Pymore Mill Company also rented a hackling shop from Richard F. Roberts and, from 1825, rented a grist mill and mill house from him as well. It would seem that Richard F. Roberts had gained control of the grist mill at the Grove at some time.

Like other mills in the area, those at Burton struggled at times to find sufficient water to keep the wheels turning, especially as Richard Roberts had ensured that the Grove Mills had the priority at set times. As a result Roberts and Darby introduced steam power to the Burton Spinning Mill around 1835. Unusually, the boiler house adjoined the warehouse on its eastern end, with the chimney rising above the nearby church.

The arrangement with the Pymore Mill Company was terminated at the end of 1835 and, instead, Roberts and Darby made a formal partnership agreement. This was to last for a period of 14 years, after which Roberts was to buy Darby's share. Although each partner had a £5,000 share in the business, Darby had also lent the concern another £2,000 and the £1,500 needed for the installation of the steam engine.

Roberts was to sell the hemp and flax on commission and had to live in Burton, while Darby would continue as a sailcloth manufacturer, but was not to venture into the spinning business and would visit Burton only when needed. To protect Darby's interest, no son of Roberts could act as the clerk to the business.

Neither partner could imagine that their venture would be so short lived. George Darby died in 1838, with his executors invoking the sale clause shortly afterward. Unfortunately Roberts had taken out certain mortgages and bonds using the mill as collateral, which meant that there were insufficient funds to buy Darby's share.

With the Burton factory valued at £8,396, Darby's executors were due to receive £4,690 in September 1839.

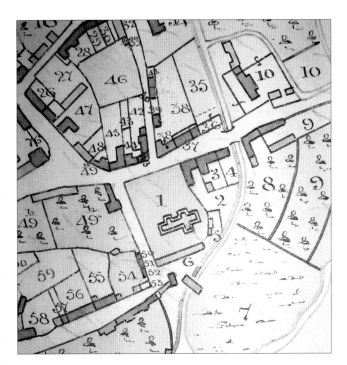

Tithe Map of 1843 showing Burton spinning mill and warehouse (6) just to the south of the church. The mill straddles the leat, with the 1794 mill to the north and the 1820s addition to the south.

This placed them in a difficult position. They realised that they would not get the full value of their share if they pushed for bankruptcy, so they made an arrangement with Roberts for the business to continue. He had to provide £1,500, secure a life assurance and borrow £1,000 from a friend to pay off one of the bonds he had taken out. The remaining debt to Darby's estate was to be paid off from the profits of the mill, with Roberts indemnifying the estate from any action taken to recover money he owed. Supervision of the Burton Spinning Mill was undertaken by John Bishop Ewens, Darby's son-in-law who was the clerk at his uncle's Bridport business. This agreement continued until 1844 when, following Roberts death two years earlier, the mill was sold to the Pymore Mill Company for £1,870.

THE GROVE SPINNING MILL

Following Richard Roberts' death the mill was run by his former foreman, Jesse Pittard, with Francis Roberts the new owner taking a back seat. In 1821, when offered for sale, it was described as a line and tow spinning mill with 212 spindles, together with a booking house and weaving shops, the last named possibly being a new use for the swingling mill now that most of the flax came already prepared.

It would seem that the mill was not sold, for Francis Roberts leased the mill out to Messrs Saunders, who operated it as the Grove Mill Company from 1824 to 1829. At this time he was applying to the Navy for a return to sea. When this was turned down, he travelled to Guernsey, where he acted as a commission agent for The Pymore Mill Company.

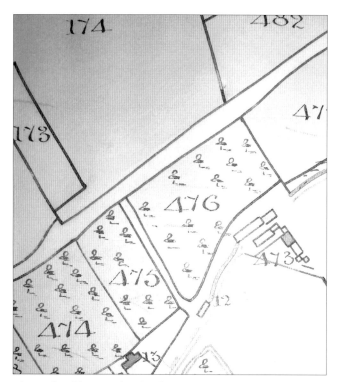

Above The Tithe Map showing the two spinning mills and swingling mill at the Grove (473), with the grist mill to the south, just across the leat.

Below An estate map of 1884 showing the rebuilt mill. The single storey mill used the stones from the original mill, the remains of which lie by the enlarged leat just to the north.

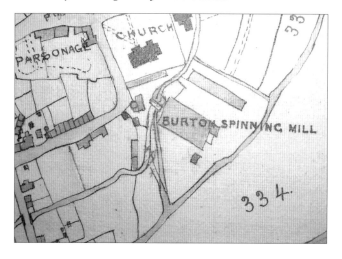

In 1845 the Poor Rates lists Francis Roberts as running the Grove Grist Mill, and both he and his son John were recorded as the millers there until 1855. While it is possible that it was the old customary mill that he was operating, it would seem more likely that he had converted the Grove Factory into a grist mill during the early 1840s. When Francis Roberts died in 1857, the mill was leased from his estate by Daniel Stone, producing an income for Robert's widow. Stone continued to run the mill until around 1870, when Joseph Rendall took over the lease; his family were still running the mill in the 1920s.

The sale of the mill in 1884 provides the first description that clearly refers to a four storey mill, thus linking it to the old Grove factory. In the late 1950s it was operating as the Burton Mills Ltd., although the water wheel was replaced in 1946 by an Armfield turbine, developing 12hp and operating the two stones.

BURTON SPINNING MILL 1844 – 1935

In 1844 the mill became the property of the Pymore Mill Company. The contemporary sale notice provided a good description of the mill, which was a typical three storey flax spinning mill, powered by two internal waterwheels and a 20hp steam engine made by Hick, which was fed by a 30hp boiler. The flax spinning machinery consisted of four flax spreading heads, 23 flax frames with 756 spindles, nine carding engines, eight tow spinning frames with 218 spindles and four twine twisting frames with 146 spindles.

The Burton Spinning Mill closed about 1860; the downturn of trade in Bridport meant that the mill at Pymore could cope on its own. The closure proved to be a hardship for the village, with many families moving to seek work elsewhere.

The American Civil War caused a shortage of cotton, restoring the need for locally spun flax and hemp. With the Bridport mills finding it difficult to supply the demand, Charles Hoare reopened the mill on his own account, complete with new machinery, in March 1865. By an odd coincidence his father was Samuel Hoare, who had been the foreman here under Richard Roberts. Charles had worked at North Mills as a mechanic and manager, taking out a patent for improvements in the flax machinery there in 1860. In 1865 he sold his Rights of Patent to William Hounsell and Co. for £200 and invested this, together with £500 of his own money, in the new venture.

The mill, with Hoare also making fishing nets, made a profit of £400 in its first year. However the end of the Civil War saw cotton yarn began to flow from the northern towns again. In consequence, although Hoare borrowed £1,756 to cover the years of 1867/8, it was to no avail and he was declared bankrupt in November 1869, with debts of £2,797. He died shortly afterwards and was buried in Burton Bradstock churchyard.

The mill was advertised to let in October 1869, when it was described as flax twine spinning mill, weaving mill, house, counting house and cottage. It was re-opened in December 1869 by William Vernon of Dorchester, with Charles Hoares' son, Thomas, as works manager.

In 1874 John Clarke Andrews, who had previously worked as a clerk for Rendall and Coombs, was running the mill with his brother Albion. They were just building up the trade when a tow carder caught fire, burning down the mill; only the walls remained. The report of the fire describes the stone built, water powered mill as having four storeys and a slate roof. There were three rows of eight windows on the longer wall, suggesting a traditional three storey mill with an attic space also being used. The dimensions given were 100ft by 30ft, which suggests that a further extension had been carried out since the 1840s.

The insurance would only pay out £813 of the estimated cost of £1,190 needed to rebuild the mill on the old plan. So it was decided to erect a single storey building, using the stones from the surviving walls laid on concrete foundations; the water wheel pinions forming the centre line of the building. The new mill, which measured 120ft by 52ft, was to the south east of the original.

The brothers resumed business, but trade did not return and they were declared bankrupt in 1879. There followed the final change of ownership; Edward Pratt Rendall, son of Henry Rendall, took over, with James Grant as manager. In the mid-1890s Edward P. Rendall moved back to Allington and the mill formally became part of Rendall & Coombs, supplying the firm with spun yarn until it closed in the 1930s. Eden Phillpots' novel *The Spinners* describes the mill around 1918. It had a lofty open roof space, with the shafting that powered the machines high up on the walls. The machines consisted of carders, spreaders and roving frames, together with gill spinners and spinning frames. Exhausters removed the dust that pervaded everywhere. Later an Otto oil engine was added and the waterwheel replaced by a water turbine. There was a separate warping shed, where the yarn from the spinning frames was wound onto reels.

Today all that can be seen of the original mill are the blocked remains of the arches leading to the pair of internal water wheels. The newer mill still stands and has been recently converted into housing.

Burton Mill has recently been converted into housing. The end walls show the location of the shafts which drove the machinery. Eden Phillpots in his novel, *The Spinners*, describes the conditions inside the mill in the early 20th century.

EMPLOYMENT

In 1838 the mill employed 153 people, but many of these were probably outworkers, as just three years later the census revealed that only 36 were employed in the mill itself. By 1851 the workforce had reached 68, falling to a low of just 7 at the closure of the mill. Its re-opening saw employment pick up; from 16 in 1871 to 35 in 1891.

ELEVEN

The Hounsell's of Bridport

The Hounsell name has a longer heritage than that of the Gundry's, going back to the 16th century. However the family was more disparate than the Gundry's and the links between the Hounsells mentioned are more tenuous, with a definite chronology only really emerging in the second half of the 18th century.

Richard Hounsell I
The earliest mention of the Hounsell name comes in 1571, when **Richard Hounsell** took Henry Stone as an apprentice ropemaker. This may be the same Hounsell who was a Bailiff for the Borough in 1596 and 1601. After which no one of that name represented the Borough for almost 150 years, suggesting that the status of the family had fallen.

Richard Hounsell II (1595-1633)
Richard was the grandson of the above and was also a roper. He had a brother, **Giles Hounsell**, who is mentioned in his will. He was the father of **Giles Hounsell** (1623-1683) a roper of Weymouth.

Giles Hounsell (1598-1660)
Giles Hounsell was the son of John Hounsell (1560-1626) and cousin to Richard Hounsell II. A roper, he lived in Bridport's South Street; at number 10 or 12. Giles had three daughters, two of whom married into the Churchill family. Stephen and Mary Churchill continued the roping business after Giles' death. Having married Ann, Richard Churchill, who lived next door at the Swan, entered the malting and brewing trade. Although Giles Hounsell left his roping tools to his grandson Giles Churchill, he too turned to the malting and brewing trade.

The Hounsells in the Woollen Trade
West Dorset had a small but significant woollen trade in the 17th and early 18th centuries. In Bridport this was much less important, with only a handful of people known to have been in the trade.

William Hounsell was a fuller, according to his will of 1700.

John Hounsell (d1776) was clothier in mid-18th century Bridport, when his property in St Michael's Lane and Allington was insured for £300.

THE HOUNSELLS IN THE HEMP AND FLAX INDUSTRY FROM THE 18th CENTURY

William Hounsell (d. 1719)
William is mentioned in the will of Susannah Hounsell in 1693. In his own will he is described as a mercer and might be the Hounsell that was the founder of the family business in 1670. He married Katharine Gundry and his son, William, was given a weekly allowance by John Gundry III in his will of 1838.

John Hounsell I (c. 1683-1759)
It is from here that the various Hounsell firms of the 19th and 20th centuries can be traced. If actually founded in 1670, then even here we are one or two generations into the business. Like most of the manufacturers at this time, much of his personal estate was in the hands of others, who prepared and made the twine. John Hounsell had his house, warehouse and counting house on the corner of Barrack Street and East Street, the site from which the family business operated into the 20th century. John had two sons, William and John, both of whom carried on the trade

William Hounsell I (1713-1752)
William married Dorothy Gundry in 1741, having two daughters before Dorothy died in 1746; Mary (b1744), who married William Downe, and Dorothy. William married

The two buildings on the corner of East Street were the site of the Hounsells' homes and warehouses. The right-hand building shows the typical warehouse loading doors in the centre, while the left hand building was rebuilt in the 1890s to the present design.

again, this time to Elizabeth who bore him a daughter, also named Elizabeth. He served as one of the Borough's bailiffs in 1748, the first Hounsell to do so for almost a century and a half.

His will of 1752 shows him to have been associated with the sailcloth trade, owning a weaving shop adjacent to 22, Barrack Street. This was left in trust to John and Joseph Gundry to provide an income for Mary, as was the land he owned, which included two plots in the Lower Ropeways in Bridport.

Also mentioned in the will were two men who worked with him, possibly as weavers, John Crabb and Anthony Lee.

John Hounsell II (1715-1803)

No mention is made of John II in his father's will, suggesting that he was already in charge of the family business. We can get an idea of the Hounsell property from the Bridport Poor Rates for 1762, which show that he has taken on his brother's weaving shop and adjoining house at 22, Barrack Street, later buying it from the executors. He also owned 59 and 61, East Street and the warehouse located behind. His will of 1802 makes it clear that he had most of his personal estate tied up in the hands of outworkers.

In 1741 he married Hannah Browne, by whom he had four children, including William II and John III. Soon after Hannah's death in 1752, he married Phoebe Collins with five more children being added to the family, of whom only Joseph I carried on the family trade.

In 1772 he leased the eastern part of the East Street property to William II, on the latter's marriage to Mary Colfox. Six years later, with John II living at 59, East Street, the western portion was leased to Joseph I, being conveyed to him in 1787, along with the Barrack Street weaving shop.

John II was described as a mercer in 1778 and, in the directory of 1784, was trading as Hounsell and Sons, makers of nets and canvas. The extent of his business can be gauged by the £400 worth of stock to be found in his warehouse in 1786. Considering that most of his estate was in the hands of outworkers, the firm's value was probably significantly higher. Even so this is far lower than the Gundry family business, and was also eclipsed by Gummer and Stone and William Fowler during this period.

Although the directory of 1793 shows that his three sons, John III, William II and Joseph I were running their own businesses as twine merchants, other records show John Hounsell and Sons trading as late as 1802.

John Hounsell III (b1747)

John III is a somewhat enigmatic character, we know even less about him than his brothers. He lived next to his father in East Street, marrying Elizabeth Lloyd in 1771. He was most likely to be the John Hounsell, twine maker, mentioned in the 1793 Directory and was the beneficiary of a house and spinning way in South Street in his father's will of 1803. However it would seem that he died in the first

Bridge House was the home of Joseph Hounsell from 1790. It was built by the Rev. Rooker as a Dissenter's Academy in the 1760s.

decade of the 19th century, with his branch of the family taking no further part in the Hounsell story.

Joseph Hounsell I (1753-1799)

Joseph was the first born son of the marriage of John II with Phoebe Collins. In 1778 he was given the lease of part of the family property in East Street. This was conveyed to him, along with the weaving shop in Barrack Street, on his marriage to Elizabeth Tucker in 1787. Six years later he leased Killingham fields from the Borough and, working as a twine manufacturer, moved into Bridge House at the far end of East Street. With his death in 1799 the business passed to his son Joseph II.

Joseph Hounsell II (1789-1864)

Joseph II was a minor when his father died and his inheritance was held in trust until he became of age. The business now included two warehouses, one leading off East Street and another behind the buildings which fronted East Street. Never marrying, he took his nephew, Herbert E. Hounsell, into the business. When he retired in the late 1850s, Herbert took charge, and he was the person who brought the traditionally-based manufacture into the machine age.

WILLIAM HOUNSELL AND COMPANY

William Hounsell II (1748-1796)

It is with William II that the story of William Hounsell and Co. really starts. Initially working in partnership with his father and brothers, William II ran his own business, following his father's retirement. In 1772 he married Mary Colfox and was given one of the family properties for his home. However five years later, when he was described as a sailcloth maker, he moved to 41/3, East Street. In 1782, as a sailcloth maker and twine spinner, he had stock and utensils, valuing £200, in a Barrack Street warehouse. The

Above 41-43, East Street was the home of William Hounsell from 1777 until his death. It remained in the Hounsell family until 1830.

Below The cottages at North Mills built by William Hounsell for the workforce in 1839.

upward rise of his business was seen by the stock doubling in value the following year. When he died, in 1796, his elder son William had just turned 21 and was able to take over the business.

William Hounsell III (1775-1833) and Thomas Collins Hounsell (1784-1877)

It was William III, along with his brother, Thomas Collins Hounsell, from 1805, who were to bring the business up to challenge Bridport's major textile firms. In 1804 William leased Joseph Hounsell's weaving shop in Barrack Street. The following year, he made a step change by purchasing Allington Mill for £2,972. Later to become North Mills, this was a water-powered grist and bolling mill, together with a mill house, several closes of land and an orchard. Completion of the sale in October 1806, meant that Thomas Collins Hounsell was old enough to become a partner in the business. Just when the mill was converted to a flax

spinning mill is uncertain, but is likely to have been sooner rather than later.

In 1810 Thomas Collins Hounsell married Mary Fowler, daughter of manufacturer and banker William Fowler. The couple moved to 46, West Street where most of their children, including William IV, were born. After the death of his father-in-law in 1824, Thomas bought Wykes Court and leased the West Street house to William Stephens, before selling it in 1837.

There followed a change of direction, the business was concentrated at North Mills, either moving the weaving shops there or giving up the sailcloth trade altogether. The Barrack Street weaving shop was let out to James Edwards in 1825, while that at Wykes Court was leased to Tucker and Whetham a year later.

William, who had not married, died in 1833 leaving his share of the business to Thomas Collins Hounsell. While William, like all his forebears, signed his will with his 'mark' Thomas was the first of the family able to write his own name.

In 1838 North Mills was described as a water powered flax spinning mill. In the same year Wykes Court, with the termination of the lease of Whetham and Tucker, was being used as a store for finished products of twine, lines and shoe thread. In 1839 four terraced worker's houses were built at North Mills

The 1830s saw expansion in other directions, beginning with the lending of £2,575 to J. Hayley in 1831, accepting Holyrood Mill, Chard as mortgage security. In 1835 he entered into a partnership, with Joseph Gundry and Co. and Samuel Gundry, to rebuild Slape Mill, Netherbury as a flax spinning mill. This may have been used as an investment since his share of the profits totalled some £3,000 between 1837 and 1849, after which John Munden took on a lease of the mill.

The 1830s also saw the marriage of two of his daughters; Caroline married the Dutch merchant William Schenk in 1833, while three years later Mary wed his brother, Reemt Schenk. William was partner in the shipping agents Hofmann and Schenk, who were based in Rotterdam and London.

It was as a result of this liaison that the firm Hounsell, Schenk and Hounsell was formed, probably to control the shipping of raw and finished materials. The first mention of the firm was in 1844, when they took over the Newfoundland shipping business of the late Daniel Fowler, a nephew of T. C. Hounsell. In the early 1850s they had offices at the Royal Exchange Buildings in London, as well as Wykes Court; although there was no further mention of them after that.

The 1840s saw **William IV** (1820-1903) and **Thomas** (1826-1884) become part of the family firm, which grew slowly over the next few years. Apart from the flax mill, they were still using traditional techniques of manufacture. It was not until the late 1850s that this changed, associated with it was the inclusion of partners from without the immediate family.

The Partnerships 1865-1914

In 1865 a partnership was formed to run William Hounsell and Co. for a period of ten years. The partners were Thomas Collins Hounsell, together with his sons William and Thomas, and **Joseph Thompson Stephens** (1842-1919). Stephens was the son of John Pike Stephens and brother of Alfred, who ran the sailcloth factory at Asker Mill. It would seem that J. T. Stephens, an apprentice twine spinner in 1861, decided his future lay outside the family concern, which also had a flax spinning mill in Bristol.

In the late 1860s Thomas Collins Hounsell's nephew **Alfred William Hounsell Dammers** (1847-1900) came to live at Wykes Court. His father, George Dammers, had been a General in the King's German Regiment and had married Emily, Thomas's sister, at Hanover in 1845. Alfred Dammers probably entered into the partnership in the 1870s, either on its renewal in 1875 or after the death of his uncle in 1877.

The death of the senior partner resulted in William IV being given the freehold of North Mills, Wykes Court and the warehouse in North Street. Thomas received the house in East Street, with the rest being divided between William and his daughters.

December 1883 saw a new partnership emerge, following the retirement of both William and Thomas Hounsell. The latter, although remaining a partner, had retired from active involvement with the firm by 1881. He moved to Hampton Wick three years later, dying there soon afterwards.

In May 1885 the new partnership, formed of **Alfred William Hounsell Dammers** and **Joseph Thompson Stephens**, leased the freehold from William for a ten year period. In 1894 when the lease was nearing its termination, and with William now in his seventies, Dammers made an offer to buy the freehold of North Mills, Wykes Court and the North Street warehouse for £8,000. In addition William was to be provided with an annuity of £903, reckoned to be equivalent to £5,661. This offer being accepted, the partnership was renewed for another ten years.

Above William Hounsell and Co.'s North Mills workforce in 1910. The elevated shafting allowed the steam engine to drive machinery in different parts of the mill.

Below Table 32. Details of the settlement received by the partners William Hounsell and Co., following its sale to Herbert Hounsell (1913) Ltd.

Freehold of North Mill and Wykes Court	£9,900	
B. F. H. Dammers	£11,050	
G. M. Dammers	£11,050	
J. A. Stephens	£7,857	(£3,007 in shares, rest in cash)
The William Hounsell & Co. name	£3,610	
	£48,310	

When A. W. H. Dammers died in 1900 the freehold passed to his executors. While his sons, **Baron Fritz Hounsell Dammers** (b1878) and **George Murray Dammers** (1880-1943), took his place in the partnership.

In May 1905, the lease for North Mills, Wykes Court and the North Street warehouse was renewed for a further 10 years, with the partnership now consisting of Baron Fritz Hounsell Dammers, George Murray Dammers and **John Augustus Stephens** (b1871), the son of J. T. Stephens. In 1912 B. F. H. Dammers bought the freehold for £9,600, on a mortgage from his father's executors.

Then two years later, with the current partnership having only a year to run, it was decided to sell the business, goodwill and freehold to H. E. Herbert (1913) Ltd. in June 1914 (see Table 32 above).

J. A. Stephens became joint managing director for Hounsells (Bridport) Ltd. Although G. M. Dammers remained in Bridport, he was no longer involved in the

North Mills, photographed around the end of the 19th century. The 1918 mill was built to the right of the chimneys.

textile industry. Baron Fritz H. Dammers moved to Reedham in Norfolk, which enabled him to continue his love of sailing. He owned a sloop called the 'Brit', which he sailed on the Norfolk Broads. His affection for Bridport is also seen in the name he gave to his house, Brit House.

B. F. H. Dammers also retained an active interest in the textile trade for he became the manager of the net factory Joseph Gundry and Co. set up in Great Yarmouth in 1920, working there until early 1925.

North Mills and Wykes Court

The story of William Hounsell and Co. is really the story of North Mills. When purchased in 1806 there were two small internal waterwheels, one for the grist mill and the other for the bolling mill. It was converted into a flax spinning mill and was employing 36 people by 1838.

Gradually the business expanded and by 1861 it was employing 108 people. North Mills was one of the few factories making machine-made twine, which, being twice polished, had a glossy appearance. The twine was sold in batches of 12 reels, either for export or to customers some distance from Bridport, very little was sold locally. Some was still put out to the walks for spinning and the foreman had his own trade in finishing the twine by hand.

The old open linewalks were replaced by covered walks. The brick walls in this one at North Mills are a recent addition.

Steam power made a belated appearance in 1861. By now its installation was vital since the fluctuating river flow, caused by the improved drainage of the farmland, made the waterwheel of less use. In 1865 a new mill with additional steam power was installed, while a second high chimney was built in 1867, suggesting that a second boiler house had been added to provide the steam for the engines. This timing coincided with the introduction of hemp spinning machines in North Mills.

When John Munden started work, at the age of eight in the mid-1860s, there were 35 working in the 'shed' department, eight in the tow room, 12 flax spinners, seven in the net room and eight who were carpenters, mechanics and smiths. Working from 6am to 6pm (2pm Saturdays), his first week's wage was 2s 8½d, while that of an adult was 17s 6d. Munden stayed there for 70 years working his way up, becoming foremen by 1891 and finishing as assistant manger in 1934.

In 1871, in an attempt to control the men's drunkenness and regulate the work being carried out, a new building was constructed for the dressing and combing of hemp and flax. By now the workforce had grown to number 340. At the same time, it was stated that the twisting was carried out using a machine running on rails that had been built by William Hounsell and Co., possibly using Charles Hoare's invention for making yarns and cordage, which he patented in 1860.

In 1876 a description of the factory appears in *The British Trade Journal*. From the warehouse the raw hemp and flax were taken to North Mills. Here some 350 tons of fibre were worked up each year, the power for which was provided by two steam engines and a 25hp waterwheel. In the first shed corrugated rollers were used to break the stems. From here they went to the heckling shop, where 30 hecklers worked to tease them into line and tow fibres. After spinning, the yarn was twisted into twine on a machine of Hounsell's own invention. The finishing processes were carried out in long sheds.

The twine passed to the weaving shop, where the **automatic** braiding machines were capable of being operated by women, unlike those normally used in Bridport. These were the only ones of their type in the country and

were the subject of constant improvements. This suggests that they were of local origin, possibly made by Thomas Helyear.

The nets, described as seines, trawls or drift nets, passed to the tanning shed before going to the drying grounds and, finally, to the warehouse at Wykes Court, where they joined the lines and twines also destined for sale.

The 1883 lease shows that these processes were housed in two spinning mills, each having their own engine house, with the heat from the boilers being used in the nearby drying house. The twine and line sheds and striking rooms were close by, as was the 1870s heckling shop. Other buildings housed the netting room and the offices, along with the tarring and tan shops and a store room for cork floats, nets and tow. There were separate shops for the smiths, carpenters and mechanics.

The following year additional buildings were commissioned, including a new shed with tan and drying houses, new offices, a hemp store and spinning mill, as well as a room for twine machinery and a hemp rolling mill.

All these buildings figure in the 1904 lease, suggesting that little changed in the ensuing 20 years. However, with the sale of North Mills to Hounsells (Bridport), a new factory was built at here in 1918, replacing the Sparacre works.

Wykes Court, the home of the Hounsell family from 1824, was on the north side of a quadrangle which housed the offices and the finished goods warehouses. The east side was occupied by the cart shed, a stable and loft while to the south was the gateway to Rax Lane. Following the sale to Hounsells (Bridport) Ltd., the use of these buildings continued until 1949.

By the 1870s William Hounsell and Co. were using automatic braiding machines which could be operated by women. The male figure in the background was probably the overseer. The lack of safety features is apparent with one operator climbing on the loom to make some alterations.

North Mills warehouses in 2006, with the 1918 factory in the background. Much of the original mill has disappeared but the site still houses two net manufacturers – Edwards Sports Products and Game Fayre.

HERBERT HOUNSELL LTD.

Herbert Eustace Hounsell (1830-1909) was the son of surgeon John Hounsell and Eliza Treble and the nephew of Joseph Hounsell (1789-1864), a manufacturer of twines, lines shoe-thread and nets. It was with his uncle that Herbert learned his trade, probably becoming a partner around 1851, when he was first described a manufacturer. Herbert had married **Juliana Wilmshurst Barrett** at

Brighton in 1856.

It seems likely that on his retirement Joseph Hounsell passed his business to Herbert, whose name first appears in the 1859 directory. At this time the business was on the corner of East Street and Barrack Street. However Herbert was clearly intent on expansion, purchasing two properties off Bedford Road in 1858; one was a house, garden and double spinning way and the other house, with a garden suitable for a spinning way.

By 1864 he had built a house, combing shop, store and outhouses to the north of this garden. David R. Hounsell moved here from North Allington, where he had been employed by Herbert Hounsell to work up the hemp into twines and lines, becoming foreman by 1871.

New investment led to the taking out of mortgages on his properties; one for £1,500 in 1866 and another for £400 three years later and a third in the same year for another £1,000. The first named was probably used to develop the land he owned in Folly Mill Lane, on which a tan-house already stood, into the Pelican Factory. Used for the machine braiding of nets, it opened in 1867. The money raised in 1869 was used to extend Sparacre, adding covered line walks and a steam engine.

The late 1860s were a difficult time for the Bridport trade and this may have extended his company somewhat, leading him to take out a loan from Charles Hill for £5,000 in 1870.

Shortly afterwards he decided to restructure the company, which became Herbert E. Hounsell Limited in September 1873. Herbert Hounsell was paid the following under this change (see Table 33 below).

The goods in-hand at this time totalled £2,709, of which £1,822 was kept in the warehouse. Of the rest only £32 was out to braid and £11 out for spinning, while £278 was at Sparacre being worked up.

However of more interest perhaps is the presence of their products at various other locations. There were goods at Billingham (£5), Yarmouth (£35), at an Industrial Exhibition (£59), as well as at an exhibition in Dublin (£10), and a significant amount in Boulogne (£290). This would suggest a wide distribution base and the appreciation of the necessity of finding markets outside the traditional ones.

The following year the first OGM was held in London. It was proposed to raise £50,000 in £10 shares on the

grounds that profits, at 10%, were giving a dividend of 5%, and that trade was being turned away for want of capital.

However the tide was beginning to turn against Herbert Hounsell; in August 1875 Williams Bank of Bridport wrote to him threatening to sell the Sparacre property if he did not pay the interest on the mortgages within three months. While in November, an Extraordinary Meeting of the Company was advertised with the motion 'that Herbert Hounsell be removed from the Board and cease to be a Director of the Company'.

Although Hounsell managed to defeat this motion, he was clearly wounded by it. He remained on the Board but was now merely the managing director. The other directors, who were engaged in a power struggle with Herbert Hounsell, were **James Alfred Hallett**, **Robert Hewitt**, **George Trenchard Cox** and **Edwin Wootton**.

In 1876 the previous mortgages were consolidated to one of £4,000, to John and Archibald Prankerd, and another of £1,000, to the Reverend B. K. W. Pearse. At an Extraordinary General Meeting of 1877, it was decided to allow a further £10,000 to be raised by the sale of debentures, with one for £1,500 being purchased by **Capt. Christopher Campbell Oldfield** in June that year. As additional security, it was set against a mortgage for the same amount.

By 1881 C. C. Oldfield, and Lord Alfred Paget had also joined the Board, the former taking Edwin Wootton's place. By now Herbert Hounsell had effectively left Bridport and was staying at the Adelphi, London. In December 1882, his house at 2, St. Andrew's Villas was put up for sale. Little more is heard of him until his death at Brixton in 1909.

In September 1882 it was thought that, with the present improved management, the Pelican Twine and Net Company Limited was capable of extension. About the same time the capital of the firm underwent a transformation. The £26,270 of 1881 was converted into 1,748 shares of £7 by 1885, giving a valuation of £12,236. It may be that these changes presaged the re-launching of the business under new ownership.

A series of account and reports for the period 1876 - 1893 show the general trend of business (see Table 34).

Sales had been increasing since 1879, initially providing a fair profit. However three years of poor fishing returns had resulted in net profits falling, which may have caused the final rift between Hounsell and the remainder of the Board.

The losses returned in the mid-1880s, with the first being shown in 1886, causing the Board to express concern for the survival of the business. This was remedied by cutting back on expenses and, in an attempt to diversify and become less reliant on the fishing trade, the firm added both cricket and tennis nets to their products. Although successful, they then found that the summer's weather affected the sales of the new products. By the early 1890s the firm was in good condition, despite the loss in 1890 caused by one district in which the fishing was poor. Around this time 59, East Street was rebuilt and was leased out to provide more

Table 33. The valuation of Herbert Hounsell Ltd. on its incorporation as a limited company in 1873.

Valuation	cash held by HEH	£1,003
	150 shares at £6	£900
	717 shares at £10	£7,170
		£9,073
Materials at Pelican Works		£2,716

Date	Capital (£)	Gross Profit (£)	Net Profit (£)	Stock (£)	Debtors (£)	Cumulative profit/(loss) (£)
1876			(-497)			
1877	24,146	4,385	2,034	7,927		
1880			1,022			
1881	26,270	4,052	888	9,939	11,912	
1885			212			212
1886			(-1021)			(-809)
1887	12,236	3,292	(-664)	5,236	5,844	(-1473)
1888	12,236	3,564	(-385)	4,803	6,437	(-1858)
1889	12,236	4,175	461	5,070	7,267	(-1397)
1890	12,236	3,627	(-102)	5,264	5,852	(-1499)
1891	12,236	3,770	120	5,488	6,474	(-1379)
1892	12,236	4,702	724	4,886	7,432	(-654)
1893	12,236	3,908	464	5,846	6,137	(-189)

Table 34. The accounts of Herbert Hounsell Ltd. covering the period from 1876 to 1893.

income for the firm.

In 1892 the auditor recommended reducing the share price from £7 to £5, a move which would wipe out the deficit, give a £1,000 reserve and make the shares more marketable. Despite legal difficulties preventing this move, the deficit was almost wiped out the following year. It was reported that the demand for lines was so great that there was a three month waiting list, with some orders having to be refused. In order to address this some £600 was spent in alterations to the plant and buildings.

This turn around in fortunes, while in part being due to the upturn in fishing, was the result the good reputation the firm gained by concentrating on the sale of superior lines. The twines, from which these lines were made, were of 40-50 lbs, and up to 80lbs, fine 12 thread flax and, not being hard laid, were pliable. The nets were tanned three times, which was followed by soaking in linseed oil, before being tanned again prior to drying. A note in the *Bridport News* of September 1883 indicated that 75% of the American fishing fleet were using their purse seine for mackerel and that gill nets were being used for the American cod. The importance of the American market was reflected by the extended visit of **Edwin James Wootton Buckpitt** to New York in 1893.

The success of the Company was due to the Board members, along with their secretary, all of whom were successful men in their own right. The Chairman was **Christopher Campbell Oldfield**, an Army Captain who was born in India and who had returned to England in the early 1870s. **James Alfred Hallet**, the managing director,

was a Navy Agent, Banker and Magistrate who was living in London in 1877. **Robert Hewitt** was a London merchant, of whom little is known.

However the most significant figure was **George Trenchard Cox** (1831-1910). Born in Maiden Newton, he was the son of a dairyman. By the time he married in 1855, he had moved to London, where he started the wholesale and retail grocers business which was to become G. T. Cox and Sons. While his involvement with Herbert Hounsell Ltd. began in 1875, the London business remained his main interest; he was one of its directors until 1900.

From 1882 the company secretary and manager was **James Buckpitt** (1845-1902). His son, **Edwin James Wootton Buckpitt** (1869-1930), took over from his father in 1901.

The death of George Trenchard Cox in 1910 set off a chain of events, which was to change the face of textile manufacture in Bridport. It involved his representatives and sons - **George Percy Cox, William Hallett Cox** and **Edward Alfred Cox**. In September 1911, they paid off the outstanding mortgages and debentures and took control of the company. The following month, Edward A. Cox lent Herbert Hounsell Ltd. £12,000, strengthening his hold on the company, which was now trading in his name. His hold was further fortified by the taking out of a trust deed in November.

His next move was to put the company into liquidation, which he initiated in December 1912. Then, in January 1913, he made an agreement to purchase the company, along with its goodwill and trade marks, for £14,000. A new company, Herbert Hounsell (1913) Ltd., was set up with his sons, **Keith Trenchard Cox** and **E. Donald Cox**, as joint managing directors. The following month, he sold the old company to the new for £14,000, which was made up by £7,678 for the buildings, plus £6,322 for the debts, rentals and liabilities. Edward A. Cox was to be paid as below in Table 35.

In reality, the shares he obtained were divided between old and new companies, 7,508 in the old company and 1,322 in the new one.

However the new company was not to have a long existence. It is likely that negotiations were already taking place for the formation of **Hounsells (Bridport) Ltd**.

Cash	£170
£1 Shares HEH(1913)Ltd 1–8830	£8,830
10 x £500 mortgage debentures	£5,000
	£14,000

Table 35. The detail of the payment made to Edward A. Cox on the formation of Herbert Hounsell (1913) Ltd.

HOUNSELLS (BRIDPORT) LIMITED

The two main events leading to the formation of this firm overlap, giving support to the suggestion that there had been collusion between various parties prior to the event. While Edward A. Cox was getting control of Herbert Hounsell Ltd, certain events were taking place at William Hounsell and Co. According to W. J. Samways, there was a row between Dammers and Stephens regarding the future of W. Hounsell and Co. It appears that Dammers

had already agreed to sell the freehold to a separate party, later known to be Herbert Hounsell (1913) Ltd., by the time the partnership was dissolved in April 1914. It has also been suggested that, following the row with Dammers, Stephens contacted Edward A. Cox, the move leading to the formation of the new firm.

Another drive towards the formation of Hounsells (Bridport) Ltd. was the opposition of T. A. Colfox, who had moved into the neighbouring Conygar House, to any expansion of the works at Sparacre. He made clear his opposition to having a factory on his doorstep in 1908, when Herbert Hounsell Ltd. wanted to increase the height of the works chimney. In the end, Herbert Hounsell Ltd., in exchange for £400 and the conveyance of a small plot of land from Colfox, agreed to rebuild the chimney further away from Conygar House. They also agreed to add a new feed water heater, a Sturtevant induced draught combined fan and a Groves Economiser, in order to reduce the emissions from the chimney.

When Hounsells (Bridport) Ltd. started trading in June 1914, E. A. Cox and his son Keith were still living in London so it was decided that Edwin J. W. Buckpitt and John A. Stephens should be joint managing directors. This lasted until Stephens left in 1918, after which E. A. Cox, in order to take a more active role in the company, moved to live at Uplyme.

The take over of W. Hounsell and Co. gave them their own spinning mill, on a site which was capable of expansion. Accordingly, in 1914, a trust deed was issued in order to raise £20,000 in £100 debentures, for a new factory adjoining North Mills. The First World War delayed the completion of the project and it was not until April 1918 that the new factory was built, allowing Sparacre to be sold to T. A. Colfox for £2,000. Hounsells (Bridport) Ltd. were to demolish the factory and clear the site, but were allowed to retain any useful machinery.

Hounsells (Bridport) Ltd. took over the lease of Fullbrooks from Richard Hayward of West Chinnock in 1916, a move which allowed them a greater production facility, and in 1918 the company took over the firm of Ewens and Turner.

The period following the end of the war was a difficult one for all the Bridport manufacturers. The decline in production, linked to the end of military orders, was matched by a depression, which the industry found hard to overcome. In 1926 most firms were working a three day week and it is not surprising to find trade agreements being set up between the main manufacturers. In 1928 Hounsells (Bridport) Ltd. and W. Edwards and Sons signed an agreement, for a ten year period, which would limit unnecessary competition. Edwards were supplied with lines at a 5% discount and in return agreed not to sell salmon nets in Canada.

The 1930s started sadly with the death of Edwin

Left Hounsells (Bridport) catalogue, dating from the 1950s, showing their dolphin trademark.

Buckpitt, after a lifetime's work for the business. The economic prospects were similarly rather gloomy, the partial recovery of the late 1920s had not lasted and a further recession took place in the 1930s. With a three-day week being re-introduced, it was the worst trading period many could remember. In 1932, to limit the effects on both the business and its workforce, Hounsells (Bridport) Ltd. started making fruit baskets. Aspen logs were imported through the harbour at West Bay, with the one shipment of 1931 increasing to three in 1934. A German machine, costing £1,000, was used to peel strips from the logs, which were then assembled into the fruit baskets. In 1935, following an improved trading position, the basket-making department was closed and machinery sold.

The Second World War saw the full cooperation between the Bridport manufacturers in the production of war materials. By the time trading returned to the peacetime

Below Aerial view of North Mills, clearly showing the 1918 mill with its 'north lights' and the array of covered linewalks.

levels, there were other clouds on the horizon. This was illustrated in January 1947, when the joint managing directors of Hounsells (Bridport) Ltd., Keith Trenchard Cox and Edward Donald Cox, reported that there was increasing competition to be met by the Bridport firms. Most of Hounsells' production was for the export market and in order to meet this competition it had been decided to re-organise North Mills and install new spinning machinery. Later that same year, Hounsells (Bridport) Ltd. merged with W. Edwards and Son to form Bridport Industries.

The basket-making workshop of Hounsells (Bridport). Open from 1932 to 1935, this was an attempt to reduce the effect of the recession on their firm and its workforce.

5, North Allington, the home of Robert Hounsell, with his net works to the rear.

ROBERT HOUNSELL AND SONS

The son of Joseph Hounsell and Jane Webber, **Robert Hounsell** (1816-1890) was another of those textile workers that started his own business in the mid 19th century. He was working as a comber/heckler, and living in Bridport's South Street, when he married Elizabeth Weaton in 1837. The family moved to North Allington in the early 1840s, where he continued to work as a heckler.

Ten years later he set up business as a twine manufacturer. Based at 5, North Allington, he was producing twines, lines, shoe thread and nets by 1855. He was probably one of the first manufacturers to employ braiding machines, selling them to Stephen Whetham and Sons in 1861.

Three of his sons, **Henry Robert Hounsell** (1842-1919), **Thomas** (b.1844) and **William Henry Hounsell** (1846-1889), were employed as factors in the business in the 1861 census. Ten years later Henry described himself as a twine manufacturer's clerk. He acted as travelling clerk for the firm for some 11 years, leaning all the aspects of the business.

In the 1870s Robert Hounsell retired from the business to become a farmer in Netherbury. In 1884, he purchased 36a, St Michael's Lane, a traditional Bridport house with its own spinning way and turnhouse. A covered twine and line walk was built on the site of the spinning way.

With the death of William in 1889, and that of his father a year later, Henry Robert Hounsell had sole control of the business. His own sons chose different paths, with the elder, **Henry H. Hounsell** (b.1874) training as an architect and combining this practice with working for the family business, while **William G. Hounsell** (1880-1949) was involved with the firm full time.

By the turn of the century it would seem that it had been decided to concentrate on netmaking, for both North Allington and St. Michael's Lane were described as net mills in 1922. However in 1910 William Gale and Sons had acquired the houses to the north of 36a St. Michael's Lane, leaving Hounsell's line walk surrounded by a competitor who tried numerous attempts to buy it. Gale's even threatened to cut off the gas supply to the house.

The early thirties was a hard time for the Bridport textile firms and Robert Hounsell and Sons were no exception to this. As with other small textile businesses, the writing was on the wall. With many fishermen giving up the trade, work was short and orders few and the firm lost money for a number of years. In 1933 Henry wrote to his sister telling her of the position in which the firm found itself, mentioning that the business might have to close. Closure seems to have taken place soon after its inclusion in the 1935 directory.

Robert Hounsell's braiding shop to the rear of 5, North Allington, in about 1900. The machines here are the old jumper looms.

TWELVE
William Edwards & Son

WILLIAM EDWARDS & SON

William Edwards was born c.1835, the son of a sailcloth weaver living in Diments Square, North Allington, where he started to manufacture rope and twine in the late 1850s. In 1874 he purchased 66, St. Michael's Lane, moving his business there. For many years it remained a small concern, employing just two boys in 1881.

The mid-1880s saw a move into netmaking, possibly as a response to the worsening economic conditions, which were not being helped by the increase in use of machine-made twine and cotton for making nets. From the 1870s, the upsurge in the popularity of lawn tennis provided a ready market for nets. It was into this sphere that William Edwards directed his business. His sons entered the firm around the same time and his workforce had grown to six.

In 1895, at the age of 60, William retired and sold the business to his elder son, William Saunders Edwards, for £1,396; while his younger son, Sidney Richard Edwards, became works manager. Sidney had started with the firm in 1886, but had worked at sea from 1887 to 1893.

The expansion had started in 1892 with the purchase of 68, St. Michael's Lane, behind which the St. Michael's Net Works was built. This was followed, two years later, by the purchase of 42 and 44, St. Michael's Lane. By 1907 the firm owned all the property in between, building the Stover Line and Twine works on the land once used as spinning ways.

This expansion was necessary to keep up with the increased production, bought about by the manufacture of football goal nets. These had been patented by J. Brodie in 1891 and were soon adopted by the Football Association. With W. Edwards and Son having been given the exclusive manufacturing rights by Brodie, around the start of the 20th Century, the firm had now become a major player in the industry and by 1914, as well as the goal nets, they were producing the majority of the nets for Gamages.

The First World War saw the Bridport manufacturers change to the production of war materials, which was co-ordinated by William Saunders Edwards. The war period also saw the death of the firm's founder William Edwards, in 1916. Full time working did not resume until 1921 and, shortly after, they were successfully prosecuted for not paying the correct rates for netting, which involved a detailed interpretation of the type of netting being worked. During this period, their attitude was the subject of much criticism by the Manufacturers Association, although it was recognised that they were probably right in doing it their way!

The letter head used by William Edwards and Son, showing the St. Michael's Networks, on the left, and Stover Works. At the time it was printed the building housing the clock tower had yet to be built.

In 1922 the company opened a depot in Manchester under the direction of A. W. Budden. Originally located in the Holmes Wright works, it moved a number of times until it settled at Lee Vale Mills, Charlesworth in 1935, by which time it was being run by Bob Myers, who had taken over following the death of Budden in 1930.

In 1928 the firm, wishing to expand further, bought Priory Mill from Gundrys. It would seem that the plan to use it as their twine mill was soon dropped, probably due to the investment needed to modernise the mill. Instead the firm made an agreement with Gundrys and the Pymore Mill Company, which saw the latter supplying their twine and, in return, Edwards agreed not to expand into the fishing market. At the same time they also made an agreement with Hounsells (Bridport) Ltd. to further limit

'Tarry' Harry Lovelace tarring nets at the St. Michael's networks of W. Edwards and Son, c1950. Tarring helped to preserve the nets but also made them more brittle.

121

Mrs Barrett tending a Zang braiding loom in the Stover Works of W. Edwards and Son, 1950.

and by 1936 they were employing some 200 workers. That same year Campbell's brother, Sidney, retired and was replaced as works manager by his son, William.

February 1939 saw another attempt at amalgamation with J. Gundry and Co. This, once again, came to nothing and, in order to produce the materials needed for the Second World War, a period of cooperation was seen between all manufacturers. During this time Campbell Edwards joined the RAF, leaving Harry Sanctuary to run the firm; representing them in the 1943 meeting regarding the eventual merger of the Bridport firms.

However, as a prelude to this merger, W. Edwards and Son took over two long-established businesses, Rendall and Coombs (1945) and William Gale and Sons (1946). In 1947, with the formation of Bridport Industries, the independent existence of the firm ended, although each firm retained their separate boards until 1954.

Figures relating to the trading activities of W Edwards and Son are few and far-between. Those that do exist cover the period from 1933 to the formation of Bridport Industries (see Table 36), and clearly show the affect of the war on the sales and profits of the company, which was mirrored by the other Bridport firms. Even so the figures held up well in the short period after the war.

competition

William Saunders Edwards died by his own hand in 1932, after being diagnosed with a long term illness. This triggered a clause in a supplemental agreement, made between Edwards and Gundry, giving the latter an option of purchasing the former within 18 months of W. S. Edwards' death. Gundry offered to pay £36,000 for the freehold and goodwill. This was refused and W. Edwards and Son continued to be run by Campbell W. Edwards and his brother-in-law, Harry Sanctuary. Expansion continued

EDWARD NORMAN/ ALBERT NORMAN

Edward Norman (1823-1882)

Devonian Edward Norman moved to Bridport, where he married Elizabeth Hockey, daughter of James Hockey the licensee of the Sun Inn, in 1844. Four years later he was the landlord of the Three Mariners public house in East Street, before moving to 96, East Street to run a beer house and a shop. He probably continued his previous occupation as a comber. Then, around 1861, he began working as a ropemaker, before becoming a manufacturer in his own right, probably as a result of the upsurge in work resulting from the American Civil War. He had his twine

Netmaking at the Stover works of W. Edwards and Son in 1930.

manufactory to the rear of the inn, by now named the Duke of Wellington

When Edward died in 1882, Elizabeth continued the business and she probably employed someone to look after the twine business, while she ran the inn and shop. However in 1893, with the staple trade of the town passing through one of its periodic recessions, she had to execute a deed of assignment. Her son Albert came to her rescue by offering the creditors 5/-(25p) in the £1.

Table 36. The sales figures and profits of W. Edwards and Son between 1933 and 1946.

	Sales (£)	Profits (£)
1933		9,484
1934		9,230
1935		10,284
1936		11,350
1937	82,273	8,281
1938	82,274	7,563
1939	112,480	15,991
1940	293,771	49,525
1941	307,398	44,027
1942	298,516	44,121
1943	363,145	60,308
1944	295,160	37,099
1945	280,230	22,582
1946	214,306	22,443

Fitting football goal nets at the works of William Edwards and Son in St. Michael's Lane around 1910.

Albert Norman (1862-1921)

Albert was working the family bakery in 1881, but when he married Elizabeth Jane Edwards there was a change of direction. In 1884 he was a net manufacturer, possibly working for his father-in-law, the manufacturer William Edwards. Three years later he was living in Irish Lane (King St.). A twine manufacturer, he was probably running the family business for his mother.

After rescuing it from bankruptcy, Albert became

The Duke of Wellington, at 96, East Street, was run by Edward Norman, who had his line and twine walks to the rear. At the time of this photograph, 1911, Albert Norman was running the pub. However his linemaking business had become bankrupt the year before.

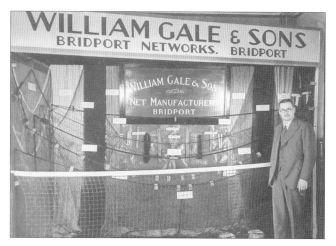

Above A William Gale and Sons' trade stand, showing the range of products the firm made.

Below Sidney Gale was the son of William Gale, founder of W. Gale and Sons. When the photograph was taken he was the town's mayor.

owner of the firm, concentrating on the manufacture of nets, mainly tennis and cricket nets. Like his mother he kept the three businesses going, with his wife running the inn and the shop. However in 1910 his business failed with net liabilities of £662. Realising that he was trading insolvently, he had managed to assign the property to William Edwards before a creditor filed a bankruptcy petition. The main cause of the failure was a bad debt relating to trade with South Africa, compounded by the cost of a failed legal submission. Like many of the small manufacturers he was trading with little capital reserve. He also had no cash record of his business, but his offer 7/6 in the £1 to his creditors was accepted by the bankruptcy court. To finance this he sold 97a, 98, and 100, East Street, which he had acquired in better times.

While the net manufacture ceased, the family retained the shop and inn, both of which continued to trade for many years. During World War One, Albert made good use of his experience in the textile trade by working for the Ministry of Defence, at their Yeovil Flax Factory. After the war, the flax factories were sold off and Albert set up as an agent for the 'Speedy Princeps' Light car. After his death in 1921, his widow continued to live at 96, East Street and was one of those killed when East Street was bombed in 1942. After the war the Norman's workshops were again used for net making, this time by Redport Nets.

WILLIAM GALE AND SONS

William Gale (b.1844) was the son of Samuel Gale, a shoemaker. He started work as a flax comber or heckler, an occupation which he continued for many years. In 1877 William Gale moved to 36-38, St. Michael's Lane, a typical spinning walk recently vacated by Walter Powell. He was working here as a twine spinner when he was widowed in 1882. Clearly the business was on a small scale, for it is not until 1885 that he started to advertise as a twine maker. By late 1897 they had opened a grocery shop for their workers. Concerns were raised a few years later that Gales were operating in contravention of the 1831 Truck Act. They countered the charge by saying that it was an old tradition to pay workers in tea and salt fish.

At the turn of the Century William's sons, **Sidney** (b.1880)**, Fred** (b.1885) **and Albert** (b.1888), were taken into the business and it is under their guidance, especially that of Sidney, that the firm started to make nets. In 1910 they bought the freehold of 30-34, St. Michael's Lane, adding 40, St. Michael's Lane in 1925. Eventually they owned all of the property from 30 to 40, St. Michael's Lane, after which they were able to build their factory, on the site of the gardens once used as spinning-ways.

In 1946 the firm was purchased by Edwards, largely to provide an entry into the fishing net business and the Zang braiding machines that Gales were using. The firm continued as a subsidiary company under the management of Albert Gale.

THIRTEEN

The Tucker Family

John Tucker (1720-c.1784)

John Tucker was a sackmaker, who married Catharine Stickland around 1747. Together they raised nine children, with all the sons entering the textile trade. In 1750, while Tucker was working as a sailcloth maker, he purchased Priory Orchard from Daniel Pring of Exeter.

Abraham Tucker (1761-1810)

Abraham went into partnership with his brother **Thomas**, but also invested in the Tuckenhay Spinning Mill, near Totnes, where he was the managing partner in 1796. In addition to his shares, he had also lent the business £2,000.

In 1793 he married Ann Creasor and had one son, John Thomas Tucker (b1795). Following Abraham's death, George Tucker and John Chilcott were appointed as trustees for his shares, which were left in trust for his son, until he reached the age of 25 years. This resulted in the move of Richard Tucker, another of Abraham's brothers, to supervise operations at Tuckenhay.

John Tucker II (1750-1782) and George Tucker (1752-1825)

It would seem that **John II** followed his father into business. In 1778 he married Jenny Hounsell and had two daughters. One, Elizabeth, married Josiah Selwood, a Bridport merchant, in 1802 while the other, also named Jenny, married **Stephen Whetham** the following year.

After the death of her husband, **Jenny Tucker** went into partnership with her brother-in-law **George**; trading as George Tucker and Company, twine spinners and sailcloth makers, in 1793. In 1785 the business was being carried out at Jenny's house, office and warehouse in South Street, with a heckling shop nearby. At Priory Orchard there was a weaving and whiting house, which was described as a Yarn Barton in 1799.

Tucker and Whetham (1803-1825; 1825-c1836)

It would seem that there were two partnerships working under this name. The first was between George Tucker and Stephen Whetham and was mentioned in the Pymore Mill records for 1803. It would seem that, shortly after his marriage to Jenny Tucker, Whetham took his mother-in-law's place in the family trade. In 1817 they took a lease on Folly Mill, which was used to drive the St. John's Spinning Mill.

The first partnership was terminated by the death of

George in 1825. His place was taken by his brother Richard I, who had recently returned from Tuckenhay and was living at 42, South Street. Although they continued to use the weaving shop in Priory Orchard, they also used out-workers as far away as Beaminster. Then, in 1826, they rented weaving shops at Wykes Court.

By the late 1820s both men had sons, who would expect to become partners in their father's businesses on reaching their majority. As a result the partnership of Tucker and Whetham was dissolved, although the exact date of this is uncertain. The first directory record of the separate firms is in 1830. Tucker and Whetham did business with the Pymore Mill Company until 1832, when the account changed to Whetham and Sons, but the lease of the weaving shop at Wykes Court continued in their joint names until 1839.

Richard Tucker I (1756-1836)

Richard Tucker was a sailcloth manufacturer by 1779 when he had stock valuing £200 in his own and two rented warehouses. Around 1792 he married Mary Cleeves Palmer, the daughter of John Palmer of South Perrott, near Crewkerne. The brewers John Cleeves and Robert Henry Palmer, who were to arrive in Bridport a century later, were also descendants of this family.

After Abraham's death, Richard moved, with his wife and young family, to run the mill at Tuckenhay. It would seem that he did not retain a manufacturing base in the Bridport, as he is not mentioned in directories of the time. He returned to Bridport in the 1820s forming a partnership with Stephen Whetham.

Richard Tucker and Sons

The partnership between Richard I and his sons, **Richard II** (1802-1898) and **William Cleeves** (1808-1856), was first entered in the late 1820s. While sailcloth was the main product, they also produced twine, lines and shoe thread, with nets being added at a later date.

After Richard Tucker's death in 1836 the business was continued by Richard II and William Cleeves Tucker. It would seem that the brothers continued the partnership with Whetham until 1839, when Stephen Whetham left to operate from the newly built Priory Mill; with St John's Mill and Wykes Court being given up soon after. In the 1840s William Cleeves Tucker moved to Greenwich to canvas support for the sale of their sailcloth to the Admiralty.

In 1844 Richard Tucker moved from South Street to 62, West Street, moving the manufacturing base there a

This warehouse was owned by Richard Tucker and Sons, until they became bankrupt in 1897.

little later. William Cleeves Tucker returned from London around 1849 and moved into Fulbrooks, North Allington, which was previously the base of James Edwards. As sailcloth is no longer mentioned, it would seem that the firm had withdrawn from this market. From this time, until the death of William Cleeves Tucker in 1856, both brothers have separate directory entries, although, as they were selling the same range of products, it is unclear whether they were in competition with each other.

Following his brother's death, Richard Tucker moved into Fullbrooks, which became the sole base of the business. In due time his sons, **Henry** (1846-1905) and **George** (1857-1918), joined the business and were the partners from 1884, following the retirement of Richard, who left his capital of £4,700 in the business, in the form of a loan.

The firm continued to prosper until 1894, when the trade with Australia ceased. From that time a trading deficit was carried over each year, until they were declared bankrupt in 1897. Over the previous 2½ years they had made a trading profit of only £150, whilst drawing nearly £2,000 in household expenses. The examination showed that they had some £9,482 worth of debts, against assets of only £7,332. However the initial cause of the failure was the fraud carried out by their brother and solicitor Richard III, who had issued accommodation bills to the value of £1,735 against them.

The firm ceased trading and Fullbrooks was sold the following year. Richard Hayward and Company of West Chinnock then leased the buildings, taking over the goodwill of Richard Tucker and Sons, using the trading name until 1916, when the site was taken over by Hounsells (Bridport) Ltd.

Thomas Tucker and Company

Thomas Tucker (1758-1847) was described as a twine spinner and sack maker in insurances of 1777 and 1779. He was living at 45, South Street, with two warehouses and a combing shop nearby. By the 1780s, like most other manufacturers, he had added sailcloth to his range of products. He continued to make these until the early 19th century, when he added the typical textile items of line, twines

and shoe thread; while from 1840 nets were also made.

By the late 18th century he was in partnership with his brother Abraham. After the latter's death in 1810, it is likely his brother **Isaac I** (1764-1834) was also involved in the business, as well as Thomas' son, **John** (1792-1860). After his father's death, John Tucker took full control, although he is also described as a grocer in the 1848 directory, as he was in his will.

By 1860 the firm was in the hands of **Robert Conway Tucker** (1830-1907) and **Isaac Tucker** (1824-1893) and it was under these two that Slape Spinning Mill was bought, after the failure of Joseph Munden in 1862. This provided them with their own yarn and allowed some degree of expansion, although they were always a small concern. One final addition was made at the turn of the century, with the building of St John's Line Shed behind their South Street headquarters.

By 1911 it was R. C. Tucker's son, **John A. Crome Tucker**, who was in control of the company. In that year he formed a partnership with **William Brown**, who was the manager and held just seven of the 197 shares. The business was valued at £12,892 and consisted of the South Street premises, a warehouse in Folly Mill Lane, old and new braiding shops at Folly House, together with Slape Mill and St. John's line shed. The freehold was retained by J. A. C. Tucker

In 1934, in common with most other firms in Bridport, Thomas Tucker and Co. were feeling the economic pinch and were approached by Joseph Gundry and Co., who offered to assist them if they were to go into liquidation. Using machinery, primarily 10 braiding machines, worth only £1,700, their turnover was some £70,000. It would seem that by then Slape Mill had been closed.

An inspection, by Kenneth Suttill, revealed that the firm made a profit in normal years and that the machinery was well maintained, but he pointed out that there was little market for second hand machinery at this time. Gundry's offer of £4,700, with the proviso that Capt. J. A. C. Tucker did not enter into any competing trade, was refused.

In 1942 Thomas Tucker and Co. became a limited company. 10,000 one pound shares were authorised, with Tucker taking 8,990, manager James Edwards taking 500 and secretary Miss D. Edwards having just 5 shares.

However, the post-war trading conditions brought the future into clear focus. In May 1946 Thomas Tucker and Co. Ltd. approached Gundry's, asking to be taken over. By now they had assets of some £23,000, including machinery worth £2,950, with an annual turnover of only £37,000 and employing just 26 people. The freehold of the property, which was still owned by J. A. C. Tucker, was not included in the sale. The advantage for Gundrys was that it would allow them entry into the sports net business, which was dominated by W. Edwards and Son. It would make up for the latter's involvement in fishing nets following their takeover of W. Gale and Sons. After some discussion the deal went through and the firm became part of Joseph Gundry and Company.

Walter Tucker (1848-1934)

Walter, the son of William Cleeves Tucker, started work with his Uncle Richard's business in 1869, staying there until December 1875, when he decided to work for himself. Initially his business was in West Street and whilst he sold twines, lines and shoe thread, he was primarily involved in selling nets.

Initially he set himself up with three of Thomas Helyear's braiding machines, but by 1881 he decided to use outworkers and sold the machines. Latterly he sold mainly tennis and fishing nets, from a building behind 79, East Street. However by 1916 he had moved back to West Allington and, after a breakdown in 1931, he severed all connections with the trade.

Slape Mill

Although there was a mill at Slape in the 18th century, the story of Slape Mill as a textile mill starts with the formation of a partnership between Joseph Gundry, J. Gundry and Co. and Samuel Gundry in 1808. They took on Henry Saunders as managing partner, who had a share in the business, but not the freehold.

The water-powered mill, which was used for swingling or dressing flax, was destroyed by fire in 1814. The sale of flax spinning machinery in 1818, both at Slape and Bridport Harbour, suggests that the mill was being converted to a spinning mill when the fire occurred. Some of the machinery that could be reused found its way back to Pymore. The partnership continued until 1820, when it was dissolved and Saunders paid his dues.

It would seem that the mill lay derelict until a new partnership was formed in the mid-1830s, this time between Joseph Gundry, Samuel Gundry and Thomas C. Hounsell. Hounsell's initial share was for £900, which was increased in later years with the building of a bolling mill and a 'new' spinning mill. He also received his one-third share in the profits from February 1835 to 1847 (see Table 37).

Decreasing profits in the early 1840s led to the mill being let out by the partners. Between 1842 and 1848 it was operated by John Gifford. In 1850, following a brief period when it was leased by John Chard, John Munden took over, running it until he became bankrupt in 1862. The mill was then bought by Thomas Tucker and Co., giving them the spinning facility they had lacked until then. They operated the mill until the 1920s, after which it again fell silent.

However the Second World War saw the need for more flax to be grown locally, which was encouraged by Rolf Gardiner of Springhead, Fontmell Magna. He formed Fontmell Industries and reopened Slape Mill in July 1939.

Above Flax retting in ponds at Slape Mill, probably during World War Two. In the Bridport area it was normal for flax to be dew-retted, leaving the pulled stalks on the ground for around three weeks.

Below Slape Mill, like many others, has been developed for housing. This 2009 photograph shows the mill to the rear of the house.

Machine-pulled flax, from both Dorset and Somerset, was brought to Slape for processing. The amount of flax grown in Dorset rose from 20 acres in 1938 to over 500 acres in 1940, the growers being paid £11 per ton.

In 1942 the Ministry of Supply took control of production, offering prizes for the best growth, which was won by Harold Huxter of Broadoak that year. The mill continued to operate through the war but peacetime conditions saw its closure once more.

Following this it became one of the early industrial estates, although on an informal basis. In 1948 it was bought by Mr and Mrs Long and operated as the Slape Laboratories and Manufacturing Chemists. A series of ventures later followed, which included a concrete block manufacturer and a car body builder and upholsterer. In 1951 the mill was used to manufacture 100,000 official badges, featuring the 'Skylon', for the Festival of Britain.

In 1955 the site was being used by Wessex Enterprises, a company with a link to Arthur Hart and Co. Hart's son had started a flock printing venture in 1952 and, employing 14 people, had moved to Slape in order to expand the business. A year later the Kingsway Trading Company was proposing to use it as an animal fertiliser factory. Finally after a period of use as a scrap merchant's yard it was redeveloped for housing.

Table 37. Thomas C. Hounsell's share of the profits in the Slape Flax Spinning Mill from 1835 to 1847.

Hounsell's	1835-6	1837	1838	1839	1840	1841	1842	1843	1844	1845	1846	1847
Profit	£152	£144	£158	£21	£160	£141	£27	£58	£55	£94	£72	£33

FOURTEEN
Stephen Whetham & Sons

Stephen Whetham (1780-1860) was the son of Stephen Whetham snr., a maltster of Netherbury. At the age of 22, Stephen married **Jenny Tucker** (1779-1825), the daughter of **John Tucker I**, the event linking the Whetham's with one of Bridport's oldest textile manufacturing families, who specialised in the woven products of sailcloth, sacks and bags.

Whetham took the place of Jenny's mother, forming a partnership with George Tucker. The two partners took a lease on Folly Mill, a corn and bolling mill, which once belonged to St. John's Chapel. They harnessed the waterwheel to drive a small spinning mill in an adjoining building. Known as **St. John's factory**, it produced most of the flax yarn for their sailcloth, although from time to time they bought additional yarn from the Pymore Mill Company.

The following year Whetham moved to 32, South Street, which he had bought from his stepfather. The house, which came with its own stables and warehouse, was to become the centre of the Whetham business. By 1823, Stephen Whetham had entered into a partnership with his brother-in-law, Josiah Selwood. They had a depot at 29, South Street, as well as a coal yard at Bridport Harbour.

After George Tucker's death, Whetham formed a partnership with Richard I, George's brother. This lasted until around 1832, when Stephen Whetham took his sons,

Above Folly Mill was a corn mill which was used to power St. John's factory in a nearby building. The mill was demolished some years ago.

Below Priory Mill, showing the lines used for drying the canvas.

128

Priory Mill, showing what was probably the original handloom building which was adapted for power looms in the 1850s. In 2009 it was being converted into housing.

The Gundry Lane warehouse of S. Whetham and Sons, which was extended to the present size in 1862. Now being used as a furniture repository, the building has been restored after an arson attack in 1997.

Stephen William Whetham (1804-90) and **Charles Whetham** (1812-85) into partnership. The new firm, Whetham and Sons, concentrated on lines, twines, shoe thread and sailcloth and were still using Folly Mill and Wykes Court.

Charles Whetham was sent to establish a branch of the business in London, opening an office and depot in the City, at 39/40, Gracechurch Street. Charles, who married Sophia Langley in 1836, soon became part of the London establishment. Charles ran the London end, while Stephen and his son, Stephen W. Whetham, ran the Bridport side of the business.

In 1838 the firm started building the Priory Spinning Mill, the first purpose-built steam-powered spinning mill in Bridport. It was built by Henry Cornick at a cost of over £2,000, with the ironwork for the building provided by Gerard Samson, a local iron founder. As with other flax spinning mills, the machinery came from Leeds, with Taylor and Company sending workers from Leeds to ensure the correct operation of the machinery. Since they stayed until the end of December 1838, it can be assumed that the mill began operating in 1839. The mill was a typical three-storey flax spinning mill. Built of Bothenhampton stone, it had the engine and boiler house adjacent to Foundry Lane.

At this stage the weaving was still carried out using handlooms. As they had given up the lease on Wykes Court, it must be presumed that this was carried out at Priory Mill, possibly in the stone building, at the top of Church Lane, which can be seen on the 1841 map.

Around the same time, the firm leased land adjoining the mill. One area, just across Foundry Lane, was bought from George Symes in 1843. Consisting of a bucking (bleaching) house and warehouse, they added a new warehouse and combing shop shortly afterwards. Two other closes of land

were used for drying sailcloth. In 1840/1 they built a bolling mill, whose set of eight stamps was made by Coombs of Beaminster.

Whethams introduced power looms in 1851, despite receiving a warning letter advising them of the consequences of doing so. Since the plant register makes little mention of any major building at this time, it must be presumed that a current building was altered. It is likely that the power looms, which came from Parker and Sons of Leeds, were housed in the old hand loom building, gradually replacing the old looms.

While the company had introduced nets to their list of products by 1840, braiding machines were not used until the 1860s. The first, a 20 score machine, came from R. Hounsell in 1861 and the following year two more were added, one from Hounsell and the other from Parris. No more were added until 1867, when one was bought from Thomas Helyear. The older machines were gradually replaced from 1870, with further expansion taking place as demand grew. The location of the braiding shop is uncertain, but may have been the single storey shed, adjoining Church Lane to the south of the weaving mill.

In 1862 the warehouse in Gundry Lane was extended by Cornick and Son, at a cost of around £4,000.

Replacement and additional machinery was ordered from time to time, coming from Taylor, Wordsworth and Company, Newton, Taylor and Company, as well as Lawson and Sons. A new engine, from Whitham and Company, was installed in 1865. New boilers were installed in 1854 and 1884, with a second boiler from Hill and Son, Manchester added the following year.

The 1860s were to be a time of change for the firm. The death of the founding partner Stephen Whetham, in 1860, was followed by Stephen W. Whetham leaving the partnership, following his marriage to Maria Button in 1863. The new partners bought out his share in the freehold of 32, South Street and the Gundry Lane warehouse.

This new partnership, formalised in 1866, was made up of Charles Whetham and his sons, **Charles Langley**

Charles Whetham ran the London operation of S. Whetham and Sons, and from 1860 was in overall charge. Here he is seen in 1878, when he was the Lord Mayor of London. He was also a director of the GWR.

Whetham (1839-1890), **William Townley Whetham** (1842-1925) and **Stephen Whetham** (1847-1923). William and Stephen Whetham were sent to run the Bridport business. William had settled in Bridport by 1865, when he married Mary Stephens, the daughter of sailcloth manufacturer **John Pike Stephens**, and was joined by Stephen soon afterwards.

The new partners started to improve the facilities, initially erecting a building for the striking machines in 1863/4. This was followed by a timber shop, bucking house and warehouse in 1867. Another bucking house was built on the 'Barton' and included a drying and gassing house.

It was during this time that the business was at its most successful, winning sailcloth orders from the Admiralty in seven of the years between 1866 and 1875. Charles Whetham was also a rising star in London, becoming an increasingly important figure. He was a director of the Great Western Railway and was elected an Alderman of the City of London in 1871. Three years later he was knighted and in 1878 became Lord Mayor of London.

Charles died in 1885, leaving Charles Langley Whetham as the head of the firm. However it was not until the sale of Lady Whetham's interest to the remaining brothers in 1892, following the death of her husband two years before, that the trading position of the business was revealed. The business had made significant losses during five of the six years up to 1891. Things were brought to a head in 1897 by a combination of the impact of the 1895 Newfoundland crisis and the absconding of their solicitor Richard Tucker III, who had fraudulently used the firm's accommodation bills for his own purposes.

The result was the bankruptcy of S. Whetham and Sons, with gross liabilities of £58,553. Campbell F. S. Sanctuary, of the solicitors Nantes and Sanctuary, was appointed by the Official Receiver to oversee the running of the business. Although William and Stephen Whetham, as bankrupts, were no longer allowed to be directors, they continued the day-to-day management of the business. 32, South Street was sold to the Town Council, in order to reduce the debt.

In 1898, with the most recent trading figures showing a net profit of £1,000 on sales of £13,000, it was decided to re-launch the concern as a limited company. A prospectus for the new company was issued in July. The proposed share capital of £15,000 was made up of £10 shares; 750 as 4% preference shares and 750 as 10% ordinary shares. On top of this £5,000 in the form of 3½% debentures could be raised, if it was thought essential to buy back Priory Mill, warehouse and cottages from the mortgagees

The chairman was to be Charles G. Nantes, while other directors included R. H. Palmer and E. J. C. Good. The Whetham family and friends pledged to take 150 preference and 704 ordinary shares. In the event the issue raised £6,070 in preference shares and £5,140 in ordinary shares. This was gradually increased, until £6,330 in preference and £5,450 in ordinary shares had been sold by 1906.

They proved to be a good investment. Buoyed up by the Boer War, they produced a dividend of 7% in 1901, although this was due to an increase in prices rather than volume. Turnover was the same in 1902, although higher wage costs meant that some goods were being sold at a loss. This trend continued the next year and was especially marked in the canvas department, which showed little profit.

The losses made in the period 1904-7 related to the loss of military work, following the end of the South African War and a cotton crisis in 1904. This led to the firm contemplating hiring out the use of the mill to other parties. That same year it was decided to authorise the creation of £5,000 debentures at 4%, of which £3,000 would be issued in the event of the company buying the freehold.

During World War One, profits rose to remarkable levels and remained high following the armistice in 1918. With the Whetham brothers now in their seventies, the firm was under the leadership of John Suttill. Previously the managing partner for J. Gundry and Co., Suttill was a director by 1911 and managing director by 1915. He provided a close link between the two firms, suggesting that J. Gundry and Co. had acquired some of the share issue.

When John Suttill died in 1919, the mill and its machinery were getting old and needed reorganisation. In 1920 shareholders were approached with an approach from J. Gundry and Co. Ltd. offering to purchase the business for £23,500. This was accepted and the firm changed hands in May 1921, but continued to trade under the Stephen Whetham and Sons name until 1931, when it was fully absorbed into J. Gundry and Co. Ltd.

Later that year Gundry's commissioned Major Stephens, joint managing director of Hounsells (Bridport) Limited, to make a report on Priory Mill. It became clear that re-organisation would be difficult, especially as much of the machinery was life-expired. However some alterations were under taken in 1922; the hackling shop was rebuilt and electric power, generated on site, was introduced.

The depression of the mid-1920s had a severe effect, with no profit being realised in the five years from 1926. Following this the mill was sold to William Edwards and Son, who were looking to expand their St Michael's Lane site. However, following a trading agreement with Joseph Gundry and Co. Ltd. and the Pymore Mill Company in 1928, Priory Mill and the Gundry Lane warehouse were sold to Northover and Gilbert. Recently the Priory Mill site has been the subject of a housing development.

THE PRIORY MILL

A description survives from 1911, when a valuation survey was carried out in relation to fire insurance by G. H. Lord and Sons of Dundee.

The **Boiler House** contained two double flue Lancashire boilers made by Thomas Hill of Manchester, probably those bought in the 1880s. The chimney, which carried the 1838 date stone, was on the north-west side of the building. Above the boiler was to be found the drying store. The **Engine House** had an 82hp overhead beam engine, with the cylinder having a 27in diameter and 6ft stroke. The beam was 18ft 6in long and the flywheel had a diameter of 22ft. From this, shafting was taken throughout the spinning and weaving mills.

In the **Spinning Mill,** the flax was prepared for spinning on the **ground floor**. There was a circular finishing card engine, together the first and second drawing frames, a spiral roving frame and tow shaker, most of which came from Lawson and Sons of Leeds. A dust extractor was a necessary piece of safety equipment to have in this environment. It was installed to prevent the dust causing an explosion, not just for the health of the workforce. On the **first floor** further preparation took place, with machinery including spread boards, spiral drawing and roving frames, again made by Lawson and Sons. One spinning frame was also to be found, along with a 3-ply cabling machine. Again dust extractors were a necessary addition. Spinning took place on the **second floor**, with one single and seven double spinning frames, made by Lawson and Sons and Newton and Sons, both of Leeds. A 3-ply cabling machine, made by the local founder Thomas Helyear, completed the equipment. The **third floor** housed the warping room, where the warp thread was wound onto reels ready for the canvas looms. There were two twisting frames and a number of reels, including a seaming reel. Two balling machines were to be found here, one for producing 8oz balls the other producing 6lb balls. Two warping mills, of 19ft 3in circumference, complete the machinery.

The **Striking Room** housed a striking and polishing machine, together with a carding roller, complete with four rotary brushes. In addition there was a steam heated saddle drying pan, made by Bowden of Bridport. The **Spooling Room** was where the shuttles were filled, using a horizontal spindle pirn-winding machine made by

In 2009 Priory Mill was being converted into housing. The spinning mill occupied the seven window bays on the right, the steam engine with the extended wall was to the left of this and has a 1838 date stone in the angle of the gable end. The boiler house was the lower roofed building on the left.

Thomas Helyear.

The **Bolling Mill** housed a variety of machines used to treat the hemp or flax prior to heckling. In order to carry out these processes, there was a heavy Beatle Hemp softener, of which only three stamps were in use. A Sharp's hemp softener and two Sharps' fluted roller softeners, together with a hemp breaker in a wooden frame completed the apparatus.

The **Factory** held seven heavy canvas looms, made by Parker, and a pirn-winding frame. While the **ground floor** housed another 10 heavy canvas looms and a pirn-winding frame, a beam stand and 11 yarn beams. On the **first floor** were the Winding Room and the Calendering Room. In the former were three winding frames, made by Parker, and a yarn beaming machine. While in the latter the canvas was pressed, using a 3-bowled compound lever and weight pressure calender.

The chlorine gas, used in bleaching, was made in the **Gas Bleaching Shed** and passed to the **Bleaching Shed**, which contained three boilers and three tanks. **The Yard** had seven vats of varying sizes, while the **Drying Ground** was studded with posts for the drying of yarn and canvas, as well as seven net drying frames.

The **Net Braiding Shop** housed twelve hand-powered jumper looms, all made by Thomas Helyear. Other buildings included the **Yarn Warehouse**, **Flax Warehouse**, **Tarring Shed**, **Hackling Shed** and **Smith's Shop**.

The **Gundry Lane Warehouse** was opened in 1863, as an extension of the older warehouse. It was 132ft long and 30ft wide and contained three floors and a garret. The ground floor contained the counting house and canvas store.

FIFTEEN

The Ewens Family

JOHN EWENS/THOMAS EWENS/ EWENS AND SON

Originally from Somerset, the family moved to the Broadwindsor area, where a Thomas Ewens is mentioned as a dyer/wool sorter at Hursey-Burstock in 1767. Shortly afterwards the family seems to have settled in the Bridport area, possibly following the collapse of the West Country woollen industry.

Thomas Ewens I (d1794) was a maltster, who married Ann Browne in 1757. Of their sons **Thomas II** (1766-1796) followed his father's trade, while **John Ewens I** (1759-1848) set up as a sailcloth manufacturer in the late 18th century. He had his workshops behind his home, which was at 26, West Street.

Ewens expanded his business, forming a partnership with John Golding who, in 1804, had built the Bridport Spinning and Flax mill, which provided the yarn used by Ewens for his sailcloth. He became the senior partner in the firm of Ewens and Golding after the death of John Golding in 1820.

The couple had six children, four of whom were involved in the textile trade; **Joseph Ewens** (1786-1836) and **John Ewens II** (1788-1821), who had married Elizabeth in 1811. Her father, George Browne, had just purchased part of the West Allington property of Robert Gummer. He built two houses on the site, in one of which John and his wife came to live. A third son, **Thomas Ewens III** (1790-1866), married sister-in-law Elizabeth after his brother's

John Ewens occupied 26, West Street (the house with the flagpole), with workshops to the rear. After Ewens death in 1848 Robert Budden worked from here. Adjoiniing to the left was a house once occupied by Joseph Gundry.

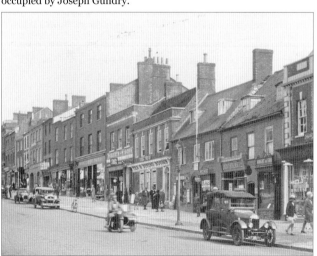

early death, while **Ann** (b1792) married John Tucker, thus linking two of Bridport's manufacturing families. By 1830 John I had retired, leaving his surviving sons, Joseph and Thomas Ewens to run the business.

Behind the house at West Allington, a yarn barton and warehouse had been built, in which was stored the lines, twines and shoe-thread made by the outworkers. Adjoining the river, further down Magdalen Lane, was a bucking house where the sailcloth was bleached, with the surrounding field being used as a drying ground.

Until John's death in 1848, the sailcloth was made and stored at the West Street site. After Joseph died in 1836, Thomas was assisted by his step-son, **George Browne Ewens** (1816-1883). They developed the business, expanding the list of products to include rope and nets. George was put in charge of the spinning mill, while Thomas looked after the rest of the business. Later Thomas's own son, **Samuel Gustave Ewens** (1835-1892), joined the firm, but not initially as a partner.

Trade continued to develop and, in 1859, the firm was being described as a considerable concern, most of whose produce was exported. Sailcloth was still being made, but from flax rather than Italian hemp as had been the case in the late 1830s. Twines for ropes and nets, which were still hand-made by out workers, were easily recognised by the three cord, eight thread construction and the colour developed from tanning, which used a mixture of barks, from oak and other species. The twines for nets were knotted at either end, prior to being let out to braid.

When Thomas died in 1866, after a long illness, there followed a period of upheaval, which was not helped by the town's trade being in a severe depression. George, who moved to run the West Allington site, was joined by his step-brother, Samuel Gustave Ewens.

Further development of the West Allington site took place around 1870, when George built a second warehouse on the east side of the lane. The bucking house and bleaching grounds were still in operation, when a 250ft line walk and a braiding shed were built near by. The tan house to be found there was in use much earlier, as the firm were tanning their own twine in 1859.

In March 1876, following some personal or financial misfortune which befell the family, George resigned his position as Alderman. In August, the West Allington property, which had been developed in the past few years, was put up for sale. It may have been this development, together with the depressions of 1868 and 1873, had overstretched the family finances. In 1879 George moved to 36, East Street, becoming the actuary of the local Savings Bank, remaining there until his death in 1883.

The Magdalen Lane site continued in operation through successive owners until 1964, when it was closed by Bridport Gundry. Today it forms the Magdalen Industrial estate, with few if any of the original buildings remaining.

Following Thomas' death in 1866, Samuel became the sole proprietor of the Spinning Mill. Shortly afterwards, with the business in decline, Samuel took **Edward Marshall Loggin** as a partner in the spinning mill, trading as **Ewens and Loggin**. Edward was the brother of local solicitor Nicholas M. Loggin, who had married Samuel's sister, Gertrude. After Loggin left in 1875, Samuel went into partnership with Fredrick Turner, forming Ewens and Turner.

At the end 1876 the spinning mill was put up for sale, but with little interest being shown in it. When the mill was again offered for sale two years later, only the mill machinery was sold.

THE BRIDPORT SPINNING AND FLAX MILL (EWENS' MILL)

This three storey mill, built in 1804 by John Golding, was at the junction of the rivers Brit and Symene. The mill race was built between the two rivers and ran through the mill itself. Wooden-framed hatches were placed in the River Brit to control the flow of water over the water wheel. These hatches were replaced in the 1830s and again in 1852-54. When they were closed, the level of the River Brit rose some 5-6 feet. In order to further increase the head of water flights were added, which caused the water to 'pond-up', preventing West Mill from operating effectively. In 1869, after being ordered to be removed, the hatches were rebuilt two to three inches higher and were fitted with a waste water weir.

The initial water wheel was located inside the mill building and was later replaced by a larger one. With the flow of water in the River Brit becoming increasingly variable, the firm introduced its first steam engine in 1834, which was replaced by a new 25hp low pressure horizontal rotary steam engine in 1859. By 1869 the water wheel was placed outside the mill and was capable of generating 20hp.

The organisation in the mill itself followed traditional lines. In 1878 the ground floor housed the tow room, with drawing and roving machines, together with breaker and carding machines. On the first floor were ten tow spinning frames, a twisting frame and a new hot water frame. The second floor held the flax spreaders, roving and drawing frames together with ten flax spinning frames, while the attic was used for reeling and winding the yarn.

Also on the site were a variety of other buildings: including a mechanics shop and a rolling house, which had been introduced in 1861 to replace the bolling mill. There was a combing or heckling shop and a weaving shed,

40, St. Michael's Lane was the workshop of James Edwards from the 1840s. It was originally three buildings which have been merged into one. It was used by Ewens and Turner from 1876 to 1918.

although most of the looms had been removed by this time. The foreman's house was also included in the sale as was the engine and boiler house, the latter housing two Cornish boilers, one being described as new.

The mill remained empty until 1889 when Herbert Nelson Harris took it over, converting it for use as a foundry. Later the water wheel was replaced with a water turbine. After his death in 1942, it was run by William Hann, on behalf of the Ministry of Supply. After the war he continued to run it as a general engineering works. For a time Harry Richards used it as a car museum, before a fire severely damaged the building, requiring the top storeys to be demolished. Today the ground floor is in use as a mortuary.

EWENS AND TURNER

In 1875, following the departure of Edward Loggin, Samuel G. Ewens formed a partnership with **Frederick Turner**, who had recently moved to Bridport. The new firm, **Ewens and Turner**, took on a 21 year lease on the spinning mill. The business had a wide range of products from canvas, twines and lines to hemp and cotton nets and shoe thread. However, with the bankruptcy of the Ewens family, they had to seek new premises from which to operate.

In September 1876 they leased 40, St Michael's Lane from George Edwards, who had been declared bankrupt two years earlier, taking over the mortgage on the site in February 1878. The property consisted of a warehouse, counting house, a new heckling shop and a weaving shed. However this partnership was also short-lived, in 1879 Samuel G. Ewens sold his share to Frederick Turner, who subsequently ran the business on his own account. Little is then heard of Samuel G. Ewens until his death in London in 1892.

Around 1882 Turner, still trading as Ewens and Turner, went into partnership with **William James**, who had recently ended his alliance with Richard Stone Major. When James left to form his own business in 1888,

Frederick Turner continued once again on his own account, producing the same lines as before.

In 1918, at the age of 68, he decided to retire and sold his business to Hounsells (Bridport) Ltd. for £1,775. As a condition of the sale he was not to set up in business within 50 miles of Bridport, unless he had the consent of Hounsells (Bridport) Ltd. In 1925 the building was sold to W. Gale and Sons for the expansion of their business.

RICHARD STONE MAJOR (b. 1830)

Richard Stone Major, the son of Richard and Ann Major of the Globe Inn, was working as a clerk for Richard Tucker and Sons by 1857.

In the 1870s he set up on his own as a manufacturer of twine. He almost certainly used outworkers for all the processes, renting a warehouse in Rax Lane behind Stag House for the storage of materials. For a brief time he entered into a partnership with William James, but this ended in 1881.

In 1884 he relocated to the Ewens' West Allington site, initially taking over one of the warehouses, before taking over the rest of the site in the following year. Leaving Bridport in 1888, Major was running the Eagle Hotel, Southampton in 1896.

WILLIAM JAMES & CO.

William James was born in London, where he joined a firm of City Brokers around 1859. Here he came into contact with Bridport-born George Knight, who was working as a wine broker in Deptford. It was this friendship that led him to move to Bridport, where he married Elizabeth Major Burden in 1870.

He began working for Messrs Ewens as a commercial clerk. When that firm closed he went to work as a twine manufacturer, in partnership with Richard Stone Major. After this partnership was terminated in 1881, William James spent a brief time on his own before forming a partnership with Frederick Turner, trading as Ewens

and Turner. In October 1888, after this partnership was terminated, he set up on his own at the Ewens' premises in West Allington.

William James concentrated on netmaking, purchasing his yarn from a number of local sources, both in Bridport and elsewhere. Twines and lines were made in the line shed at West Allington, while netmaking was likely to have been carried out both on site and by outworkers. William James was one of the first manufacturers to enter the sports net market, selling tennis nets to Slazenger among others.

Around 1896 the firm changed its name to William James and Company. Presumably he took on a partner, either to help finance expansion plans or to assist him when the life-long malady, which afflicted him, became too much. In 1910 he formed a partnership with Leonard Whetham, which lasted until he retired at the outbreak of World War One. William James died in December 1915. He had taken an active interest in the life of Bridport, occupying the positions of both Mayor and Alderman. He was also the Commander of the Fire Brigade.

Leonard Whetham (1870-1923) was the son of William Townley Whetham, a partner in Stephen Whetham and Sons. He ran William James and Co. until he was joined by his cousin Edward Albion Whetham.

Edward Albion Whetham (1892-1972), the son of Stephen Whetham, had joined the family firm prior to serving in the First World War. In 1916 he joined Leonard Whetham as a partner of William James and Co., owning a one-third share. The business was valued at £2,700, with £1,500 for the goodwill. When his cousin became ill, Albion Whetham ran the firm, taking over on Leonard's death.

Albion Whetham continued in charge and, when it was taken over by Rendall and Coombs in 1939, was given a place on the Board. Albion Whetham retired in 1945, following the take-over of Rendall and Coombs by William Edwards and Son.

With the formation of Bridport Industries, the William James name was retained. Unlike many of its companions, it survived the formation of Bridport-Gundry and it was not until the 1971 re-organisation that the name was dropped. However the William James brand has been revived in recent times.

SIXTEEN

Rendall and Coombs

The story of Rendall and Coombs starts in the 18th century when John Rendell moved from Somerset to Bridport. A cooper by trade, he set up a business manufacturing the barrels in which nets were packed prior to being transported.

His son, **John Thorn Rendall** (1789-1861), was initially apprenticed to a carpenter before going to sea for a short while, an experience which included a voyage to China. On his return in 1810, he married Elizabeth Saunders (1788-1848). His father-in-law was Henry Saunders, the landlord of the Greyhound and a person who had some connections in the textile trade. The couple moved to live at the Marquis of Granby, where John set himself up as a sack manufacturer. In 1815 he moved to 13, West Allington, behind which was his warehouse, adding twine to his portfolio. The property was extended in 1848 with the purchase of 11, West Allington, previously the Ship Inn, from the assignees of Samuel Gundry. These were to be the headquarters of the business for many years.

By 1839 he also owned six houses in Mount Pleasant, North Allington, using them as his manufacturing base. There were four spinning ways and turn-houses, combing shops and a weaving shed with nine looms, on which his tenants wove the sacks and bags.

In 1849 John Rendall retired and sold his business to his son, **Henry Rendall** (1813-1901) for an annuity of £50 p.a. Immediately, after taking control, Henry set up in partnership with **Charles Abbott Coombs** (1809-1855), a sailcloth manufacturer of Stoke Abbott.

The son of a Beaminster wheelwright, Charles Coombs jnr. was in partnership with **David Bugler** (1801-1872), who was a bag and sack maker by trade. By the 1840s Coombs and Bugler were running flax spinning mills at Hooke and Horsehill Mill, Stoke Abbott. These provided Coombs with the line flax for his sailcloth and Bugler with the tow flax for his bags and sacks.

With the formation of Rendall and Coombs, the latter moved to West Allington to take an active role in the business. Interestingly David Bugler also moved there, but it is not known whether he had any interest in the firm. Horsehill flax mill was sold to George Macey, while **Charles Coombs snr.** (1783-1869) took over the Hooke Flax Mill.

From the start Rendall and Coombs were making a variety of woven goods, probably using yarn from Hooke Mill. As with most of the Bridport businesses, sailcloth

This single storied flax spinning mill, Horsehill Mill at Stoke Abbott, was worked by Bugler and Coombs in the 1840s. It was then occupied by George Macey until the 1870s.

was soon dropped and the firm added lines and nets to the twines, sacks and bags already being produced.

In 1851 there was a double marriage within the Rendall family; Henry married Julia Pratt, whose father ran Bickley Mills, Glastonbury, while Henry's sister, Sarah, married Edwin Coombs Pratt, Julia's brother.

Charles Abbott Coombs died in 1855, after which his widow and family moved to live with his parents in Beaminster. It would seem that Charles Coombs snr. and **Edwin Coombs** (b1814) retained the family interest in Rendall and Coombs, thus providing an income for Sarah Coombs and her children.

In 1858 Henry Rendall bought five houses at 51, West Allington, taking out a £1,300 mortgage to pay for them. This was previously the works of George Darby and, after his death, those of John Bishop Ewens, Darby's nephew.

Following the death of John Rendall there was a re-alignment of the company's finances, with Henry Rendall taking over his father's mortgages and property. The business was shaken by the burning down of Hooke Mill in 1867, and the death of Charles Coombs two years later. It is possible that the active involvement of the Coombs family ceased around this time, as Edwin Coombs described himself as millwright and draper in the 1871 census.

In 1881 Rendall and Coombs were employing 127 people and had become involved with the Burton Spinning Mill, which had been recently run by John Clarke Andrews. **Edward Pratt Rendall** (1853-1930), Henry's son, moved to live in Burton Bradstock to oversee operations, employing James Grant as manager. Initially they were

A linewalk at Rendall and Coombs' West Allington works. In the photograph the strands have been hitched to the 'cogs' of the 'lower end' and twisting has begun. The spinning wheels are being turned by electric motors.

trading as the Burton Mill Company but, by the end of the century, it was formally part of Rendall and Coombs.

In 1883 Henry and Julia took out a £1,600 mortgage on their property, possibly to finance the Burton business. Four years later, for some unknown reason, Henry signed the business properties over to his wife Julia.

By 1893 the partnership, which included Henry and his two sons, Edward and **Henry Arthur Rendall** (b1859), took out a £2,500 loan against their property. This may have been used to develop the covered line walks built at 51, West Allington. Around this time Edward Pratt Rendall moved to live in 48, West Allington.

After Henry Rendall died in 1901, Julia transferred ownership of some of the properties occupied by the firm to her daughters. This provided them with an income, as Rendall and Coombs, now run by Edward and Henry A. Rendall, leased them back. By this time the property included line sheds, three warehouses, bucking house, gas house and combing shops.

A new partnership agreement was made in October 1917, but the only known partner was Henry A. Rendall. Edward Pratt Rendall was known to be in Ireland in 1922, where he gained commission for trade done for Joseph Gundry and Co. However as he retained his West Allington house, it is uncertain whether he had left the business or not. Other partners may have included some of Henry's sisters, since they owned some of the firm's property.

Mortgages were taken out in 1915 and 1919, in order to guarantee a banking account for the firm. This suggests that trading conditions were not as they would hope, which is unusual as wartime conditions usually helped the Bridport industry. Henry Rendall is credited with inventing the modern line-walk and may have used up all his money in doing so, in which case this financial arrangement may have related to his invention. A new warehouse was built in 1922.

Edward Pratt Rendall died in June 1930 and it was shortly after that Rendall and Coombs became a private limited company, with an issue of 5,000 shares of £1, which were divided into 4,000 preference and 1,000 ordinary shares. Henry A. Rendall was to be a permanent director, while other shareholders included Miss H. Rendall and Mrs M. Stubbs. This arrangement was short-lived, for the partnership of 1917 was dissolved in the following year, when Henry A. Rendall assigned his interest to Rendall and Coombs.

The 1930s trade recession caused many problems, leading to Rendall and Coombs closing down their Burton Spinning Mill. Another significant change occurred in 1939, when Rendall and Coombs took over the neighbouring firm of William James and Co., with the latter's principal, Edward Albion Whetham, becoming managing director of the new Rendall and Coombs.

By 1944 Fred Kenway was also involved with the firm, when they were approached by William Edwards and Son with a take-over offer. There had been a previous increase in the capital of Rendall and Coombs, which now consisted of 14,000 "A" preference, 3,500 "B" preference and 6,000 ordinary shares, giving a total capital of £23,500.

Virtually all of the shareholders were members of the Rendall family, the only exceptions being Edward Whetham and Fred Kenway. There was to be an exchange of shares, with the preference shareholders getting Edwards and Son preference shares and each ordinary share being converted into six ordinary shares of Edwards and Son. At the same time there was to be a further increase in the capital of Rendall and Coombs, to which the shareholders had to agree.

Edward Whetham retired after 40 years in the industry, leaving Fred Kenway to become chairman and a member of the Edwards board. In the following years Rendall and Coombs was run as a separate business within the Edwards and Son group. Even when Bridport Industries was formed in 1947, it remained as a separate business until 1954.

SEVENTEEN
The Powell and Gale Families

The inter-relationships of many of these families make it sensible to treat them together. Many can be described as manufacturers, despite not being listed in a contemporary directory.

MATTHEW POWELL AND HIS FAMILY

Matthew Powell (1753-1834)

Matthew Powell, who worked for Joseph Gundry as a twine spinner, was one of the first to be associated with St. Michael's Lane. From the 1790s, he was lived at what is now number 36/38.

Thomas Powell (1780-1840)

Thomas, the son of Matthew, was also a twine spinner. Initially based at 36, St. Michael's Lane, he moved up the lane to N⁰· 20 in 1815. In 1834 Thomas bought the land on which was built 42/44, St Michael's Lane.

Robert Powell (b.1800)

Robert was the nephew of Thomas and seems to have inherited the use of 20, St. Michael's Lane. He was described as a line maker in the 1851 and 1861 censuses. In the latter he was employing 14 people, including his sons, Daniel and George. He had retired by 1871.

Ambrose Powell (1803-1884)

Ambrose, the brother of Robert, was a hemp comber in 1841. However he had set himself up as a twine manufacturer in West Allington by 1851.

ROBERT POWELL AND HIS FAMILY

Robert Powell (b.1785)

Robert was a twine spinner, who lived behind 60/62, West Street in the 1840s, before moving to Bradpole towards the end of the decade. It was his children who were to become manufacturers.

Mark Powell (1816-1866), Maria Powell (neé Budden) (1817-1872) and Henry Powell (b.1844)

Mark Powell was running the Hope and Anchor public house by 1830. He took over the house and spinning way next to the pub from his father, when the latter moved to Bradpole. His first entry in a directory was in 1851,

when he was making twines, lines, shoe-threads and nets, although his primary occupation was still as an innkeeper. In 1858 he bought 36a, St. Michael's Lane and extended the spinning-ways there.

In 1837 Mark married **Maria Budden** from Portsmouth, who carried on the business after his death in 1866, together with their son **Henry**. By now canvas had been added to the portfolio. The partnership did not last long, being dissolved in 1867, after which Henry continued on his own account. Henry was producing twines, lines and nets and was employing six people, whom he took on a works outing to Seaton in 1871. By now he was leasing out the Hope and Anchor to Edwin Gale, who was also described as a twine manufacturer.

In 1873 the property, which was next to the Hope and Anchor, included a counting house, warehouse, stores, combing shed, yarn room, ruling room and thread room. It was held on mortgage to the Bridgwater Building Society and was the subject of another mortgage in 1881. It was repossessed by Williams Bank when Henry became bankrupt. In 1882 the Hope and Anchor was sold to John Groves and Co., the Weymouth Brewers, who converted the textile manufactory into housing, while 36a St Michael's Lane was sold to Robert Hounsell.

WALTER POWELL AND SONS

Walter Powell (1825-1912) was the younger son of Robert Powell. In 1853 he bought 38, St Michael's Lane

The Hope & Anchor was run in the 1850s by Mark Powell. The adjoining car park occupies the site of the spinning walks he used.

137

from Ann Powell, the great grand-daughter of Matthew Powell (1753-1834)

Although he described himself as a twine spinner in 1861, he could have been classed as a manufacturer, since he was employing 10 men, four spinners and two wheel turners. However it was not until the 1870s that he was listed as the directories, producing twines, lines and nets. By this time he was in partnership with his sons **George Powell** (1850-1907), **Robert Powell** (1853-1913) and **Daniel Powell** (1855-1899). Daniel emigrated to Canada around 1870, only to return eight years later. Robert left the business in the 1880s to move to Nottingham.

In 1876 Asker Mill became vacant, following the Stephens Brothers' move to Bristol. It was taken over by Walter Powell, who sold the St. Michael's Lane property to William Gale. After Walter's retirement in the 1880s, the business was run as a partnership between George and Daniel. They introduced net making machines into Asker Mill, with George taking responsibility for that side of the business, while Daniel looked after the twine manufacture. After Daniel's death in 1899, George continued on his own account until 1904. When he became ill, Asker Mill was sold to the Gourock Ropeworks Company.

BENJAMIN GALE AND HIS FAMILY

Benjamin was a twine spinner living in South Street and it was his children Silvester, Walter, James and Edwin who were to become manufacturers.

Silvester Gale (1818-1870), George (b1846)

Silvester Gale was a twine spinner living at 22, St. Michael's Lane. He married Mary Powell, daughter of Robert and Charlotte Powell. Whilst he continued to be a twine spinner all his life it was his son, **George** (b1846), who set up as a twine manufacturer around 1880. This seems to have been a short lived, for the 1881 census has him as a twine spinner. Ten years later he was working as a rope and twine finisher, whilst his own son, **Alfred** (b.1868), was a line maker.

Walter Gale

The directory entries for this business are complicated by there being separate father and son firms.

Walter Gale (1827-c.1873) was living at 32/34, St. Michael's Lane in 1851, working as a twine spinner. In the late 1850s he moved to 84, East Street, the house once occupied by the linemaker Edward Crabb. It is here that Gale had set up as a twine and line manufacturer by 1861. Following his death in the mid 1870s the manufactory was continued briefly by his widow, **Grace**.

Walter Gale (b.1845), having married Elizabeth, moved to 20, St. Michael's Lane, where he worked as a twine and rope manufacturer from c.1871 until the early 1890s.

James Gale (b.1829)

James Gale was a hemp dresser in 1851, living in the Rope Walks area of Bridport. Ten years later he had moved to 32, St. Michael's Lane, setting up as a twine and rope manufacturer. There was no mention of him as a manufacturer in the 1871 census, suggesting that his business must have ceased, explaining his move to Barrack Street in the late 1860s.

Edwin Gale (b.1831)

Edwin was a musician in the 1851 census, living with his father in South Street. By 1861 he had married Caroline and was living at 86a, East Street, being employed as a twine spinner. He set up as a manufacturer of twine and rope in the mid-1860s.

With the dissolution of the partnership between Henry Powell and his mother, Edwin moved from East Street to take over running the Hope and Anchor. He was still describing himself as a manufacturer in 1878, so it seems likely that he was helping to run Henry Powell's business. Powell's bankruptcy saw an end to this, causing Edwin to move from the Hope and Anchor and, in 1891, he was again working as a twine spinner.

EIGHTEEN

John Pike Stephens / Stephens & Co.

John Pike Stephens

In 1788 **William Stephens** (1755-1837), a Truro-born Quaker, married Ann Dawe, who had set up in business at 13/15 East Street, Bridport. After Ann died in 1795, William married Amy Metford, the niece of Joseph Pike. William was primarily a draper but it is likely that he was involved in **Stephens and Salter**, the sailcloth manufacturers mentioned in the 1814 directory.

Following that he formed a partnership with his son, **John Pike Stephens** (1798-1872), initially storing the materials in a warehouse near Barrack Street. When this was dissolved in 1824 John Pike Stephens continued the business on his own. By 1832 he was using a warehouse on the corner of Downe Street and Rax Lane, behind the family draper's business.

Bridge House Easternmost Meadow had housed a bucking or bleaching house and a tan house belonging to William Hounsell and Co. After leasing the land from the Borough Council in 1835, John Pike and **Isaac Stephens** (1811-1895) built Asker Mill, a water-powered flax spinning mill, on the site. The finished yarn was taken to the Rax Lane warehouse for storage, before being was sent to Beaminster, where it was made into sailcloth. On their return the pieces of sailcloth were stored at the Rax Lane warehouse.

Walter Stephens (1809-1872) was the works manager for the Pymore Mill Company in 1834. He moved to Bristol in 1842, to join his brothers, who were planning to build a flax spinning mill there. While the Bristol concern was known as **Stephens Brothers**, the Bridport branch continued to trade as **J. P. Stephens and Co.**, adding lines, twine, shoe thread and nets to their list of products by the late 1840s.

Power looms were installed in Asker Mill in June 1861 and were producing over 80% of their canvas by the following year. As more looms were installed, the Bridport and Bristol businesses were re-organised, with Bristol doing all the spinning, sending the yarn to Bridport for processing.

The re-organised mill was now steam-powered, using a high pressure steam engine, which was linked by shafting to the rest of the mill. The weaving room held 12 power looms, three leaf twilling looms and two canvas looms and, in another room, there were three swifting machines. Bleaching was carried out in two vats, using chlorine gas produced in lead retorts. In the steeping room were two tanks, together with yarn squeezing machines. Other rooms or buildings were used as a drying room, warehousing and offices.

Stephens and Co.

When John Pike Stephens retired in the early-1860s, the Bridport business was renamed **Stephens and Co.** with his son **Alfred** (1838-1874), who started working for the firm in 1856, becoming a partner in both the Bridport and Bristol businesses. **Walter Langrish Stephens** (1838-1910) moved to Bridport in the late 1860s, to look after Walter's interests at Asker Mill, before returning to Bristol in 1872, after his father's death. When Alfred died in 1874, the business was concentrated at Bristol. The manufacture of sailcloth at Asker Mill ceased in June 1875 and, although it was intended that bleaching should continue, the factory was advertised for sale the following month.

John Pike Stephens' younger son, **Joseph Thompson Stephens** (1842-1919), chose not to work in the family business, becoming instead a partner in William Hounsell and Co.

Asker Mill after 1875

The following year saw the firm of **Walter Powell and Sons** moving from St. Michael's Lane to take occupation of the mill. They were twine and net makers and re-equipped the mill accordingly, probably using steam power since the steam engine was included in the sale. By 1904, the site consisted of a combing shed, braiding room, stores and warehouses; complete with three houses built by the owners.

The **Gourock Ropeworks Company** of Scotland was an old, established rope-making firm who, with a full order book on ropes and cloth, usually left the net-making to smaller companies. However this changed with their acquisition of the New Lanark Mills in 1881, when they imported machinery and workers from other areas, including Bridport - this was a time of hardship in the Dorset town and migration of workers to other areas became significant.

As the Scottish Herring fleet was beginning to fish further from Scotland, the 'Gourock' decided to take-over a number of small net-making concerns further south. The illness of George Powell allowed them to establish a base in Bridport, probably in 1904. Asker Mill was now using jumper looms to turn out mackerel nets, 'Dutch' nets and

Scottish drift nets. In 1907, following the death of George Powell, the 'Gourock' took on the lease from the Borough.

The 'Gourock' remained in Bridport until 1912, when their resources were concentrated at their Clyde base.

The factory was leased to **Robert Budden and Sons**, apart from the carding/combing room, which was leased to the Parrett and Axe Vale Dairies. In 1918 the Borough Council offered to sell the property to the tenants, however Robert Budden and Son moved to 54, West Street instead, allowing English Dairies, as they were now called, to take over the whole of the site.

Today the site is a small trading estate and, after a break of some years, the net-making tradition returned in the 1960s with the establishment of Knowle Nets, who currently make fruit, garden, sports, game and pest control nets.

NINETEEN

The Wessex Flax Factory at Allington

In November 1917, the Yeovil area of the British Flax and Hemp Growers Society set out to increase the area of flax grown in West Dorset. Linen was in short supply and, as well as the usual shirts, collars and cloth, it was much needed for covering the frames of the aircraft of the newly formed Royal Flying Corps. A factory was set up in Yeovil, which was taken over by the Ministry of Agriculture in January 1918. Later the Allington factory was opened, with R. Suttill, of the Pymore Mill Company, as the local administrator. Built on land owned by Hounsells (Bridport) Ltd., it had a capacity of 750 tons. Locally grown flax was taken to here for retting and scutching before being passed on to the manufacturers.

In March 1920 the Ministry of Agriculture disposed of the factories to the investment bankers Pinners Hale. Wessex Flax Factories Ltd. was formed to take over the business, which was being run by Messrs. A. Michaelson & Co. Ltd. The new company had a share capital of £200,000, made up of 140,000 preference shares of £1; 1,130,000 ordinary shares of 1/- and 70,000 staff shares of 1/-, while the Government held £32,500 in 6% debentures. The directors were F. Shearman (chairman) of Tiverton, W. Harvey-Blake of Norton-sub-Hamden, T. Selby-Down of Castle Cary, J Crumple (managing director) of West Coker and Archibald Michaelson, chairman of the Anglo-Continental Guano Company.

After the war flax was still in short supply. Nationally the industry used 100,000 tons, of which 80,000 tons came from Russia. In 1920 the expected shortfall led the company to advertise for farmers to grow flax under contract, offering £16 per ton for straw and seed. At the same time they estimated the profit on their 'Wessex Crown' brand products to be £40,000 per year.

At the share-holders meeting in July, it was revealed that the cost of the enterprise was to be reduced to £28,000, in lieu of £97,000, due to the incomplete nature of the factories. The company wanted to improve the Allington factory by building 5,000 gallon retting tanks, but were refused planning permission. In 1922 the factory suffered a fire in a Dutch barn, destroying two ricks of flax by-products, machinery and flax straw, causing work to cease until replacements were found.

In 1923 the company went into receivership, following which a meeting of flax growers was held in Beaminster. These growers were of the opinion that the company ought to have gone into liquidation, since they felt that they would have had a greater chance of getting more of the money owed to them. A further meeting was held in February 1924, but without any results.

In April 1925 the lease on the Allington Flax Factory was purchased by Frederick Bromfield, although Hounsells (Bridport) retained the freehold.

TWENTY

Other Textile Firms

Ackerman, Henry (d1879)
Ackerman was the landlord of the Five Bells at 85, South Street and was working as a twine spinner in the walks behind. He was mentioned in directories from 1865. After his death his widow took over, in association with her brother-in-law. This was probably George Kenway, since he was advertising as working from Ackerman's premises in 1880.

Bartlett, Joseph I (1781 – 1869) and Joseph II (b1818)
Joseph Bartlett I was working as a twine manufacturer in Bridport from 1820. Bartlett and Son were at 56, West Street between 1841 and 1853, before moving to 53, East St. They also had a warehouse at West Allington, which was given up when 7, Barrack St and the adjoining warehouse, previously the Independent chapel, were bought in 1859. The business ended in 1871, with the house and warehouse being sold the following year.

Baker, Samuel (1807-1896)
Samuel started as comber in Barrack St. He is mentioned as a twine manufacturer at 113, East Street from 1855, before moving adjacent to the vicarage in South Street ten years later. His last directory entry was in 1875 and he died in Ilford, Essex in 1896.

Balston, George (1781-1849) and Joseph (1791-1862)
Making lines, twines, shoe thread and nets, by 1833 they were operating from 10, Barrack St., later taking over 22,

7, Barrack Street was the home of Joseph Bartlett. Between 1859 and 1871 he used the adjoining chapel as a warehouse.

Barrack St from James Edwards.

Balston, William (d.1821) and Sarah
William was a twine, line and shoe thread manufacturer operating from East Street. After his death the business was carried on by his widow Sarah.

Bridgeman, John (b1815)
Born in London, Bridgeman arrived in Bridport and took over 22, Barrack St from his brother-in-law Joseph Balston in the late 1850s, presumably due to the latter's poor health. He ceased trading in 1862, following Joseph's death.

Robert Budden and Sons
This firm had its origins in the late 18th century with **Robert Budden** (1737-1807), who owned three houses and a triple spinning way in Gundry Lane, indicating that he was more than just a twine spinner. His own house was at 36, South Street, with another house to be found in Gundry Lane. After his death, the property was divided amongst his wife and children.

John Budden (1783-1856) followed in his father's footsteps and was living at 40, South Street. He married Frances Smith in 1811 and the parish records show that he was a twine spinner, as well as a bag and sack maker.

John's eldest son, **Robert** (1813-1889), started work as a comber. He married Amelia Crabb in 1834 and was living with his uncle, William Budden, at 36, South Street. Sadly Amelia died in 1843, leaving Robert to look after his young family. He soon remarried and Elizabeth, his new

54, West Street was the foundry of Thomas Helyear, who was renowned for his braiding machines. It later became the base of Robert Budden and Sons after his move from Asker Mill in 1919

wife, may have been well connected, as his fortunes show an upturn shortly afterwards.

In 1848 Robert Budden took over the lease of 26/28, South Street, following the death of sailcloth manufacturer John Ewens. Consisting of a house, weaving shop and warehouse, it was here that he set himself up as a sack and canvas manufacturer. Two of his sons, **Albert** (b.1835) and **Charles** (b.1858), followed him into the trade, becoming sack weavers for their father.

In 1862 Robert seems to have given up the lease on the warehouse. Like most manufacturers he moved away from woven goods, such as webbing and sacks, to concentrate on producing twines and ropes.

When Robert died in 1889, his widow, Elizabeth, took over the business, probably helped by Albert, who was working as a sack and rope maker.

Thomas Charles Budden (1847-1913), was another of Robert's sons and had been working as the head brewer of the Old Brewery since 1871. He joined the family firm in 1898, although he might already have had an administrative role. It was his influence that resulted in the introduction of net making to the portfolio. Shortly before his death, the firm took over the lease on Asker Mill from the Gourock Ropeworks Company, using it for their net making operation. With Thomas becoming increasingly unwell, it seems likely that it was his son, **Eustace Budden** (1883-c.1929), who was the guiding principle behind this.

Eustace was about to buy the freehold of Asker Mill in 1919, when 54, West Street came onto the market. Once the workshops and offices of Thomas Helyear, the iron founder and braiding machine maker, it was to here that Budden moved his net making operation. The firm seems to have ceased trading in 1925-26, when 54, West Street was sold to Fenwick for use as a shop.

Coppock, John jnr. (d.1806)

In the 1793 directory John Coppock jnr. was a twine spinner. In 1769 his father had built the Marquis of Granby, on the site of St. John's Chapel, at the bottom of East Street. The workshops behind were probably used by him, as well as being leased to others, including Punfield, Gummer and Stone. He also had a weaving shop in Stake Lane, which was leased by Robert Gummer.

Crabb, Andrew, John and Edward

Andrew Crabb was spinning for Joseph Gundry during the period from 1780 to 1795, at which time he was living at the northern end of the Higher Alms Houses in South Street.

John Crabb, who was a seaman in 1816, returned to shore to work as a twine spinner living at 84, East Street. His son Edward followed in his footsteps, working as a line maker at the same address. In the late 1850s, when Joseph Gundry and Co. set up a new line walk at The Court, Edward became the foreman and moved to live at Chardsmead. By 1871 he was the foreman of a department of 26 men, but was still calling himself a manufacturer. He remained in this post until his death in 1873.

The Marquis of Granby Hotel was built, by John Coppock in 1769, on the site of the old St. John's Chapel. In the later 18th century the workshops behind were leased to a number of manufacturers.

George Darby (1775-1838)

George was a web manufacturer, who married Rosina, the daughter of Samuel Davie of Lyme Regis. He was working at 51, West Allington from c.1815. In 1820 he moved some of his work to North Street. In 1823 he formed a partnership with Richard Francis Roberts, relating to the Burton Spinning Mill. After his death in 1838, his executors carried on the business until R. F. Roberts died in 1842.

Denziloe, Matthew and Son

Matthew was recorded working as a sack and sail cloth manufacturer between 1813 and 1816.

Denziloe, John and Edwin.

John Denziloe was producing twines, lines and shoe thread in East Street in 1830 and 1840, while his son Edwin was working in Allington in 1838.

Messrs Denziloe and Company

The *Bridport News* mentioned that they had a store in Rax Lane in 1855.

Dunn, Silvester (c.1839-1920)

Formally a twine spinner, Silvester took over the old Ewens line walks at West Allington, when he set up as a rope maker in 1879. At the same time he entered the licensed trade, running the Woodman in South Street. He soon moved to the Baker's Arms in the Ropewalks, which was run by his family until it closed in 1960.

Elliott, John and James

James Elliott, a twine spinner, bought some land from Joseph Gundry in 1822. It was sold on to John Elliott, who built a number of houses on the site, which became 50, St. Michael's Lane. He emigrated to Newfoundland in 1841.

There was also a John Elliott (b.1796) living at 50, St Michael's Lane, working as a weaver during the first half of the 19th century.

Ewens, John Bishop (b1796)
J. B. Ewens was the nephew of George Darby. From 1827 he was described as a web manufacturer and bleacher/dyer, living in Bridport.

He moved to Allington in the mid-1830s, working as his uncle's clerk. When Darby died in 1838, he moved to run the Burton Spinning Mill, remaining there until the mill was sold in 1844. He returned to Bridport, living near West Bridge, and continued to run his late uncle's West Allington business. In 1857 he gave up the textile trade, working as an accountant until the 1870s.

His son, **John Henry Ewens** (b 1834) started work as a bleacher but soon moved on to become the foreman for Joseph Bartlett and Son, later becoming clerk of a textile business. However, by 1881, he was the school attendance officer and was living in Bedford Place.

Edwards, James and George
James Edwards was running the Tiger's Head in Barrack Street from 1829. Four years earlier, following William Hounsell's move to Wykes Court, James and Thomas Edwards had leased 22, Barrack Street, which consisted of a warehouse, weaving workshop, counting house, combing shop and stables. They manufactured lines, twines and shoe-thread, while sacking and sailcloth were also occasionally made.

Accounts of the Pymore Mill Company suggest that he was in partnership with Thomas Edwards until late 1838, when he moved the business to Fullbrooks, North Allington, adding net production to the list of manufactures. In 1841, by now living in West Allington, he took over part of 40, St. Michael's Lane, for use as a warehouse. As his business expanded he bought up all three properties which made up No. 40.

His sons, George and Henry, worked with him as clerks

The Tiger's Head in Barrack Street was run by James Edwards from 1829, shortly after he had leased 22, Barrack Street.

and when James retired, in the late 1860s, George took over. However the trade recession of the 1870s resulted in the firm's bankruptcy, after which Ewens and Turner took over the St. Michael's Lane warehouse. James moved to live in Downe Street, dying there in 1878, while George moved to Cardiff, before returning a few years before his death in 1913

Gifford, Henry
In 1801 Henry Gifford had taken a lease on a Borough Council property in St Michael's Lane, which was immediately behind 62, West Street. From here he ran his sailcloth manufactory, purchasing his yarn from the Pymore Mill Company. However by 1807 he had moved to Plymouth, with the lease passing to John Symes.

Golding, George, John and John
George (1749-1831) was a draper living at 18-20, East Street. In 1778 and 1780 he was in partnership with John and Nicholas Bools, as sailcloth makers and twine, line and net-makers.

In 1802 John (1774-1820) was in partnership with his father, George. However, during the following year, he built a flax spinning mill on the western edge of Bridport, where the river Symene joins the river Brit. He was in partnership with John Ewens, either at that time or soon after.

John (1791-1842), who lived at 23, South Street, was a merchant by 1815. In 1820 he took over his uncle's share in the spinning mill, now operated as Ewens and Golding. In true Bridport tradition, John was also operating on his own account, using the yarn produced at the spinning mill for making lines, twines, shoe thread and nets.

Joseph Golding (d1777) was also a twine spinner. Another Joseph appears in the 1793 directory as a twine merchant.

Gummer, Robert, Robert jnr. and William P. (1769-1835)
Robert Gummer was a sailcloth manufacturer living at 71, East Street. He was in partnership with William Stone, running a carpet weaving firm in addition to the twine and sailcloth businesses. The combined concern was substantial, leasing a number of properties and having stock worth around £2,000 in 1783. These properties included a yarn barton in Walditch, a carpet weaving shop in Stake Lane, Bradpole, warehouses in and near Pink Mead, along with combing shops and offices. During the late 18th century, Robert Gummer built a warehouse to the rear of a house that he leased adjoining The Court. They also leased a weaving shop, behind the Marquis of Granby, from John Coppock.

Robert Gummer retired from the business around 1793, passing control to his two sons, Robert jnr. and William Puglsey Gummer. However they did not have his business acumen and the business folded early in the 19th century. The bolling mill they built in 1794 was sold in 1809, being converted into a foundry. W. P. Gummer was declared bankrupt the following year.

Haydon, Joseph and Thomas

Joseph Haydon was operating from West Street in the 1823 directory, but it was Thomas Haydon who was listed there by 1830. Both were producing twine, shoe thread and lines. In 1803 Thomas Haydon obtained a mortgage on 29, East Street, which had been occupied by the family before 1781. It is possible that the money raised was used to finance the business. Thomas Haydon, like many others, bought his yarn from the Pymore Mill Company.

Hinde, John (b 1787)

John Hinde was bag maker in the 1841 census and a bag manufacturer in the 1851 census. In the latter he was living in St Michael's Lane.

Hinde, Thomas (b 1822)

Thomas was described as a manufacturer in the 1841 census.

Hinde, John (b 1819-1903)

John Hinde was a flax manufacturer, who emigrated to the United States in 1841.

Hockey, Robert (b1807)

Robert Hockey came from Chard and was possibly related to the family who formed the Chard Engineering Company. He was married in Bridport in 1831, when he was working as a mechanic. By 1842 he was listed as a bag, twine and line manufacturer, living at 66, St Michael's Lane. His name continues to appear in the directories until 1851.

Hodder, James and John

James Hodder was mentioned in the 1823 directory as a twine, line and shoe thread manufacturer of Allington. It would seem likely he was one of the partners in Knight and Hodder, who were based in St. Michael's Lane from 1809 to 1820. John Hodder had taken his place in the 1830 directory.

Hood, John (1738-1803), Samuel (b1777)

John Hood was born in Mosterton, but had moved to South Street, Bridport in the 1760s, where he set himself up as a sailcloth manufacturer. By the 1790s he had passed the reins of the business on to his son, Samuel, who took full control after his father's death in 1803.

Samuel formed a partnership, trading as Gundry, Hood and Symes. From 1801 to 1804 they received yarn from Pymore Mill, with Samuel Hood supplying the Mill with hemp oakham between 1803 and 1805.

In 1806 Samuel moved to London to work as a canvas inspector at the Naval Dockyard at Deptford.

Kenway and Sons

This was an old-established business, with James Kenway (1742-1833) recorded in partnership with Gawen Ball in the

The Bridport Foundry was originally a bolling mill built by Robert and William Gummer in 1794. It later became the Grove Iron Works, where the extension housed Richard Samson's braiding machine manufactory and networks from the 1880s.

88, East Street was the home of the Kenway family. The warehouse at the rear was in use by Kenway and Fox from 1833 until c1850, when J. Seymour Kenway moved to Batheaston.

1793 directory.

Initially based in West Street, Kenway and Sons first appears in the 1823 directory but had moved to 88, East Street by 1830. The senior partner in the firm was James' son, Peter Kenway (1771-1844), together with his sons; John Seymour Kenway (1797-1867), William Kenway (1798-1844) and Henry Kenway (b1801).

The business had a rather chequered history. In 1824 they took over a field by East Road, in which they built a cottage brewery. In October 1832 the partnership was dissolved as a result of them becoming bankrupt. They owed some £4,000 to creditors, mostly for raw material for their textile trade. After the bankruptcy William was practising as an accountant.

Kenway and Company (1833-c.1850)

The new company seem to have been formed in 1833, straight after the bankruptcy of the Kenway and Sons. It was run by a partnership of John Seymour Kenway and Joseph Gundry Fox, a grandson of Joseph Gundry. The firm operated from the warehouse at the back of 88, East Street.

In 1843 there was a change of partners, with Joseph Gundry Fox being replaced by his older brother Baruch Fox (1808-1863). This partnership lasted until 1849/50 when the firm was closed. John Seymour Kenway moved to Batheaston, where he died in 1867, while records suggest that Joseph Gundry Fox had moved to the Channel Islands by 1848. The warehouse at 88, East Street was used by Joseph Gundry and Co. until 1852.

George Kenway (1846-1918)

The son of an Allington sackmaker, George was working as an accountant and commercial traveller in 1871, living at Mount Pleasant, North Allington.

In 1880 he took over the business of Louisa Ackerman, who was his sister-in-law, which was based at the Five Bells in South Street. He moved to the top part of St. Michael's Lane in the late 1890s. He continued to run the business until the early 20th century, the last directory entry being 1903.

Knight, Matthew I, John, Matthew II (1767-1830), Matthew III (b.1803) and John T. (1793-1839)

Matthew I and John Knight were merchant manufacturers, who bought 62, West Street in 1792. Matthew built a new house on the site, which passed to Matthew II on his death.

From 1809 to 1820 Matthew II was in partnership as Knight and Hodder, having a warehouse behind 62, West Street on land leased from the Borough Council. In 1820 Matthew II took on the lease of the old Town Brewhouse, near West Mill. This was used as a sale room and weaving shop for their sailcloth business. However by this time, it would seem that the textile trade was gradually being overtaken by their work as auctioneers.

From 1817 John Thomas Knight was buying yarn from the Pymore Mill Company, which suggests that he was working on his own account. In 1820 the name changed to Knight and Sons, from which it would appear that Matthew II went into partnership with his sons John Thomas and Matthew III.

The business probably ceased trading some time after

The Brewhouse and Malthouse was used by the Knight family from 1820. Initially was used as a warehouse and later as an auctioneer's room. It became Mrs Gundry's School by 1841, and was destroyed by fire in 1906.

The New Brewery was built by Thomas Rose around 1814. Previous to becoming a brewer he was a sailcloth manufacturer in partnership with his father in law, Samuel Taylor. After he became bankrupt in 1817 the brewery was taken over by Thomas Cole, once the managing partner at Pymore Mill.

the death of Matthew II. Parish records show that Matthew Knight III was a manufacturer from 1828-1831, while John Thomas Knight was a merchant from 1829-1831 and a sail cloth manufacturer in the 1831 Allington census. Since George Knight was in possession of both the Town Brewhouse and 62, West Street in 1833, it would suggest that J. T. Knight continued trading only for a year or so after his father's death.

Thomas Rose (1765-1847)

Thomas, the son of a publican brewer, married Sarah, the daughter of Samuel Taylor, a sailcloth manufacturer with whom he formed a partnership. After the death of Samuel, Thomas carried on for a short while, before entering the brewing trade in 1807. Initially leasing the Town Brewhouse and Malthouse, he later opened the New Brewery in Gundry Lane. He became bankrupt in 1817, after which he left the area for some years, later returning to live in Chideock.

Richard Samson (1852-1922)

The Samson family ran the Grove Iron Works, formally the bolling mill of Robert Gummer, from 1833 to 1922. Richard Samson developed his braiding machines in the early 1880s, selling them to local manufacturers; some even found their way to Russia. While developing these machines, he decided to use them to manufacture and sell his own nets, usually those for herring, mackerel and sprats. He was listed in the directories from 1889 to 1903.

Seymour family

The Seymour family was one of Bridport's old established textile concerns. John Seymour (1682-1767) passed the business to his three sons, Peter, Richard and Edward, all of whom lived at 80-82, East Street. The partnership changed regularly, as fathers were replaced by sons, with Richard replaced by Seth (1757-1828) in 1779 and Henry taking over from Peter in 1789.

The partnership seems to have been dissolved sometime in the late 18th or early 19th century. From this time we see three separate businesses, those of Seth, Richard jnr. and Henry jnr.

Seth moved to work on his own account at 25, South Street in 1785, with his place in the partnership taken by Richard (d 1806). It was this partnership which was mentioned in the 1793 directory.

Richard Seymour (1787-1856) was based opposite St. Mary's Church, near 85, South Street from the early 19th century. Around 1830 he seems to have retired from the business and moved to Bradpole, becoming a farmer.

Henry Seymour (b1789) was the only one to remain at the family home, 80-82 East Street, and it is here that he worked as a rope-maker with his son, Edmund (1819-1890), who carried on the business after his death. However by 1881 Edmund was no longer a rope-maker, merely a twine spinner, so one must presume that the business failed in the 1870s, which was a time of hardship for Bridport's staple trade.

In 1785 **Seth Seymour** married Elizabeth Stoodley, licensee of the Five Bells at 25, South Street. From 1819 he leased the nearby spinning ways in Mortarhay. After he died in 1828 his widow leased the spinning ways to John Golding. After her death in 1840 her nephew James Stoodley took over the properties.

Stone, Joseph
Joseph Stone was a sailcloth manufacturer working in East Street. He is mentioned in an insurance of 1783 and in the 1793 directory.

Stone, William
William Stone was in partnership with Robert Gummer, manufacturing twine and sailcloth and having a carpet weaving concern.

The combined business was substantial, leasing a number of properties and with stock worth around £2,000 in 1783. These properties included a yarn barton in Walditch, a carpet weaving shop in Stake Lane, Bradpole, warehouse in and near Pink Mead along with combing shops and offices. They also had a weaving shop at St. John's, behind the Marquis of Granby, leased from John Coppock.

Stoodley James (b1777) and James jnr. (b1815)
James was the nephew of Seth and Elizabeth Seymour who, on the death of the former, took over the business at 25, South Street. Following the death of his aunt in 1840 he also took on the properties as well, including the spinning ways at Mortarhay, which were sub-leased to John Golding. The business continued until the early 1850s, with John Symes leasing the spinning ways by 1856.

Symes, Daniel (b1797), James Dyke (1824-1910) and Henry (b1851)
A Daniel Symes occupied 90-92, East Street in the late 18th century. Although the business had been in existence

Richard Samson made braiding machines from around 1880 until the early 20th century, a number of which were exported to Russia.

80, East Street was the home of the Seymour family, who had their walks leading off behind the house. Rope making was carried on here until the 1870s.

before the 1830s, the first we really hear of the family is in the 1841 census, when Daniel and James Dyke Symes were working as line makers. James continued that occupation until the mid-1850s, when he set himself up as a rope and twine manufacturer, being joined by his son Henry in the early 1860s. By the later 1870s he had built up a significant property portfolio, which included four houses complete with combing shops and eight spinning ways. He owned another five houses to the east of these, as well as 90/92, East Street, with its three sheds, open rope walks, combing sheds and store.

The business suffered a serious fire in 1878, from which it did not recover. The firm went into liquidation soon after, and the property was offered for sale the following year. However in April 1879 his son, Henry, started as a rope and twine manufacturer at 90/92, East Street and was employing 10 people two years later. In February 1889 the property was described as a house, store, stables and a 340ft long shed. Although sold to Mr Spencer, a builder it was used as a ropewalk by H. T. Symes, until it was advertised to let the following month.

The 1889 directory has H. T. Symes as the manager of the rope and twine business of Charlotte Rouning. One must presume that when the business was failing Mrs Rouning came into finance a form of rescue. In April 1890 the property was again advertised to let, but with no more success. Four months later, Mrs Symes sold the rope-making machinery of H. T. Symes, which included twine jacks, wheels, tarring apparatus, rollers and winders.

Later James Dyke Symes seems to have worked for Joseph Gundry and Co. and, at the time of his death in 1910, was living at 21 Victoria Street

Samuel Taylor

Samuel Taylor was a sailcloth manufacturer who lived at 63, East Street, with a warehouse next to The Court, which had previously been occupied by Robert Gummer. He formed a partnership with his son-in-law from 1797 until his death in 1806.

Turner, Robert (b1789)

Robert Turner was recorded as a twine merchant living at 29, East Street, the lease of which he took out in 1839. For some years he had been a junior partner in the Greenham Spinning Mill, along with James Hayden and Josiah Flight, the senior partner. On Flight's emigration to New Zealand in 1841 each junior partner took over Flight's shares in the concern. Turner continued in business until 1859, when he gave up the lease on the East Street property.

Vivian, John (b1824)

John Vivian was listed as a line-maker in the 1841 census and as a rope-maker in the 1851 census. In the directories from 1855 to 1865, he was a rope and twine manufacturer living in East Street.

Webb, Edward

The parish records for Allington show Edward to be a sailcloth manufacturer during the period 1810-1817.

Webb, Henry (b.1802)

Henry Webb is mentioned as a line-maker in the 1841 census and a rope-maker in the 1851 census, this time with his son James. He makes one appearance in a directory, in 1855.

Webb, W. and Company

W. Webb and Company is mentioned in the 1907 directory.

Welsford, John (b.1840)

The son of twine spinners William and Sarah, John was mentioned in the 1891 census as a manufacturer of fishing nets, based in Allington.

APPENDIX

Family Trees

THE EWENS FAMILY TREE

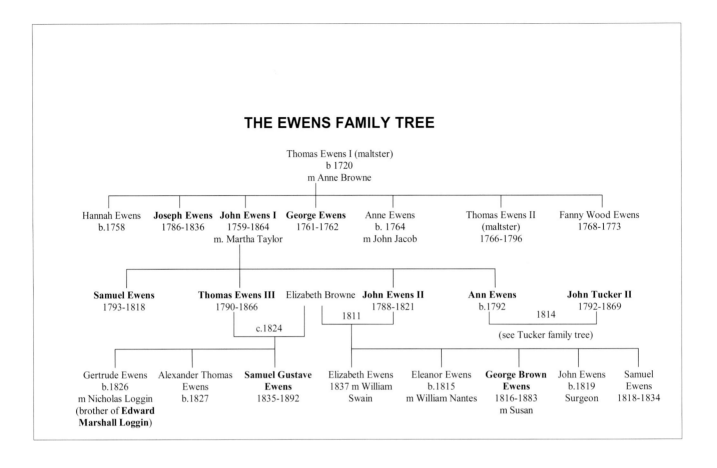

Thomas Ewens I (maltster)
b 1720
m Anne Browne

Hannah Ewens b.1758	**Joseph Ewens** 1786-1836	**John Ewens I** 1759-1864 m. Martha Taylor	**George Ewens** 1761-1762	Anne Ewens b. 1764 m John Jacob	Thomas Ewens II (maltster) 1766-1796	Fanny Wood Ewens 1768-1773

Samuel Ewens 1793-1818   **Thomas Ewens III** 1790-1866   Elizabeth Browne   **John Ewens II** 1788-1821   **Ann Ewens** b.1792   **John Tucker II** 1792-1869

c.1824   1811   1814

(see Tucker family tree)

Gertrude Ewens b.1826 m Nicholas Loggin (brother of **Edward Marshall Loggin**)   Alexander Thomas Ewens b.1827   **Samuel Gustave Ewens** 1835-1892   Elizabeth Ewens 1837 m William Swain   Eleanor Ewens b.1815 m William Nantes   **George Brown Ewens** 1816-1883 m Susan   John Ewens b.1819 Surgeon   Samuel Ewens 1818-1834

THE GALE FAMILY TREE

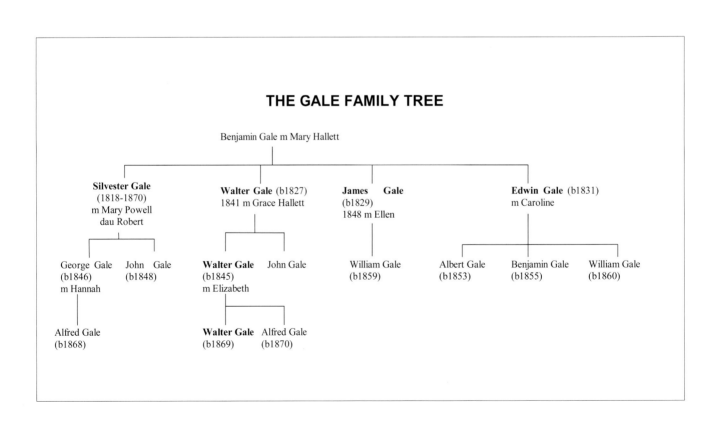

Benjamin Gale m Mary Hallett

Silvester Gale (1818-1870) m Mary Powell dau Robert   **Walter Gale** (b1827) 1841 m Grace Hallett   **James   Gale** (b1829) 1848 m Ellen   **Edwin Gale** (b1831) m Caroline

George Gale (b1846) m Hannah   John Gale (b1848)   **Walter Gale** (b1845) m Elizabeth   John Gale   William Gale (b1859)   Albert Gale (b1853)   Benjamin Gale (b1855)   William Gale (b1860)

Alfred Gale (b1868)   **Walter Gale** (b1869)   Alfred Gale (b1870)

THE GUNDRY FAMILY TREE (part 1)

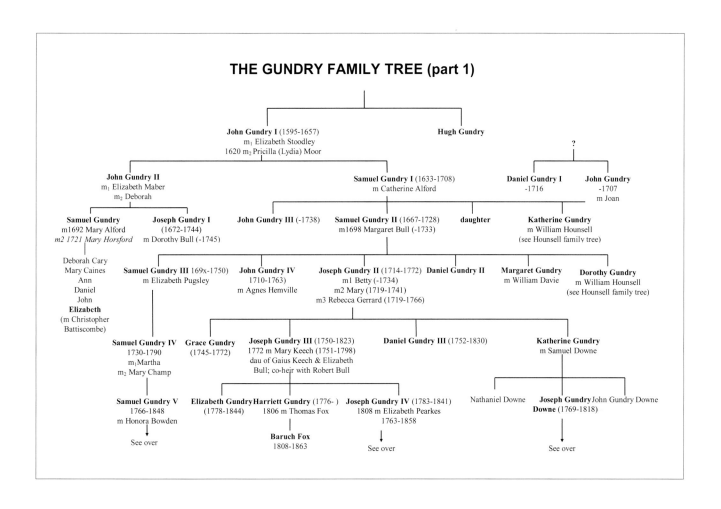

THE GUNDRY FAMILY TREE (part 2)

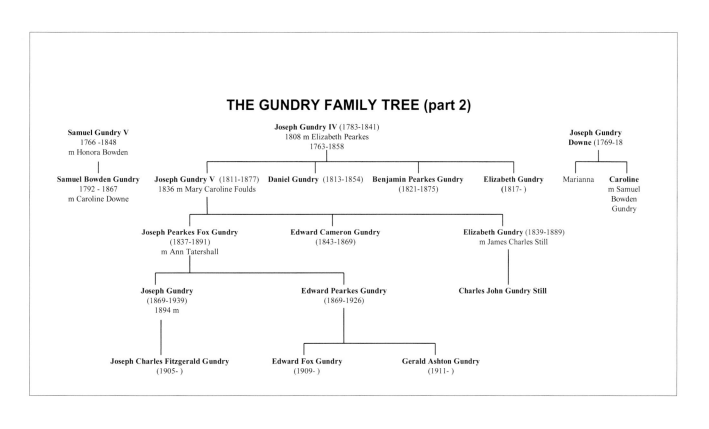

THE GUNDRY FAMILY TREE (occupations)

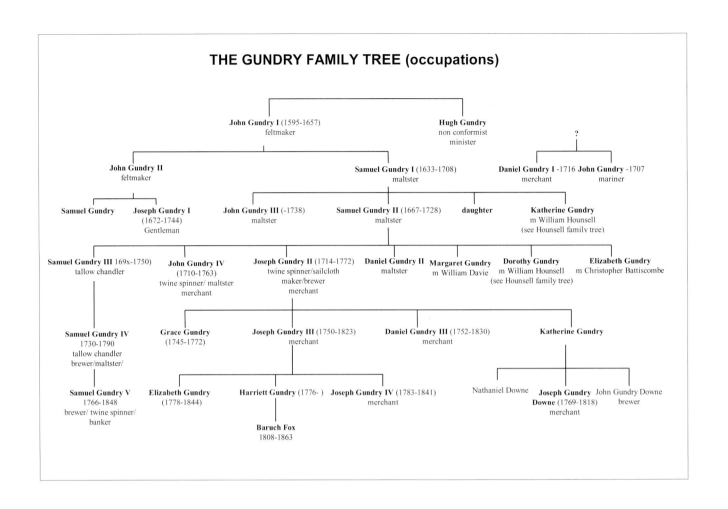

THE HOUNSELL FAMILY TREE

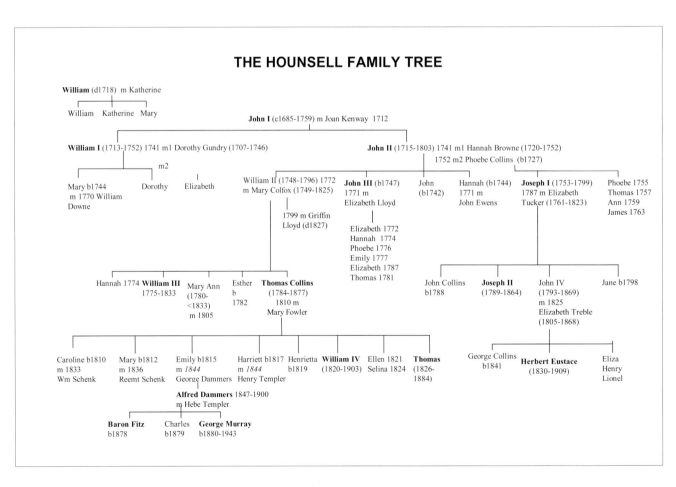

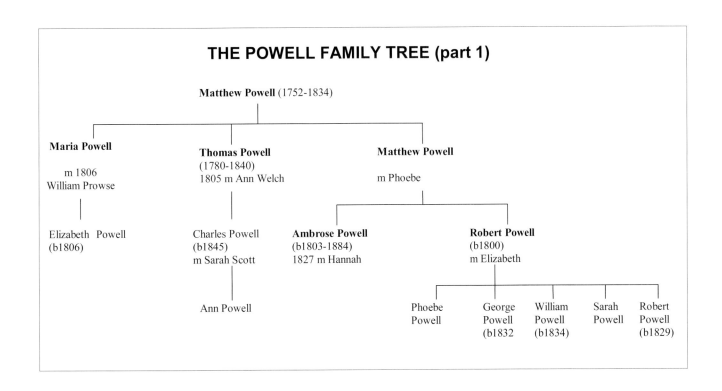

THE POWELL FAMILY TREE (part 1)

Matthew Powell (1752-1834)

Maria Powell

m 1806
William Prowse

Elizabeth Powell
(b1806)

Thomas Powell
(1780-1840)
1805 m Ann Welch

Charles Powell
(b1845)
m Sarah Scott

Ann Powell

Matthew Powell

m Phoebe

Ambrose Powell
(b1803-1884)
1827 m Hannah

Robert Powell
(b1800)
m Elizabeth

Phoebe
Powell

George
Powell
(b1832

William
Powell
(b1834)

Sarah
Powell

Robert
Powell
(b1829)

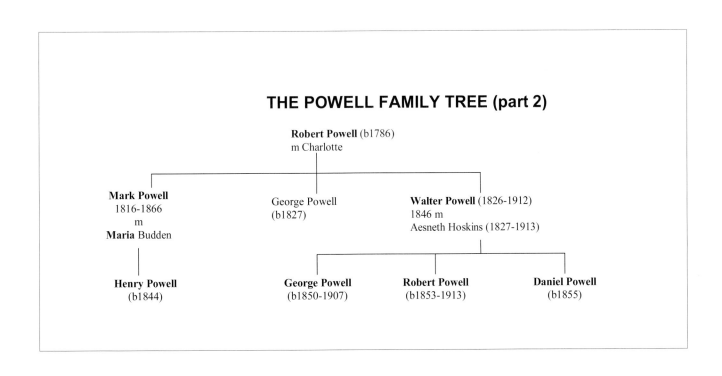

THE POWELL FAMILY TREE (part 2)

Robert Powell (b1786)
m Charlotte

Mark Powell
1816-1866
m
Maria Budden

George Powell
(b1827)

Walter Powell (1826-1912)
1846 m
Aesneth Hoskins (1827-1913)

Henry Powell
(b1844)

George Powell
(b1850-1907)

Robert Powell
(b1853-1913)

Daniel Powell
(b1855)

THE STEPHENS FAMILY TREE

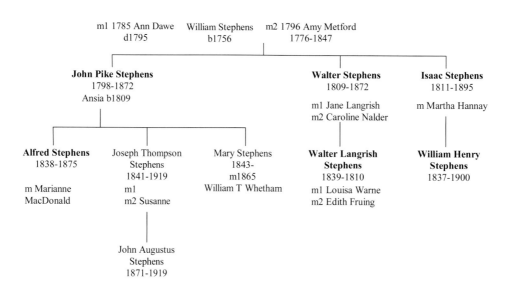

m1 1785 Ann Dawe d1795 — William Stephens b1756 — m2 1796 Amy Metford 1776-1847

John Pike Stephens 1798-1872, Ansia b1809

Walter Stephens 1809-1872, m1 Jane Langrish, m2 Caroline Nalder

Isaac Stephens 1811-1895, m Martha Hannay

Alfred Stephens 1838-1875, m Marianne MacDonald

Joseph Thompson Stephens 1841-1919, m1, m2 Susanne

Mary Stephens 1843- m1865 William T Whetham

Walter Langrish Stephens 1839-1810, m1 Louisa Warne, m2 Edith Fruing

William Henry Stephens 1837-1900

John Augustus Stephens 1871-1919

Abridged version showing only those involved with Bridport Textile Industry- those in **bold** relate to Stephens family business

Other children of **William Stephens** - William in Guernsey by 1837; Eleanor m1835 James Clark; Rebecca m1836 Francis Thompson; Silvanus (1799-1879) draper Bridport; Henry b1801; Samuel emigrates to N Zealand in 1840s

THE TUCKER and WHETHAM FAMILY TREE

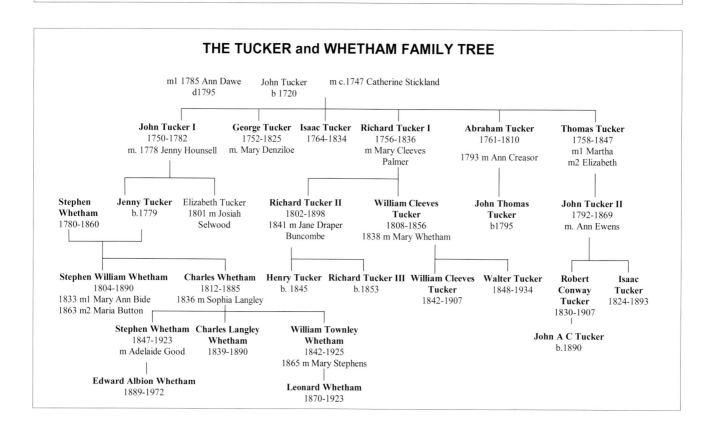

m1 1785 Ann Dawe d1795 — John Tucker b 1720 — m c.1747 Catherine Stickland

John Tucker I 1750-1782, m. 1778 Jenny Hounsell

George Tucker 1752-1825, m. Mary Denziloe

Isaac Tucker 1764-1834

Richard Tucker I 1756-1836, m Mary Cleeves Palmer

Abraham Tucker 1761-1810, 1793 m Ann Creasor

Thomas Tucker 1758-1847, m1 Martha, m2 Elizabeth

Stephen Whetham 1780-1860

Jenny Tucker b.1779

Elizabeth Tucker 1801 m Josiah Selwood

Richard Tucker II 1802-1898, 1841 m Jane Draper Buncombe

William Cleeves Tucker 1808-1856, 1838 m Mary Whetham

John Thomas Tucker b1795

John Tucker II 1792-1869, m. Ann Ewens

Stephen William Whetham 1804-1890, 1833 m1 Mary Ann Bide, 1863 m2 Maria Button

Charles Whetham 1812-1885, 1836 m Sophia Langley

Henry Tucker b. 1845

Richard Tucker III b.1853

William Cleeves Tucker 1842-1907

Walter Tucker 1848-1934

Robert Conway Tucker 1830-1907

Isaac Tucker 1824-1893

Stephen Whetham 1847-1923, m Adelaide Good

Charles Langley Whetham 1839-1890

William Townley Whetham 1842-1925, 1865 m Mary Stephens

John A C Tucker b.1890

Edward Albion Whetham 1889-1972

Leonard Whetham 1870-1923

154

Sources and Further Reading

Sources

The main lines of written evidence come from two sources: the Sanctuary Collection at the Museum of Net Manufacture and the Bridport Gundry (D/BGL) Collection at the Dorset History Centre (DHC).

Also consulted at the DHC were the following files from the Pitt Rivers Estate (D/PIT) - E19, M45, M46, T44, T45, T64, T74, T85 and T87, relating to Burton Bradstock. Reference was also made to D1/MC92 (Slape Mill); D141/B3 (1911 Thomas Tucker agreement); D/152/1 and 2 (Richard Roberts letters); D/ASH/A/F29 (the will of George Tucker) ; D/BTM/B1/2/1 (the 1865 agreement relating to W. Hounsell and Co.); D/BTM/B1/4/1 (an inventory of the Stephens Brothers); D/VIZ/8 (the agreement between R. F. Roberts and George Darby); D/NWS, an uncatalogued collection providing documents relating to the Gundry interest, together with documents and wills relating to Bridport manufacturers.

The rates returns for Bridport (MIC/R/1437; D/BTB/MN8), together with the leases for Borough property (D/BTB/Q15 and 16), have allowed me to pinpoint the location of many of the early firms' premises.

The tithe maps of Loders, Bradpole, Allington, Bridport, Symondsbury and Burton Bradstock. The Pitt Rivers Estate map of 1884 (D/PIT/P4).

Bridport Museum has provided the sources for parish records, census data, and directories as well as recently acquired material on the Gundrys businesses. The Museum has copies of the Annual Reports and accounts for Bridport Gundry from 1963-1997, along with copies of the Bridport Gundry house magazines. They also provided many of the photographs included in the book.

The past editions of the *Bridport News* are on microfilm at Bridport Library, with the gaps in these being filled from the Bridport News archive. The *Sherborne Mercury* was consulted at the DHC.

Bridport Library has also been the source of the journals of the D.N.H.A.S., Somerset & Dorset Notes and Queries and other articles in their local history collection.

Past chairmen and managers of Bridport Gundry, along with those of the current businesses provided information on their firms, either through interview or correspondence.

The Sun Insurance records from The Guildhall Library, London.

Use was also made of internet sources, including Dorset OPC, Family Search and Antiquity. While Google books provided access to number of early 19th century texts on the industry.

Published texts consulted were the following:

Angerstein R. R., Berg, T. and P. *R. R. Angerstein's Illustrated Travel Diaries 1753-1755: Industry in England and Wales from a Swedish perspective*, 74-75, Science Museum, 2001

Bernard, T., Case of the Salt Duties, 242-243, J Murray, 1817

Bone, M., Bridport Textile Industry 1814-1944, *Somerset & Dorset notes and Queries*, vol xxxi, 141-154, 1981.

Bone, M., The Bridport Flax and Hemp Industry, *Bristol Industrial Archaeology Society Journal*, vol 18, 19-31,1986.

Claridge, J., *A general view of the agriculture of the county of Dorset*, 26-39, W Smith, 1793.

Clark, R. S., A report on a visit to Bridport Manufacturers of small meshed nets, The Marine Biological Association of the United Kingdom, 1914

Crick, M. M., The Hemp Industry, *The Victoria History of the County of Dorset*, vol 2, 344-353, Constable, 1908.

Hayward, A. R., The manufacture of Coker sailcloth in Somerset, *The Somerset Year Book*, 94-97, 1936

Mease, J., On the manufacture of sailcloth, *The Archives of useful knowledge*, 1811

Nathan, M., *The annals of West Coker*, 401-425, C.U.P. 1957.

Pahl, J., The Rope and Net Industry of Bridport: Some Aspects of its History and Geography, *Proceedings of the Dorset Natural History and Archaeology Society*, vol 82, 143-154, 1960.

Perry, P.J., Bridport Harbour and the Hemp and Flax Trade 1815-1914, *Proceedings of the Dorset Natural History and Archaeology Society*, vol 86, 231-234, 1964.

Phillpott, E., *The Spinners*, Heinemann, 1918.

Runyan T. J.(ed), A fourteenth century cordage account for the king's ships, *The Mariner's Mirror*, vol 60, 311-326, 1974

Saunders, H., letter in *A treatise on hemp* by Wissett R., Somerville J. S. S., Riviere and Son, 284-286, J Harding,1806

Short, E Basil, Bridport Textile Industry, *Somerset & Dorset Notes and Queries*, vol xxxi, Sept 1986, 205-209

Stevenson, *A general view of the agriculture of the county of Dorset*, 287-303, W & G Nicol, 1812

Way, H.B., On the preparation of hemp in Dorsetshire and on the growth of sea cale, *The Transactions of the Society for the encouragement of Arts, Manufactures and Commerce*, 346-353, 1812

Rowson, J. W., *Bridport in the Great War, its record at work, at home and in the field.* 105-116, T Werner Laurie, 1923

Further Reading

Buchanan, C. A., *From field to Factory, Flax and Hemp in Somerset's History after1750.* Somerset Industrial Archaeology Society, 2008.

Martin, Celia, *The Bridport Trade, Rope & Net: Hemp & Flax.* Constanduros Press, 2003

Sanctuary, Anthony, *Rope, Twine and Net Making.* Shire Publications, 2008.

Stanier, Peter, *Discover Dorset: The Industrial Past.* Dovecote Press, 1998

Stanier, Peter, *Discover Dorset: Mills.* Dovecote Press, 2000.

Williams, M., *Bridport and West Bay, the buildings of the flax and hemp industry.* English Heritage, 2006.

The Subscribers

The publishers would like to thank all those whose names are listed below, as well as
the subscribers who chose to remain anonymous.
Their support and interest helped make this book possible.

A.F.W. Budden
Alan G.E. Bailey
John A. Bennett
Mike Bone
John Bowden
Amsafe Bridport
John F. Brown
C.A. Buchanan
Mr & Mrs I. Cochrane
Maurice Cole
J. Brian Crawford
Martin Davies
Casper M.A. de Boer
G.W. Dilbey
Geoffrey W. Dilbey MBE
Mrs Helen Doble
   (née Crabb) Bridport Gundry 1978-1985
Mick Edgeworth
Kenneth F.M. Farrance
Roger Ffooks
William Gove
Hampshire Industrial Archaeology Society
Giles Harvey

Roger N. Holden
Graham Jolliffe
Jenny Jones
Christopher John Louden
A. Elizabeth MacGregor
Mrs Hilary Malaws
John McGuinness
Rod & Ann Morse
Michael Norman
Des Pawson MBE
R. J. Roberts
Joachim Rother
John Russell
The Revd Canon Gordon Sealy and Mrs Marilyn
   Sealy (née Chubb)
Peter Stanier
Brian C. Stidwell
Marion Taylor
Michael Tighe
A.J. Warren
Gavin Watson
Mike Williams